United States Marine Corps
Generals of World War II

ALSO BY GEORGE B. CLARK
AND FROM McFARLAND

*The United States Military in Latin America:
A History of Interventions through 1934* (2014)

*The American Expeditionary Force in World War I:
A Statistical History, 1917–1919* (2013)

Battle History of the United States Marine Corps, 1775–1945 (2010)

*The Second Infantry Division in World War I: A History
of the American Expeditionary Force Regulars, 1917–1919* (2007)

Decorated Marines of the Fourth Brigade in World War I (2007)

*The Six Marine Divisions in the Pacific:
Every Campaign of World War II* (2006)

*Hiram Iddings Bearss, U.S. Marine Corps:
Biography of a World War I Hero* (2005)

EDITED BY GEORGE B. CLARK
AND FROM McFARLAND

*United States Marine Corps Medal of Honor Recipients:
A Comprehensive Registry, Including U.S. Navy Medical Personnel
Honored for Serving Marines in Combat* (2005; softcover 2011)

BY JOHN W. THOMASON, JR. AND
EDITED BY GEORGE B. CLARK

*The United States Army Second Division Northwest of
Chateau Thierry in World War I* (2006)

United States Marine Corps Generals of World War II

A Biographical Dictionary

GEORGE B. CLARK

McFarland & Company, Inc., Publishers
Jefferson, North Carolina

The present work is a reprint of the illustrated case bound edition of United States Marine Corps Generals of World War II: A Biographical Dictionary, *first published in 2008 by McFarland.*

LIBRARY OF CONGRESS CATALOGUING-IN-PUBLICATION DATA

Clark, George B., 1926–
United States Marine Corps generals of World War II :
a biographical dictionary / George B. Clark.
p.   cm.
Includes bibliographical references and index.

ISBN 978-0-7864-9543-6
(softcover : acid free paper) ∞

1. United States. Marine Corps—Officers—Biography—Dictionaries.
2. Generals—United States—Biography—Dictionaries.   3. Marines—
United States—Biography—Dictionaries.   4. World War,
1939–1945—Biography—Dictionaries.   I. Title.
E745.C43   2014   940.54'13730922—dc22 [B]   2007049393

BRITISH LIBRARY CATALOGUING DATA ARE AVAILABLE

© 2008 George B. Clark. All rights reserved

*No part of this book may be reproduced or transmitted in any form
or by any means, electronic or mechanical, including photocopying
or recording, or by any information storage and retrieval system,
without permission in writing from the publisher.*

On the cover: General Graves Blanchard Erskine;
flag background © 2014 Shutterstock

Manufactured in the United States of America

*McFarland & Company, Inc., Publishers
Box 611, Jefferson, North Carolina 28640
www.mcfarlandpub.com*

As always, for my dear wife, Jeanne,
who is always there when I need her

Acknowledgments

With special thanks to Thomas Fitzgerald, author of that splendid biography *A Character that Inspired: Major General Charles D. Barrett, USMC, Amphibious Warfare Pioneer.* Tom has always been there when I needed help and answers. Army officer, airborne and ranger, and retired as a special agent from the Federal Bureau of Investigation, Tom is now writing a biography of the late, lamented Marine commandant, Lemuel Shepherd.

Thanks to Ms. Lena Kaljot, a valued member of the Historical Reference Branch staff, the History Division, now at Quantico. Without her help I would lack many of the photographs that appear in the text. Patricia Mullen, archivist on the staff of the U.S. Marine Corps University, Quantico, VA, has, as always, been of help, no matter when I've requested her assistance.

Frequently I have burdened members of both information groups at Quantico with my multitude of needs, and nevertheless they have always responded as best they could. They, like everyone else at that Marine Corps Base, have been extremely busy helping to prepare for the grand opening of the Marine Corps Museum, which now has met with great success.

Semper Fidelis to all.

Table of Contents

Acknowledgments vi
Abbreviations 1
Preface 3
Introduction 5

Biographical Dictionary 17

Appendix A. Summary of Generals 177
Appendix B. Generals by Birthplace 181
Selected Bibliography 183
Index 189

Abbreviations

ABF   Advanced Base Force. Pre-FMF development.
ADC   Assistant Division Commander.
AWC   Army War College. At Fort Humphrey, then Fort McNair, Washington, D.C.
C&GS   U.S. Army Command & General Staff School. Always at Fort Leavenworth, Kansas.
CinCPAC   Commander in Chief, Pacific.
CinCPOA   Commander in Chief, Pacific Ocean Areas.
CG   Commanding General.
CO   Commanding Officer.
CoS   Chief of Staff.
DB   Defense Battalion(s). There were twenty in all, nos. 1 through 18 and nos. 51 and 52.
DMO   Division Marine Officer. Senior Marine officer in a naval division (battleships, cruisers).
DoP   Department of the Pacific.
EO   Executive Officer.
FMF   Fleet Marine Force. The land units which successfully projected the USN across the Pacific, taking bases and eliminating the enemy.
FMO   Fleet Marine Officer. See Division Marine Officer, above.
HQMC   always means Headquarters, U.S. Marine Corps, Washington, D.C.
IMAC   First Marine Amphibious Corps. Activated October 1942.
IIIAC   Third Amphibious Corps. IMAC was redesignated IIIAC on 15 April 1944.
JCS   Joint Chiefs of Staff.
MAG   Marine Air Group.
MarFairWest   Marine Fleet Air, West.
MAW   Marine Air Wing.
MB   Marine Barracks. Any, anywhere.
MCI   Marine Corps Institute, an educational unit formed post–World War I, mainly to promote education, often by mail, for the enlisted Marines. Various courses were established and they were graded at the MCI headquarters, usually based at Eight and Eye.
MCS   Marine Corps Schools. The primary educational system for Marine officers, developed post–World War I. Its instructors were generally Marine officers recently educated at one of the courses offered there, usually based at Quantico.

Abbreviations

MD   Marine Detachment, usually aboard ship though often refers to small groups of Marines anywhere on the face of the globe. Detachment has no numeric limitation.

MGC   Major General Commandant (or LGC = Lieutenant General Commandant).

MOS   Marine Officer's School. This usually applies to what eventually became the Basic School, which after reception every modern day Marine officer has "endured." The school, no matter what its name might be, and it changed several times over many years, endeavored to make Marine officers of educated individuals.

MTC   Marine Training Camp (or School) established for the arriving World War I officers, as opposed to previous "Basic" schooling. Much later would be called "OCS."

NAS   Naval Air Station.

ONI   Office of Naval Intelligence. Original intelligence agency to which Marine officers were assigned.

Quantico   always means the USMC base at Quantico, Virginia, although frequently for aviation persons it might also mean Brown Field, the attached airfield.

SMO   Squadron Marine Officer. See Fleet or Division Marine Officer, above.

VAC   Fifth Amphibious Corps. Activated 25 August 1943.

Many entries show a rank and name followed by brackets. This means that Lieutenant Colonel Rea (29 June 1938), for example, became that rank on that date.

Preface

This is a biographical history of all the men who would attain flag rank (general officers) in the United States Marine Corps and serve as such during the Second World War. Most attained the rank, sometimes temporarily, after the war had begun and had weighty roles in the prosecuting of that war, usually in senior positions as commanding generals or as the commanding general's immediate subordinates, as assistant division commanders or as chiefs of staff. The end date used for my research was 31 December 1945, and only one man was promoted right after the war. He is Samuel Lutz Howard, commanding officer of the Fourth Marines at Corregidor, who went into captivity as a colonel. He was, however, promoted to major general upon release in August 1945 and was at the head of the major general lineal list because he would have been promoted very early to flag rank had he not become a prisoner of war.

Some entries may cover quite a bit of information about the individual, but I tend to lean more heavily that way, rather than to leave out even modest details. Some entries are sparse, mainly because the individual served primarily stateside, and most often in an administrative post. Such posts were generally not very active, and not much could be added to the biography. If the men served with the quartermaster or paymaster department, they usually had daily tasks that changed but little during the course of the war. A few had additional roles, always of an administrative nature, that included such tasks as development or extension of bases.

Some men who were of flag rank when the war began were at that rank because they had been in the Corps long enough and served well in peacetime. Some proved not quite competent for wartime tasks. Since most were of permanent rank, space and tasks had to be found for them in the United States. They, unintentionally, of course, held other men back from promotions. In reading through, you may decide which they were.

The record of awards received for courage, leadership, or administrative ability is extensive in some cases while in others it is basic. The reasons are simple: Most awards were general in nature. Most were for being there, few were for outstanding courage (exceptions include Edson), some for leadership (Vandegrift at Guadalcanal) or many for administration (as chiefs of staff, for instance).

Many of the generals had served in World War I, sometimes in company ranks as platoon leaders or even as company commanders. Occasionally the men rose from the enlisted ranks and with additional education in the Corps (Army and Navy schools included) attained the ultimate rank, general, before or upon retiring. Two became commandant of the Marine Corps: Cates and Shepherd, in that order.

Introduction

This book contains biographical sketches of all the Marines who were flag officers during any period of World War II (December 1941 to December 1945). Most had a part in the fighting in the Pacific against the Japanese Empire, with a few noncombatant administrators included who served as quartermaster or paymaster at various stateside posts and occasionally overseas. Some officers were recalled from retirement and most of the ranks were temporary appointments. The criterion for inclusion in this biographical dictionary was simply having worn a general's star or stars during the period.

Most officers had served in various interventions in the Caribbean, the Philippines or China; some in France during World War I; and many with Marine detachments aboard U.S. Navy ships. Unless you are or have been a Marine and know a smattering of Corps history, you may well puzzle over what various generals were doing at HQMC or in China, Haiti or Santo Domingo, or at various schools or aboard ship. If they served aboard a ship, it is always identified in italics and without the usual "USS."

What follows is some general information about what is in the biographies. This will be especially helpful for readers whose knowledge of the what, when, how, and where of the Marine Corps is limited. Each category summarizes in general terms rather than trying to cover the entry in detail.

Amphibious warfare: Soon after the Marines returned to the United States from occupation duty in Germany, following World War I, the senior Marines were looking for a reason for the Corps' continued existence. Their experiences of command in France made them realize that the Marine Corps had only one way to go and that was to enlarge: increase personnel (thereby creating more rank, which was considered desirable) and to find a future task commensurate with a larger Corps—a task which would continue the close association with the Navy. Otherwise, they would constitute a second Army, which all realized was a major problem.

The then–Commandant, MG John A. Lejeune, and his closest advisors (as well as most naval officers) recognized that the next war would be with Japan. If that were true, the Navy would be in the forefront, and they would need protected support bases in the far Pacific. Who better to support the Navy on the ground than the Marine Corps? It was decided to develop the old concept of taking advance bases, and soon some of the minds began to consider creating defense battalions to protect those bases once taken. That idea was bypassed by others who considered assaulting and conquering islands held by an enemy as the primary focus of the new Corps. Both plans were under development in the 1930s.

There was an active element within the Corps that considered and studied the requirements of aggressive amphibious landings. With the help of naval officers of a like mind, they experimented with landing craft and came up with numerous examples crafted by several manufacturers. Testing began in the 1920s, became serious in the 1930s and continued even after World War II was being fought. Eventually, the whole thing came together and vessels and vehicles were created for the successful completion of the war in the Pacific.

Aviation: For many years following World War I, Marine flyers were required to resume ground duty after five years in aviation. As planes became more sophisticated, and the expense of training flyers increased with sophistication, a decision was made to keep men flying if they so desired. Most did and only a few eventually left aviation. Some, like Roy Stanley Geiger, eventually became full-fledged infantrymen.

Land-based service: The earliest Marine air officers, mainly those who served in Europe, did not have an opportunity to serve Marine ground troops in France but realized that would be their requisite in any future wars. Postwar Marine aviation became almost entirely ground-based as they were assigned to Marine ground forces in Haiti and Santo Domingo. Between the wars, close combat skills were developed in both interventions as well as later in Nicaragua and then China. Dive bombing (actually, glide-bombing) plus other close ground support techniques evolved by Marines were copied by Germany and later used most effectively. When the Marines went to war at Guadalcanal, Marine air soon provided them with superior reinforcement in various techniques learned at the expense of native rebel groups. Getting the planes to where they would be needed, however, was a problem only solved when the troops conquered ground for the planes to land; Henderson Field is a very early example.

Carrier-based service: Navy and Marine officers felt that planes flying from carriers with the fleet would be in a better position to support troops in their landing phase. There was a great deal of controversy between individual and groups of Marine aviators concerning flying from carriers. The first Marine flyers aboard carriers were members of VS-14M under the command of Capt. William J. Wallace aboard the USS *Saratoga* in 1931. They were closely followed by VS-15M under 1st Lt. William O. Brice aboard the USS *Lexington*. Carrier support became much more feasible later in the war, when carriers were developed and built for Marines.

The more authoritative (those Marines in charge) aviators were inclined towards serving with the Navy and flying from carriers. The others were instead more interested in supporting the ground troops in their landings, without a Navy distraction. Geiger was with the former, and Ross Erastus Rowell with the latter. Rowell was out of the mainstream, so he was sent to Peru (as was Ford Rogers).

Basic School: From 1891 to today, the incoming Marine officers' basic educational unit, now known as the Basic School, has undergone numerous changes in name, location, and in structure.

Basic School was originally called the School of Application and located at the MB, Washington, D.C., on 1 May 1891. Deactivated during the Spanish-American War, it was reactivated at the MB, Annapolis, MD, in July 1903, then deactivated from June 1907 until December 1909.

It was reactivated at the Naval Station, Port Royal, SC, as the Marine Officer's School; then it relocated to the MB, Naval Station, Norfolk, VA. Relocated to the MB, Quantico, VA, in July 1917, the structure and program greatly lessened and was redesignated Marine Officers' Training School.

Postwar the school was redesignated the Basic School in March 1922 and relocated to the MB, Navy Yard, Philadelphia, PA in July 1924. From September 1940 until June 1942, detachments were located at the State Military Reservation, Indiantown Gap, PA. It was deactivated at Philadelphia and Indiantown Gap, on 20 July 1942. Basic School was absorbed by Officer Candidate Class, the Platoon Leader's Class, and Reserve Officer's Class at the Marine Base, Quantico, VA from July 1942 until October 1945.

Postwar the Officer's Candidate School was redesignated on 17 January 1945 the Platoon Commander's School, Marine Corps Schools, Quantico, VA. It was redesignated The Basic School on 3 October 1945. The Marine Corps Schools were redesignated on 1 January 1968 as the Marine Corps Development and Education Command, Quantico, VA, with the Basic School placed under the operational control of the Education Center.

Colonial soldiers: For over a hundred years, the Marines were used nearly exclusively as colonial soldiers. That is, the Navy Department, at the direction of the State Department, moved troops into small nations to protect American citizens or help with the selection of a leader whom Washington would accept. The Marines were always chosen, mainly because they were on the scene, and were very good at knocking heads together at very little cost. Many of the hard-charging Marines were convinced that the Corps would always be a valued tool for intervening and would never have to change their modus operandi. There were, however, some Marines who were thinking about the future—and were in a position to alter it.

Lejeune was one of them. He made changes that affected the staid and settled and set into motion plans for the study for a war against Japan in the Pacific. Though not serious ground-pounders, Ben Fuller and John Russell made more plans and began efforts to create a Fleet Marine Force (FMF) for the Navy and to project the Corps across the Pacific, which became a reality. The time was ripe for the termination of the Old Corps. To save money the Hoover administration determined to end American occupation of Haiti and Nicaragua, which was satisfactorily completed soon after by the incoming Roosevelt administration. Only Shanghai, China, remained occupied by American Marines. The age of the colonial soldiers was over.

Department of the Pacific: This unit was seemingly formed especially for the former commandant George Barnett after World War I to give him a suitable command until he decided to retire. Eventually its purposes and value became widespread and included responsibility for supplying the necessaries for all Pacific-based Marine installations. It was a shipping terminal and quartermaster depot and the officers in charge oversaw other Marine installations on the West Coast including the San Diego Marine Base, Mare Island, Bremerton, as well as Pearl Harbor.

It was also a place which one officer described as having large-scale "inefficiency and corruption." He also found it an ideal spot for the "sick, lame and lazy," especially the latter, until there was a shakeup in the mid–1930s. Many senior Marine officers served at the facility and may very well have been included within that description.

Depot of Supplies, Philadelphia: Most products required for everyday Marine living, especially clothing, shoes, etc., were manufactured on site. The DoS was in operation for many years and provided especially good services during World War II until it couldn't hire sufficient civilian help to adequately run that kind of manufacturing organization. It was also found to be much less expensive to subcontract to commercial companies for generic products (shoes, underwear, etc.). Undoubtedly some congressmen suggested alternate commercial subcontractors, especially within their own districts.

Fleet Landing Exercises (aka FLEX): Soon after the end of World War I, the Marine Corps and Navy began making efforts to prepare for what most thinking officers anticipated: a naval war with Japan. Preparing, planning, and training for amphibious warfare required much more effort and money than either service was then ready to provide. Severe budget cuts, especially after the financial failure of the early 1930s, limited what could be done, other than concept development. Fortunately the latter was prevailing no matter how much money was lacking.

Marines landing from USN ships had a long history prior to the post–World War I period, and landing examples during the early 20th century were plentiful. Nonetheless, many naval and Marine officers could see the future required serious experimentation for that next war: landings against defended beaches. What eventually became known as Fleet Landing Exercises first took place between January and April 1922 when a Marine expeditionary detachment under the command of Lt.Col. Richard M. Cutts (he of the famous compensator) participated in the exercises held at Guantánamo Bay and Culebra Island. In the beginning, heavy emphasis was placed upon landing heavy guns from small landing boats. One can imagine the lack of success in the early days when the old French "seventy-fives" were the weapon of choice then available.

In 1923–1924 a much larger group of Marines, about 3,300, commanded by BG Eli K. Cole participated in Flex IV at Culebra. Half the Marine complement landed and the other half under command of Col. Dion Williams defended the island. The exercise utilized various modern components including gas, engineers, signal, aviation, anti-aircraft guns, and even balloons. Fleet exercises were for training troops but also for testing various equipment, with emphasis on boats to carry the then important .75 mm. For many years after, the Flex continued and exercises changed to the Pacific and as far west as Hawaii in 1925.

Though the landing boats continued to provide the most headaches, eventually, after a long struggle with the Bureau of Ships, several satisfactory landing craft were made available by Andrew Higgins and Donald Roebling. (The latter had created a waterborne vehicle for use in Florida's swamps.) See also Amphibious Warfare.

Fleet Marine Force (aka FMF): The concept originated in 1934: a landing force in readiness for service with the fleet. It was then composed of two skeleton brigades, the First (at Quantico) and the Second (at San Diego), but in effect they were two under strength regiments, perhaps as many as 4,000 officers and men total. It was developed when the assistant commandant, MG John H. Russell, suggested the discontinuance of the old expeditionary force and the creation of a Fleet Base Defense Force or Fleet Marine Force (the latter title was accepted) to stand ready for tactical deployment with and to assist the Navy. Other than the earlier Advance (aka Advanced) Base Force of the early part of the twentieth century, it was the first standing landing force ready to do battle with the Navy. That pleased the officers of both branches of the naval service.

The FMF served throughout the coming war in the Pacific, making many satisfactory landings against Japanese defenders and *never* losing a battle.

Interventions: During the period covered in the following biographies, especially before World War I, there were numerous times when the State Department called for an intervention, usually somewhere in the Caribbean. President Woodrow Wilson was exceptionally concerned, perhaps upset is a better word, with the elected or nonelected heads of the various Latin American nations. As he proclaimed, "We'll teach them to elect good men." Each of the countries had something special about them that brought about the interventions by the United States, mostly American investments. Armed forces intervened in Haiti and Santo Domingo, in particular, because each might have provided submarine bases for Germany and because of potential money losses by American investors; in Panama and Nicaragua because of the canal or, in the case of the latter, the potential canal, plus American investments and money; in Cuba, for money reasons, also because we had a standard right to intervene, based upon the Platt Amendment, signed under duress by Cuba (then the need for sugar during World War I caused a serious intervention and occupation).

The nations and interventions involved in this time frame were Honduras, Panama, and Santo Domingo, 1903; Santo Domingo several times in 1904, plus Panama; Panama again in 1905; numerous landings in Cuba, beginning in 1906 and occupation, plus Panama again; an attempt to stop a war between Honduras and Nicaragua in 1907; back to Panama in 1908; Nicaragua in 1909; and again 1910; Cuba and China in 1911; very active in Cuba during 1912, and China, and especially in Nicaragua where there was a major brawl; Mexico, China, Panama in 1913; Haiti, China and a major intervention in Mexico in 1914; Haiti for twenty years beginning in 1915, followed by a serious but shorter term intervention (nine years) in Santo Domingo (these two were of such substance that large numbers of Marines were required for both, making the large manpower commitment to the forces in France extremely difficult at times); Cuba again (big time) in 1917; France in 1917. Many or all interventions were detested by the subject nations' inhabitants.

Post-World War I interventions were mainly limited, for the first few years, to the Haiti (First Brigade) and Santo Domingo (Second Brigade) occupations. However, more trouble brewing in Nicaragua in 1926–1927 "forced" the State Department to "call in the Marines." That was a major intervention, involving two regiments (5th and 11th, or the 2d Brigade) chasing "bandits" when the total available Marine population was notoriously low. Then in early 1927, the State Department required the Third Brigade to go to the aid of threatened American citizens in China. Two regiments (the 4th and 6th) plus combined arms including many vehicles and airplanes made this the largest between-wars military involvement. In modern terms, it was also the first time that "combined arms" were utilized: ships to bring the brigade to China; infantry with armored vehicles and an aircraft service including a fighter squadron plus an observation squadron. It lasted two years, and all that time the Corps, with two brigades active, was struggling to live within its very modest budget. With the 1932 election, all occupations of foreign lands became a thing of the past.

Meanwhile, during that entire period, our Marines also landed in nations such as Korea, China, Morocco, Abyssinia, and the Philippines, plus taking up a permanent station at Hawaii and Peking, China.

Over there, France: The Great War was for Marines, like the Army, the greatest opportunity for advancement. Therefore many officers were willing to get to France and command a Marine unit. The first senior officer to be selected was Col. Charles A. Doyen, a colonial soldier with modest credentials but long service. What the Marines and Army didn't realize at that time was this war was different than anything any of them had ever witnessed. Worse, though the war had been going on since 1914, few American military persons were prepared for what they would soon face. Doyen went to France in June 1917 with the 5th Regiment which, after arrival, was selected to labor for the AEF until another Marine regiment (6th) could be trained and shipped to France.

The officers selected to go over were generally those with a modicum of experience, with the senior officers retained in the United States to train them. Those who became company grade officers were usually enlisted men with much experience in "little wars" and were promoted for the occasion. The newcomers, usually platoon leaders, were most often college-educated with little if any training other than the minimal training at Quantico as Marines. Later, including those enlisted men promoted for bravery or skills shown in battle, most officers came from the ranks. Some, but not many, had a modicum of education. Their specialty was courage and individual fighting skills. Those who fought in France and remained Marines generally were well-represented in flag rank during World War II. Some attained general rank (see Appendix A).

Many of the Marines sent to France were recipients of medals of various kinds, most being U.S. Army medals like the Distinguished Service Cross and the Silver Star citation (later a medal). After the war, the Navy developed the Navy Cross, a medal to rank with the DSC, and most of the Marines and Corpsmen who received the DSC also were awarded a Navy Cross for the same reason. The 4th Brigade was, as a unit, awarded the French Fourragere, which entitled members to wear the so-called "pogey rope." It was actually the Croix de Guerre awarded to the unit and its subordinate units, such as both the 5th and 6th Marines and anyone that served in either regiment "forever." The ultimate medal, the Medal of Honor, was awarded by the United States Army. Later the Navy also issued their version of that medal, for the same action, to the same men.

One honor, a ribbon (scarlet and gold), was for expeditionary service and prescribed in 1919 by Marine Corps Order No. 33 "for which service no campaign badge has been awarded." The ribbon could be worn for expeditions previous to 1919, and by 1921 included 37 landings all told, going as far back as Hawaii in 1874. A medal was created and authorized in 1929, to be worn by recipients, which by World War II included 52 expeditions. In 1931 two or more expeditions were represented by bronze stars, rather than numerals, for each additional campaign. A brief description: The obverse shows a Marine charging with a fixed bayonet; the reverse has an eagle perched on a branch and anchor between the words "For Service."

After the war, two boards were created to determine which men should be retained as officers in the greatly reduced wartime Marine Corps. The Russell Board decided against retention of most of the courageous enlisted men, for the educated (naval academy) officers. It so happened that many of the latter were not veterans of the Great War, while most of the former were. A second board, the Neville Board, refuted most of the findings of the Russell Board and selected the wartime heroes instead. Loyalty and performance rather than education prevailed. Unfortunately, later events proved that neither was a perfect solution. Some members of both groups proved to be superior and when the selection system came about (1934), the so-called cream of the crop rose to the top.

Police forces, foreign: Officers, and some enlisted men, were selected to form or head up several police-military type forces in Haiti, Santo Domingo, and Nicaragua. Usually, the Marine officer's rank, in the police force, was increased by at least one, and they received additional salary from the police forces' nation. Their names were, as expected, in the language of the nation: Haiti was the *Gendarmerie d'Haiti*, to later be changed to the *Garde d'Haiti*. The force in Santo Domingo was called the *Policia Nacional Dominicana*. The Nicaraguan was called the *Guardia Nacional de Nicaragua.*

Most of them functioned as planned by their Marine creators. However, in later years, following the withdrawal of Marine supervision, most went to pieces. In the Dominican Republic, Rafael Trujillo, the first native officer of that police force, had fine efficiency reports when he went from second lieutenant to major in only two years. It wasn't long before he dominated that force and became the "president for life."

Postings: Officers and enlisted Marines could expect duty, foreign or domestic, almost any place on Earth and on the high seas. Before World War I there was a great deal of intervention in the affairs of other lands, and especially our near neighbors in the Caribbean, including Mexico, Nicaragua, Honduras, Panama, Haiti, and Santo Domingo (now the Dominican Republic). There were other hot spots including the Philippines, China, and the numerous small islands of the Pacific. It was almost always entirely a landing of Marines, which kept that relatively small force very busy.

The many Navy bases in the United States always needed a covey of Marines to provide guards. So did, for that matter, many of the ships of the Navy. In the early years, most Marines could expect numerous postings at sea. Some postings were more desirable than others and duty at the American Embassy in Peking, China, was considered the ultimate. After the intervention of the 3d Marine Brigade into China from 1927 to 1929, the 4th Marine Regiment was left in Shanghai. That duty became even more of an attraction for Marines and sailors, because it was the crème de la crème of foreign service. Ten years later, when the 15th U.S. Infantry, always stationed in Tientsin, was withdrawn, a segment of Marines from Peking (then Peiping) assumed their place and duties. There were numerous Marine officers that were considered to be among the "Old China Hands." That was not always a complimentary salutation because they were frequently considered to have an inordinate, and undue, amount of power in the old Corps.

Post-World War I, the postings in the United States were versatile to an extreme. During two periods the U.S. mail required Marine guards to protect the mail from the ever-increasing bands of criminals stopping trains en route. The Corps was always looking for a "few good men" and recruiting duty in most major cities was prevalent.

Numerous officers with combat credentials were sidetracked into administrative roles. Even Holland McT. Smith served several years in the Quartermaster's office. Some fighting men, like Frank Whitehead, were assigned to the QM and eventually selected the noncombat track as best suited for them and their future career as Marines.

Officers, and some enlisted Marines, were diverted to schools—many to the Army—to learn trades and skills necessary for the modern Corps. Officers were also sent to staff schools, USA or USN, to increase and perfect their skills. The Corps was always big on schooling.

Lastly, officers and senior noncommissioned Marines often could have their families with them when stationed in places mentioned above and especially China. Frequently the latter was considered extremely desirable duty, especially when the wife was along and could purchase (with American dollars, even Depression dollars, converted to Chinese dollars) expensive items that would have been unheard of for any but the wealthiest people. Having numerous servants (even the enlisted Marines) at a fraction of usual American cost was also a major factor in the overall experience.

Promotions: Each service had their own particular problems insofar as promotions were concerned, especially post–Civil War. They paled to nothingness compared to problems of the officers of the Marine Corps. Some Marine officers served as captains from the 1860s until the Spanish-American War and then, even though company grade, were too old for active service, therefore unusable and not eligible for promotion. The First World War changed many problems into new ones, especially when noncommissioned officers were directly selected as captains. They fought the war, some were very good, some good, and a few were less than adequate. Postwar they were, however, retained, some at their temporary rank, and many for a very long period.

After the war, the position of permanent captain built up until most officers were captains. It remained that way until the process of selection (see) came about and the logjam was partially broken. Rank just seemed to expand until the required berths were filled, then World War II came along to cause more headaches. Expansion of the Corps required many officers in field and flag ranks (major to colonel and brigadier general to major general). The lower field ranks were easy to fill but the upper flag ranks required so many that most officers, of necessity, were promoted on a temporary basis.

Postwar provided a whole new set of problems. Who would be a permanent major general? The multitude of brigadier generals, most of whom were just temporary appointments (many still permanent colonels, but more lieutenant colonels), caused a multitude of problems not settled for many until postwar. The serious problems were settled when most BGs took early retirement in late 1945 and early 1946. Numerous colonels also retired in December 1946 and were promoted to what was called "Tombstone Promotions" as brigadier generals, but these are in a time considered too late for inclusion in this book.

Schools, education: During the early years of the Corps, most officers came off the street. They were frequently accepted mainly because they were the sons of notables or people with political pull. Some were useless, but there were enough good, courageous and hard-charging men amongst them to continue a viable military force. A force frequently used, in the early days, before the Spanish-American War, to intervene wherever the U.S. State Department wished to project national power. In the latter years of the nineteenth century, several commandants made great efforts to encourage Naval Academy graduates to accept Marine Corps commissions. Some later notables did, and they were among those slated to lead the Corps in the early twentieth century, and through the world war.

The first important group from the academy, five cadets in 1890, included three who would become outstanding members of the Corps. John A. Lejeune, Eli K. Cole, and Theodore P. Kane all attended the first School of Application at Eighth and Eye, on 1 May 1891. The next seven years, each incoming group of second lieutenants attended until April 1898 when, because of the Spanish-American War, the school was deactivated.

When World War I ended, the new commandant, Lejeune, decided to create a school system to train officers for the future. Marines could only guess at what tomorrow would include; but, like the USN officers, most considered war with Japan as absolute, therefore an amphibious war. In 1921 the MCS at Quantico offered three courses: field officer's course, the company officer's course and the basic course. The latter was transferred to the Philadelphia Navy Yard in 1924.

Incoming officers had to serve for a year at Basic School, which increased all college graduates' and academy graduates' education for a fifth year. No other military force required that additional education. The other schools continued for many years. The Marine Corps enhanced a reputation for increasingly developing educated officers and men. Another school that trained enlisted men was Sea School. The first one was at Norfolk, Virginia; a second was later established at San Diego. The curriculum was solely to prepare for service aboard ships of the USN. It included conduct, dress, and naval weapons training. For a period, at least post–World War I, there was even a separate school at Norfolk called Officer's School for Service Afloat to prepare officers for sea duty.

Other, non–Marine Corps schools attended included the venerable Fort Leavenworth Command and General Staff School course; the equally esteemed advanced course at the Newport, RI, Naval War College; Army War College in Washington, D.C.; Fort Benning's Army Infantry School; and various U.S. Army specialty schools.

Sea service: Until very recently, Marines have served aboard most if not all capital ships of the USN. That was their original base, especially when needed to fire down upon sailors, or Marines, on enemy ships, and it lasted for well over two hundred years. Occasional attempts were made (one by President Theodore Roosevelt) to remove Marines from ships, but Congress always intervened. Later in history, especially after ships of the line began to be propelled by steam, and conditions aboard ship were much better for the crew, guards to protect the ships' officers were no longer required.

Marines were nothing if not adaptable. They remained aboard and assumed responsibility for some of the secondary batteries and later for anti-aircraft artillery. In later years their service was mostly ceremonial and (when in port) for display purposes. Most of the officers listed herein at one or more times served as the Marine Detachment (MD) commanding officer (skipper) and their service aboard usually lasted a bit over two years.

Conditions aboard most ships were reasonably comfortable, and generally a Marine officer was made to feel at home. Nevertheless, there are exceptions to every rule and occasionally he, and frequently his command, was treated with less than civilized courtesy by the ship's captain. Frequently the Marine officer would be assigned legal duties and have responsibility for court-martial administration.

Selection of officers: Until May 1934, the USMC promoted its officers according to seniority. That is, the official day an officer accepted his commission was his place in the ranking and promotions. Unless he committed a heinous crime, he remained in that position until he retired or died. Several commandants made great efforts to alter that state of affairs and to use the system the U.S. Navy had introduced: selecting officer promotions based upon performance, as perceived by their peers.

Many enlisted men were promoted to the officer ranks during World War I. In fact, after the initial collection of newly arrived, usually university-trained officers in 1917, most new officers came from the ranks. Many were superb fighting men and earned numerous awards. There were so many, in fact, that following the end of the war, it was obvious that most would never advance beyond the rank of major when they were old enough to retire. Two boards were effected to find a solution, the first eliminating most of the enlisted promotions, the second continuing the status quo. By the late 1920s, only a very few officers had been promoted since the end of the war. There was an overwhelming number of Marines holding the rank of captain. Money was not readily available and as the Depression worsened, presidents Hoover and Roosevelt cut the Corps' budget drastically.

Soon after becoming commandant in May 1934, General John Russell managed to have Congress accept legislation to adopt selection as opposed to promotion by seniority. Promotions for those officers examined by peers, and not found wanting, were moved up to the next rank. That is why there was a great promotion "explosion" on 29 May 1934.

From that date to the end of World War II, many deserving officers were further promoted up to field and possibly flag rank and thus appear on this list. Unfortunately, some of the greatest "hard-charging" Marine officers were dropped by the wayside. Many anticipated being passed over and being forced out and therefore took early retirement, usually if they had performed fittingly in combat at the next highest rank.

Tentative Manual for Landing Operations. After much effort by Marine officers, with input from USN officers, a manual was developed in 1934 at Quantico to guide the FMF. Although it went through several alterations, including title changes, mainly the original concept remained. Changes in wording occurred every year, sometimes several in each; however, it eventually became a standard manual for both the USN and USA, even being used in the Atlantic war and the Pacific war.

The contents essentially provided the pattern to be used for command relationships ashore and afloat between the naval commander and the landing force commander. Naval gunfire support: how and until when the ships would provide gunfire for the landing force. Air support: included both Marine and Navy air for close-support as well as reconnaissance. Ship-to-shore-movement: problems inherent in transferring troops and equipment to landing craft. Combat loading: loading ships in such a way as to unload the most necessary items first. Shore parties: to keep the material landed moving to the troops.

Command relationship was a major problem in the early days of the war. The admirals, who commanded afloat, also believed they should command ashore. The generals resented and refuted that notion. After some serious problems, the matter was resolved satisfactorily, for the most part.

Units: The largest Marine Corps unit during World War II was an amphibious corps; there were three of them but only two were active at any one time. A corps usually consisted of two or three divisions, each of approximately 28,000 officers and men. At times a corps might also include a U.S. Army division or divisions.

Division was the next congregate size downward and there were six of them during World War II. Smaller yet was a brigade. "Brigade," as utilized prior to World War II, was usually (maximum) two moderate-sized regiments (each about 1,000 officers and men, plus or minus). A post–World War I brigade would also have service-type troops, plus artillery and often including aviators and their ground service men and, in the case of the Third Brigade in China, armored vehicles.

I have found records of six actual pre–World War II brigades. The 1st started in 1912 as the Advanced Base Force out of Philadelphia and later served in Haiti between 1915 and 1933. The 2d was in Santo Domingo between 1916 and 1924. Then it became the brigade that intervened into Nicaragua in 1927, remaining there until 1933. The 3d Brigade went to China, while the 1st was still in Haiti and the 2d in Nicaragua; this meant that a large portion of Marine Corps personnel was committed at the same time and concurrent for several years in three brigades. The 4th Brigade served nobly in France as the 5th attempted to do, with minimal luck.

The next smallest unit was a regiment, and that, depending on the period, could consist of as few as several hundred Marines or, as in France, up to 3,000 officers and men. (The Marine Corps was required to accept the newly created U.S. Army regulations pertaining to unit sizes while part of the AEF in France.) Battalions were a third the size of a regiment, often much less; and a company could consist of 75 (or even less) or, as in the 4th Brigade, an absolute 250 officers and men. Below that, on a regular basis, was a detachment which could consist of any number, hundreds or a handful.

Between the two World Wars, the numeric size of the Corps was minimal, down to perhaps as few as ten thousand active officers and men. It was difficult to maintain three brigades plus service aboard the USN's ships of the line; guard detachments at most Navy and all Marine posts; and numerous other duties. But they managed, as always.

Biographical Dictionary

AMES, Major General Evans Orchard was born 12 April (or 12 January) 1895 in Boston, MA. Schooling was local, and then Ames studied law at the University of San Francisco. It was obvious that war with Germany was coming so he applied for and was appointed from California as a second lieutenant of Marines on 6 February 1917. During a stint at the Marine Officers' School (MOS), Port Royal, SC, he was promoted to captain on 23 May 1917. Ames' first foreign duty was with the Marine Barracks (MB) on Guam on 29 April 1918, from which he returned to the MB, Mare Island, on 26 August 1920. In the meantime Ames received his permanent captaincy on 4 June 1920. On 6 December 1921 he went to Salt Lake City, UT, for recruiting duty.

Two years later, on 23 October 1923, Ames served overseas in Haiti with the First Brigade, at a time when strife was continual. Marines were performing several tasks: rounding up "troublemakers"; establishing a training program for a national police force (*Gendarmerie d' Haiti*); and serving as officers within that organization. Ames was reassigned to the States on 25 November 1925 and arrived at MB, Quantico, on 2 December 1925. While there, he attended and graduated from the Company Officers' course.

His next assignment was with the recently reactivated 6th Marines, at San Diego. It soon after became a part of the 3d Brigade, with BG Smedley D. Butler, Commanding. They arrived in China in late March 1927 and remained there until 1929. It was a period of showing the flag, but not much more. He and some other officers and men were, however, transferred back to the U.S. in January 1928 where he once again was assigned to the MB, Mare Island, CA. On 14 June 1929 he received his first seagoing assignment: to command the Marine Detachment (MD) aboard the USS *California*. He was transferred back to Quantico on 21 August 1931. Following this he was ordered on 13 June 1932 to the MB, Norfolk. On 15 November 1934 Major Ames (29 May 1934) was back at MB, Quantico, where he completed the Field Officers' course.

Upon graduation and leave, on 3 November 1935 he was at San Diego with the 6th Marines. On 17 February 1938, now a lieutenant colonel (7 May 1938), he arrived at Olongapo, the Philippine Islands, remaining there until July 1940 when he was made Fleet Marine Officer (FMO), Asiatic Fleet. A latter record shows that date as being February 1940. Ames was transferred to shore duty in January 1941 and assigned as an instructor at Marine Corps Schools (MCS) until December 1942.

With war came many promotions. Col. Ames' (1 January 1942) next assignment was as commanding officer (CO) of the recently formed 21st Marines, Third Marine Division (3dMarDiv), which berth he held from January 1943 to March 1944.

He relieved the CO, Col. Daniel E. Campbell, who had taken ill. Ames brought the regiment to New Zealand where they resumed training. His first experience in combat, beginning on 1 November 1943, was with his regiment at Cape Torokina, Empress Augusta Bay, Bougainville. By midmonth the Marines were advancing well into the island. Ames led his regiment admirably and the infamous "Hellzapoppin Ridge" was occasionally called "Snuffy's Ridge" in "honor" of Col. Ames. The island secured, the 3d Division was relieved by various U.S. Army units, the 182d Infantry relieving the 21st Marines, and on 9 January 1944 the Marines left the island. Ames was then assigned as Chief of Staff (CoS) and deputy commander of Supply Service, Fleet Marine Force (FMF), Pacific, from March 1944 until January 1946. While in this position, he was promoted to the rank of brigadier general on 9 May 1945.

Upon retirement in February 1947 he was promoted to major general. His decorations included two Legions of Merit, one for Bougainville and the other a Gold Star in lieu of a second medal, for service as CoS of the Supply Service, FMF; and the Bronze Star; appropriate World War II campaign medals and several expeditionary medals from Haiti and China.

Major General Evans O. Ames died on 17 March 1982.

BARRETT, Major General Charles Dodson was born on 16 August 1885, in Henderson, KY. His family, led by his Episcopal priest father, moved to Alexandria, VA in 1896. After primary schooling in that town for four years, he attended a private Episcopal school from 1900 until 1902. At age 17, he began work for the Southern Railway Co. It is said that a family friend, Ralph S. Keyser, already a Marine officer, got Barrett interested in becoming a Marine. After passing the necessary exams, Barrett was appointed a Marine from Virginia and commissioned a second lieutenant on 5 August 1909. His first assignment beginning on 15 September 1909 was at the MOS, Port Royal, SC. That schooling usually lasted a year or so in length at that time, depending upon situations and needs of expeditionary duty, which frequently interfered. Educated as a Marine officer, on 20 December 1910 he was on his way to the MB, Boston after fifteen months grueling experiences under the martinet (those students believed) school commandant, Lt.Col. Eli K. Cole. He spent but four months at the MB, Boston and soon after, on 25 May 1911, he assumed command of the MD aboard the *Indiana*. This ship was part of the U.S. Naval Academy Squadron that sailed the seas in northern Europe and the Mediterranean for summer cruises. On 29 August 1911 he was detached for duty aboard the *New Jersey* with the MD on his second cruise.

Charles Dodson Barrett.

His ship served mainly in nearly the same way as had the *Indiana*, that is, in taking Naval cadets to sea for further training. This went on until the fall of 1913 when

New Jersey took up station off Vera Cruz, Mexico. That nation's revolutions had caused serious concerns for American interests and would continue for several more years. Barrett's first serious action occurred when he was at the occupation of Vera Cruz in April 1914. Barrett landed on 22 April as part of the ship's MD under the command of Capt. Frank F. Robards. They became part of the command led by Major John Russell at the pumping station at El Tejar, which came under some severe scrutiny in later years. On 30 April, Robards, Barrett, and their command re-boarded the *New Jersey* which remained watchful off-shore until 13 August when she plied the Caribbean looking for un–American activities anywhere else. On 13 December he was detached and on 19 December arrived at his new station, the MOS, Norfolk, VA.

From there he was transferred directly to the MB at Norfolk on 19 December 1914. Capt. Barrett (29 August 1916) was still there when, like so many other second and first lieutenants, he was promoted to captain. While there, he was an instructor at the MOS, which school was newly transferred to Norfolk from Port Royal. For a limited period he was detached as an aide to the commandant in 1917 after which he was assigned duty at Quantico with the 5th Marine Brigade, Headquarters Detachment. The Brigade went overseas in late September 1918 and when they arrived they were welcomed by their fellow Marines but not by the rest of the AEF. They were mainly allowed to vegetate on the sidelines while most of the officers scrambled for a combat assignment. He like so many other surplus Marine officers, had been unable to find employment with the U.S. Army in France. He was, probably at his own request, transferred to command of the 2d Battalion, 367th Infantry, 92d Infantry Division, and fought them in the Meuse Argonne Offensive. The Division had recently arrived in France, and, unfortunately, was considered an eminent disappointment becoming, at Pershing's request, the first of the AEF units to return home.

Major Barrett (1 July 1918) was assigned to the 4th Brigade and wound up during the occupation, from April until July 1919, at Nieder Bieber, Germany. Upon his return to the United States he received a brief leave and a return to Quantico. He had, like so many other temporary ratings, now been reduced to captain. He was at Quantico but a short time when he was selected to return to France with ten other Marines to prepare a relief map of the Belleau Wood area.

In September 1919 his party (which also included Lem Shepherd) did all that was necessary and in January 1920 left France for home. They spent the following six months at Philadelphia making the map, which until about 1946 found a home at the Smithsonian Institution, after which it was returned to, and stored at, Quantico. In the meantime, Barrett had been assigned as a department head at the MOS, Infantry, now at Quantico. His fellows were two outstanding intellectual Marines; Majors Ralph Keyser and Edwin H. Brainard. Barrett's promotion to major occurred on 6 April 1921.

In a few months, from 8 August 1921, Major Barrett was with the 2d Brigade in Santo Domingo. While the war in France had kept many Marines busy, the troubles in Hispaniola (Haiti and Santo Domingo) had kept nearly as many Marines chasing "bandits" all over the island. Brigadier General Harry Lee, formerly CO of the 6th Marines, 4th Brigade, had recently assumed command of the 2d Brigade. At that same time, Lt.Col. William Harllee, who had also just arrived, was appointed to command the 15th Marines (infantry) and delegated to ride roughshod over all bandit activity.

On 1 February 1923 Barrett was back at Quantico and on 5 April 1924 was assigned duty with the American Battlefield

Monuments Commission in Washington D.C. He led two Army officers to France to study war-time locations in order to establish cemeteries, and then they came back to the States. That berth terminated on 23 February 1927 and he immediately prepared to go back to France. He had requested assignment, and was approved, as a student at the Ecole de Guerre in Paris, France, and arrived there on 5 March 1927. This school was highly esteemed and accepted few American students. He graduated in 1929 and returned to the MB, Quantico, on 29 August 1929.

For the next four years, until 1933, he was an instructor at Marine Corps schools. It was during this period that he came to the attention of the schools' directors, BGs Randolph C. Berkeley and James C. Breckinridge, and became, along with Lt.Col. Ellis B. Miller, the guiding hands in developing the *Tentative Manual for Landing Operations*. He was reassigned to Headquarters, USMC (HQMC), Washington D.C. on 2 June 1933. Lt.Col. Barrett (29 May 1934) and on 30 March 1936 assigned as Division Marine Officer, (DMO) Battleship Division 4, aboard the *California*. Col. Barrett's (1 February 1937) next duty was in the war plans section of the Office of the Chief of Naval Operations (CNO) on 12 January 1937. There were other Marines whom he had followed on the lineal list for years who were now beginning to fall behind him in grade. This was the time of selection, rather than just seniority.

His post with the CNO ended in July 1939 and he next was CO of the 5th Marines, First Marine Brigade, from 4 August 1939 until 3 May 1940. On 17 June 1940 he was assigned duties at HQMC as Director of the Plans and Policies Division and then as Assistant Commandant of the Marine Corps, from November 1941 to March 1942. Brigadier General Barrett (7 November 1941) became the CG of the Third Marine Brigade between March and September 1942. The brigade's task assignment was to provide protection for the Samoan Islands.

Major General Barrett (26 August 1942) assumed command of the newly created 3dMarDiv. He retained command between September 1942 and September 1943, leaving that post while at Guadalcanal to go to Noumea, New Caledonia, as CG of the First Marine Amphibious Corps (IMAC).

Barrett would only command that unit between September and October 1943: He was accidentally killed on October 8, 1943 when he died from a broken neck as the result of a fall from the porch of his quarters. Termination of his career at this time has always been considered a disaster since he was so well regarded by those who served under and over him. In fact, he undoubtedly had a serious chance for the ultimate role: that of Commandant. He was considered to be a brainy individual who had many years of exceptional service still lying ahead of him. Major General Barrett now rests in Arlington National Cemetery.

His decorations included a posthumous Distinguished Service Medal plus an assortment of campaign medals: the Mexican Service; Victory Medal, France; Army of Occupation, Germany; Santo Domingo Expeditionary Medal; American Defense Service Medal; Asiatic-Pacific Campaign Medal; and the Victory Medal, World War II.

BLAKE, Major General Robert was born on 17 August 1894, in Seattle, Washington. In June 1917 he graduated from the University of California and was appointed from that state a second lieutenant in the U.S. Marine Corps on 10 August 1917. Like numerous other appointees, he was immediately promoted to first lieutenant the following day. Blake shipped over to France, arriving on 19 November 1917. Soon afterward he was assigned as a platoon leader in the 17th Company, 1st Battalion, Fifth Regiment of Marines. With his regiment he served at Belleau Wood, Soissons, and St. Mihiel. He received a temporary promotion to captain effective on 1 July 1918. On 24 October 1918 he was promoted to command of the 66th Company also part of 1/5. He went on to serve notably during the Meuse River campaign and led his company across the bridge during the last night of the war, 10/11 November. In fact, his company advanced further than any other on the 11th, reaching the village of Moulin before being ordered to withdraw back to the Marine lines.

During his service in France he was awarded a U.S. Army Distinguished Service Cross, later followed by the Navy Cross for heroics on Hill 142 at Belleau Wood on 6 June 1918. Additionally he was awarded two Silver Star citations and two Croix de Guerres, a Gold and a Bronze. Following the end of the war he served with the Army of Occupation in Germany from December 1918 until July 1919.

Upon his return to Quantico, Blake made the decision to remain a Marine. His first postwar assignment was with the MB at Mare Island, CA, arriving there on 1 October 1919. He was assigned duty as an Instructor at MCS on 3 January 1920, remaining in that post until April 1922. He had received his permanent captaincy on 4 June 1920. On 11 September 1922 he was once again assigned duties at Mare Island. He was appointed to his first sea duty on 14 June 1923 as "skipper" of the MD, aboard the *Pennsylvania*. Two years later, on April 1925, he was aboard the receiving ship at San Francisco, CA.

On 16 January 1928 he was assigned to command 2/5 of the 5th Marines as part of the 2d Brigade in Nicaragua. During this period (10 February 1929 through 30 June 1929), he was awarded a Gold Star in lieu of a second Navy Cross. He remained there, later serving with the electoral mission in Nicaragua, 1929 and 1932. Between those periods he also served at Quantico and then at HQMC, and for a short stay at the American Embassy in Madrid, Spain and Paris, France, beginning in May 1931. Later he completed the Field Officers' course and remained to serve as an instructor at MCS at Quantico from December 1932 until June 1934. Major Blake (1 June 1932) reported to the Special Service Squadron on 10 July 1935 as Squadron Marine Officer (SMO) and a month later, 1 August 1935, he was promoted to lieutenant colonel. That service included patrolling between Panama and Nicaragua. He had also picked up a newly issued Silver Star medal for his service in France.

From there he was assigned duty with the Office of Naval Intelligence in September 1937, remaining at that post until June 1940. His next appointment was with the Naval War College (NWC), Newport, in July 1940, from which he graduated in May 1941. Col. Blake (8 July 1940) assumed command of the Fifth Marine Regiment on 27 May 1941. On 1 April 1942, he assumed command of the Tenth Defense Battalion which terminated in June 1943. His next promotion was to the command of the Marine Defense Group, June to August 1943. This was followed by the role of CoS of the 3dMarDiv from 15 September 1943 through 1 February 1944. At this time he planned the successful landings and operations on Bougainville for which he was awarded a Legion of Merit. This was followed on 1 February to 20 April 1944 by command of the 21st Marines. He was awarded a Gold Star in lieu of a second Legion of Merit for this service. Col. Blake would be promoted to brigadier general retroactive to 2 October 1942.

Brigadier General Blake (2 October 1942) was assigned duty as deputy island commander of Guam from 1944 until May 1945. He then became Marine Deputy CoS of the Tenth Army on Okinawa between June and November 1945. During that period, on 27 September 1945, Blake was designated Prospective CG, Occupation Forces, Truk and Central Carolines. His mission was to occupy and develop Truk as a U.S. Navy fleet anchorage and for the support aircraft. This was followed by his assumption of the role of CG of occupation forces, November 1945 through June 1946.

Returning to the States he became President of the Postwar Personnel Reorganization Board from June to October 1946. Assignments after the war included inspector general, U.S. Marine Corps, 1946–1949. He was promoted to major general upon retirement in June 1949.

His decorations included the Navy Cross and a Gold Star in lieu of a second, the Distinguished Service Cross, Purple Heart, Silver Star, Legion of Merit and Bronze Star, plus expeditionary medals for services in Nicaragua and the usual campaign medals for World War I, and World War II in the Pacific.

Major General Robert Blake died on 2 October 1983.

BOURKE, Lieutenant General Thomas Eugene was born on 5 May 1896, in Severna Park, MD. He earned a Bachelor of Science degree from St. John's College in 1916. Upon graduation he joined the Maryland National Guard for enlisted service on the Mexican border. Shortly afterward, on 18 November 1916, he accepted a commission as a Marine second lieutenant then promotion to first lieutenant on the same date and then to captain on 23 May 1917, but all were temporary rank. In fact, his and the six other Marines commissioned on that date in November 1916 were subject to be "fixed upon completion of competitive examination."

His first overseas duty was to have been at Santo Domingo, but beginning on 27 April 1917 he and fifty recruits were diverted to the naval station at St. Croix, in the newly acquired Virgin Islands. He was permanently promoted to captain on 12 July 1919 and by then had returned to the MB,

Thomas Eugene Bourke.

Quantico on 9 April 1919. On 2 February 1922 he was transferred to the MD, American Embassy, Managua, Nicaragua where he served until April 1924. Back in the States his next posting on 28 April was at the MB, Washington D.C.

On 2 September 1927 he attended the U.S. Army Field Artillery School, Fort Sill, OK, from which he graduated the following June. His next assignment was as "skipper" of the MD, arriving aboard the *West Virginia* on 23 June 1928 and back on dry land in July 1930 and on 25 August he was at the MB, Quantico. Next year, on 30 July 1931, Major Bourke (1 September 1931) was assigned to the war plans division at HQMC.

Lt.Col. Bourke (30 June 1935) had graduated from the Army Artillery School, the Marine Corps Field Officers' course, and in June 1936 graduated from the Army War College (AWC). From there he returned to the MB, Quantico, as CO from 30 July until 5 September of the 1st Battalion, 10th Artillery (there was but one battalion of that regiment on each coast). Bourke would command the battalion off and on, returning to his battalion on 25 May 1937, continuing as CO until 2 May 1938.

Bourke served at the Navy Yard at Pearl Harbor beginning on 10 June 1938 until he returned Stateside in July 1940, taking a post at MB, San Diego on 1 August 1940. Col. Bourke (1 November 1939) remained at San Diego until assigned duties as the first CO of the newly reactivated and reconstituted as a regiment, 10th Marine Artillery on 27 December 1940. The regiment, but lacking the 3d Battalion, moved to Camp Elliott in January 1941.

He served as CO of the regiment at Tarawa, going ashore with the CG of the 2dMarDiv, MG Julian C. Smith, on 22 November 1943. Brigadier General Bourke (back to June 1943) was detached to serve the U.S. Army in their originally planned assault upon Yap, which later changed to Leyte. This was the only time the 10th Marines was commanded by a flag officer. During that period he was the CG of 24th Corps Artillery (U.S. Army) 1943–1944, and his command included, besides scores of U.S. Army troops, 1500 Marine artillerymen. They landed on 20 October 1944 and successfully provided fire with their 155mm guns for the Army's advance. The Marines left Leyte on 13 December for Guam where Bourke reattached to VAC.

In the meantime, Bourke had become the first CO of the newly formed 5thMarDiv at Camp Pendleton on 21 January 1944 but he was soon after relieved by MG Keller E. Rockey on 4 February 1944. Major General (1 February 1944) remained with the 5th and served on Iwo Jima as the ADC. General Bourke assumed command of the 5thMarDiv on 25 June 1945 and led it in the occupation of Japan. He and his division landed at Sasebo in September 1945. With the disbandment of the 5th Division he became Deputy Commander and Inspector General of FMF Pacific. He retired in November 1946 and upon retirement was promoted to lieutenant general. John Letcher, and able BG and a long-time subordinate of Bourke, stated in his biography that Bourke was the finest gentlemen that ever wore a Marine uniform that he knew.

His decorations included the Legion of Merit (23 December 1940 to 10 December 1943) plus a Bronze Star with Combat V and a Gold Star in lieu of a second. His expeditionary medals included those from Santo Domingo and Nicaragua, and the campaign medals from the war in the Pacific, plus the World War II Victory Medal.

Lieutenant General Thomas E. Bourke died in Santa Clara, CA, on 5 January 1978.

BREWSTER, Brigadier General David Lukens Shoemaker was born on 31 December 1887 in Washington D.C. and attended the Army and Navy Academy in that city. He was appointed from Virginia and commissioned a second lieutenant of Marines on 15 November 1910 after which he attended the MCS at Port Royal, SC. His first assignment after graduation, on 4 January 1912, was at the MB, Charleston, SC. A few months later on 13 May 1912 he reported to MB, Philadelphia. He was next transferred on 11 July 1913 to the prestigious post at the MB, American Legation, in Peking, China. He arrived back in the States in May 1915 and on 21 October reported for duty at the Marine Corps Rifle Range, Winthrop, MD.

Capt. Brewster (29 August 1916) reported the following 10 January 1917 as CO of the MB, Pensacola, FL. "Big Dave" Bourke as Brewster was known, was assigned to the Naval Aeronautic School, Pensacola, FL following which he was designated a naval aviator number 55 and USMC aviator number six on 5 July 1917. That date he became a flying instructor at Pensacola and in January 1918 he was ordered to the Azores with the First Marine Aeronautic Company.

On 24 July half the company was recalled to the U.S. to become instructors and Brewster became the new CO of the remaining Marines. With his comrades, he flew anti-sub patrols, retaining command until the end of World War I. Brewster had been promoted to temporary major on 1 July 1918, which rank he lost postwar. The company returned to the States, arriving at the Marine Flying Field, Miami, on 15 March 1919.

After a brief leave, on 13 June 1919 Capt. Brewster reported at MB, Quantico, VA. On 5 March 1921 he reported for duty with the 2d Brigade in Santo Domingo. Brewster remained there until he reported back to the MB, Quantico on 17 July 1922. It was time for him to resume his required return to field duty after five years in aviation. On 3 June 1924 he was returned to his rank of major and at Quantico graduated from MCS's Field Officers course. He then was appointed an instructor at MCS, 1925–1926. His next post, as of 3 May 1927, was aboard the *Rochester* as the Special Service Squadron's Marine Officer in Charge. This was during the Nicaraguan Campaign of 1927 to 1929 and occasionally the Squadron's Marines would be called upon to land at designated hot spots in Latin America. Brewster led a force of 300 Marines from the *Rochester* at Corinto, Nicaragua on 25 March 1928 to assist in establishing order during activity by Sandino's troops.

On 22 April 1929 he reported to HQMC, at which post he remained until being transferred to the 4th Marines in Shanghai, China in December 1933. He assumed command of 3/4 on 6 March 1934 and relinquished command on 18 December 1934 but remaining with the regiment. While there Lt.Col. (1 June 1935) "Big Dave" Brewster served as Executive Officer (EO) of the regiment. Returning to the States, on 1 June 1936 he reported to MB, Philadelphia. Two years later, 11 July 1938,

David Lukens Shoemaker Brewster.

he returned to Quantico to become EO of the 5th Marines. Then on 4 May 1940 Col. Brewster (retroactive to 1 October 1939) became the CO of the regiment, followed by relief of command of Lt.Col. Alfred H. Noble on the following day. This was a time when officers were taking turns every few weeks or months commanding an infantry regiment.

The war altered many things. Brewster was assigned command of the Barracks Detachment at New River, NC, (part of Camp Lejeune) on 9 September 1941 and rose to brigadier general on 16 September 1942. He was assigned to First Marine Amphibious Corps (IMAC) 1943–1944 and became CoS of Administrative Command 1944–1945 during the operations in the Marianas. Relieved of all duty due to illness in June 1945 he was returned to the States and entered the Naval Hospital Bethesda, MD. Brewster died of multiple myeloma on 10 July 1945 and was buried with honors in Arlington National Cemetery.

He was awarded a Legion of Merit for

his staff duties with the FMF from June to August 1944. He was also awarded the World War I and World War II Victory Medals, campaign medals from his service in the Second World War, and expeditionary medals for service in Santo Domingo, Nicaragua, and China, plus several foreign decorations.

BRICE, General William Oscar was born on 10 December 1898, in Columbia, SC. He attended Mt. Zion Institute at Winnsboro, SC, from 1913 to 1917, then served in the Army in the latter part of World War I. After the war, he resumed his education, graduating in 1921 with a Bachelor of Science degree from The Citadel at Charleston, SC. On September 25th of that year, he accepted a commission and reported for active duty as a Marine second lieutenant to the Company Officers' School at Quantico. Graduating from the school in July 1922, he was stationed at the MB, Parris Island, SC, until 8 May 1923, when he joined the 1st Marine Brigade in Haiti. He returned from that country in January 1924, to enter flight training at Pensacola, FL, where he was designated an aviator that August. His next posting on 11 November 1924 was at Quantico's Brown Field.

In 1925, after further instruction at Pensacola and service with Observation Squadron 3 at Quantico, Brice began another tour of overseas duty, beginning on 3 June, this time with Scouting Squadron 1 on Guam. First Lieutenant Brice (26 May 1926) was ordered to China in April 1927, when most of the squadron as part of the 3d Marine Brigade was sent there to help protect Americans and other foreigners during the Chinese civil war. Apparently his squadron's service in China was over almost as soon as it had begun. The squadron was withdrawn to the Philippines in May while arrangements for a flying field were made with the Chinese government, and the next month it returned to China to begin oper-

William Oscar Brice.

ating from Hsin Ho in support of the 3d Brigade. They flew observation flights, keeping an eye upon the advances of both Chiang Khi-sek's army and the various warlord armies he was going against.

Returning to the United States in December 1927, Brice was assigned on 16 January 1928 to Fighter Squadron 9-M at Quantico, remaining there until October 1931. Following his return, to Quantico, he, and fellow aviator Capt. William J. Wallace were the first Marine aviators to take station aboard U. S. Navy carriers. On 2 November of that year he and his Scouting Squadron 15-M, reported aboard the aircraft carrier *Lexington* and thus began its service as one of the first two Marine squadrons to be based on Navy carriers. (The other unit, Scouting Squadron 14-M, with Wallace in command boarded the *Saratoga* the same day.)

Brice remained on the *Lexington* until December 1932 when his squadron landed at San Diego, sea service ended. That 1 June, after six months at San Diego, he returned to Quantico. Capt. Brice (29 May 1934) remained there during the next three years; he served on aviation duty; completed the Junior course at MCS; and was a member of the War Plans Section.

He next entered the Army Air Corps Tactical School at Maxwell Field, Montgomery, AL, in August 1936. Upon graduation in June of the following year, Brice returned to Quantico on the 28th to serve as EO and later, Commander, of Scouting Squadron 1. After that he was an instructor at Pensacola from July 1939 and served there until June 1941, when Major Brice (29 June 1938) went back to Quantico on 21 August as Operations Officer of Marine Aircraft Group (MAG) 11.

With that group Major Brice moved to San Diego in December 1941, and there, in March 1942, now lieutenant colonel effective on 1 January, he assumed command of MAG 12. He headed that unit until September 1942, when Col. Brice rejoined MAG 11 on 20 October and as its commander. The following month he sailed with it (via New Caledonia) for the New Hebrides Islands, where the group began feeding planes and pilots into Guadalcanal. In December 1942, he moved up to Guadalcanal to take command of MAG 14. He also commanded all U.S. Army, Navy, and Royal New Zealand Air Force search, bombing and torpedo planes based on that island until April 1943, when he departed for New Zealand with the group.

He also headed MAG 14 during its support of the New Georgia and Bougainville invasions. He returned to the Solomons with that unit in August 1943, to support the New Georgia and Bougainville operations and directed all Solomons-based Army, Navy, Marine and New Zealand fighter operations against Rabaul, Japan's biggest base in the Southwest Pacific. The group became the nucleus of the Solomons Fighter Command, and that October Brice was assigned additional duties as head of that organization. He relinquished his command of the group in January 1944, but continued to head the Fighter Command until he returned to the United States that March.

In September 1944, after service in various capacities at the Marine Corps Air Station, Cherry Point, NC, Brice reported to HQMC, where he served as EO of the Division of Plans and Policies until June 1945. Brigadier General Brice (25 January 1945) was promoted at the age of 46, which made him the youngest general officer then in the Marine Corps, and that July he arrived in Hawaii to assume the role of CoS, Air, FMF, Pacific. Holding that post until May 1947, and the following month, returned to as Assistant Director of Marine Aviation.

Leaving in May 1949, the general's next tour of duty was at Glenview, Illinois, as a Commander of Marine Air Reserve Training from that July until April 1951, when he left for Korea to become Assistant Commander of the 1st Marine Aircraft Wing (MAW). Promoted to major general that August, he returned to Hawaii in October as Deputy Commander, FMF, Pacific, serving in that capacity until March 1952, when he returned to the United States. He became Director of Aviation the following month, and on 28 August 1953, when that post was elevated to a lieutenant general's billet, he was promoted to that rank. He left Washington in July 1955, and assumed his final command on September 9th of that year. He retired in 1956 and was advanced to the rank of general.

In addition to the Distinguished Service Medal, Legion of Merit, Bronze Star Medal, Air Medal and Order of the British Empire, General Brice holds the Marine Corps Expeditionary Medal with one bronze star; the World War I Victory Medal; the Yangtze Service Medal; the American Defense Service Medal; the Asiatic-Pacific Area Campaign Medal with three bronze stars; the American Area Campaign Medal;

the World War II Medal; the National Defense Service Medal; the Korean Service Medal with two bronze stars; the United Nations Service Medal and the Korean Presidential Unit Citation Ribbon.

General William Oscar Brice, a veteran of pre-war expeditionary duty in Haiti and China, the World War II fight for the Solomon Islands, and the Korean conflict, died 30 January 1972 at the U.S. Army Hospital, Fort Jackson, SC.

CAMPBELL, Major General Harold Denny was born on 30 March 1895, in Middlesex, VT. He was awarded a Bachelor of Science degree from Norwich Military University, Northfield, VT, in 1917 following which he was commissioned a second lieutenant of Marines on 10 August 1917 and the following day promoted to first lieutenant. Campbell was assigned to the 23d Company, 5th Marine Regiment, and after schooling at the Lewis Gun school in Syracuse, NY, went to France arriving on 19 September 1917. His 23d Company, along with the 15th, were, on 15 January 1918, detached from the 5th Marines to fill out the (formerly 1st Machine Gun Battalion) 6th Machine Gun Battalion. Campbell served with the battalion throughout the war: at Verdun, Belleau Wood, Soissons, Marbache, St. Mihiel, Blanc Mont, and the Meuse River Campaign. On 14 June 1918, amidst the battle at Belleau Wood, he was transferred to the 81st Company. Capt. Campbell (1 July 1918) at St. Mihiel, he was a casualty at Blanc Mont, like so many others, being wounded on 5 October while again with the 23d Company. Nonetheless, he survived the war and took part in the occupation of Germany, returning to the U.S. on 19 June 1919.

After a short leave he returned to the MB at Quantico where he was stationed effective 17 August 1919. Like so many others, his war-time temporary appointments and promotions were reduced in rank effective 4 June 1920. Meanwhile First Lieutenant Campbell applied for training as an aviator and upon graduation on 28 June 1921 was designated Naval Aviator #2988. His first duty as an aviator was briefly in Haiti with the First Brigade, and then at the Naval Air Station (NAS) in Pensacola, FL in December 1922. Following which he was with the Second Brigade in Santo Domingo on 12 May 1923. Capt. Campbell (17 April 1923) was, in July 1924, operating out of the Marine Corps Base at San Diego where he remained until being reassigned for instruction at the U.S. Army Tactical School, Langley, VA in April 1927.

In the meantime, Campbell was the recipient of the Schiff Award in 1926 for the world's record number of air hours (839.5) without an accident. To accept the award he flew from San Diego to Washington D.C. then still considered a feat of endurance and skill. His graduation from the Air Corps Tactical School took place in 1929. This was followed by duty at the MB

Harold Denny Campbell.

in Guam beginning in December 1929 but he was back at San Diego one year later. On 15 April 1931 he reported for duty at the MB, Quantico. When the Purple Heart medal was issued for the wounds suffered at Blanc Mont, Campbell received his.

During this period, while still a captain, he headed up an aviation group in the development and writing of the famed *Tentative Landing Operations Manual*. Vernon E. Magee was one of his four lieutenants. While stationed at Quantico on 15 December 1935 Major Campbell (29 May 1934) was transferred to San Diego once again there to be the air officer for the FMF 1935–1939. Now Lt.Col. Campbell (5 September 1938) he was promoted over many officers that had preceded him. In July 1939 he was once again transferred to Quantico. On 6 December 1941 Campbell commanded MAG 11 based there at Brown Field. Sometime during this period, he was promoted to full colonel, there not being a record in the registers showing the actual date.

His next assignment, beginning on 25 May 1942, included being advisor to Lord Louis Mountbatten for air cover in the Dieppe raid on 19 August 1942. Following this assignment, he was promoted to brigadier general in April 1943 and given command of the 4th MBDAW (later 4th MAW). In August 1943 he assumed command of the Aircraft Defense Force, Samoan area. Campbell was then assigned as CG of the 2d MAW which command he retained until 6 July 1944. Following which he was called to Pearl Harbor by Gen. Geiger to organize a headquarters for Geiger's forthcoming role at Peleliu. The Peleliu Island Command was organized on 16 July with Campbell in command of the 3d Island Base Headquarters. On 13 January 1945, MG Paul J. Mueller, USA, became Army Ground commander at Peleilu, and on 16 November 1944 BG Campbell was promoted to CG of Island Command, Peleliu. As Island Commander his force included the 81st Division, USA, and the 12th Antiaircraft Artillery Battalion. An unexpected landing by Japanese soldiers on 18 January was met and defeated with the death of 71 Japanese and the capture of two more. Campbell, as CG of the 2d MAW was also charged with bringing Marine air in to utilize the airfield on Peleliu. Campbell was relieved on 19 March 1945 by BG Christian Schilt. Returning to the U.S., Campbell commanded Marine Corps Air Bases and the 9th MAW until his retirement, as a major general, in November 1946

His decorations included the Legion of Merit for the period 16 June 1942 through 26 April 1943 and Purple Heart in addition to the various campaign medals for his service in World War I, and World War II both in Europe and in the Pacific war. Earlier he also was awarded campaign medals for his role in the Dominican Republic.

Major General Harold D. Campbell died on 29 December 1955.

CATES, General and 19th Commandant Clifton Bledsoe was born on 31 August 1893, in Tiptonville, Tennessee. His early education was primarily derived from the Missouri Military Academy followed by matriculation at the University of Tennessee, from which he obtained a Bachelor of Law degree in 1916. Cates was awarded a commission as a second lieutenant of Marines on 24 May 1917. He graduated from the Marine Officers Training Camp at the MB, Port Royal, SC in August 1917 and was shipped to Quantico. There he joined and became a platoon leader in the 96th company, 2d Battalion, 6th Marine Regiment. It was the battalion's fate to be last of the 4th Brigade to arrive in France in January 1918. They combined with the balance of the regiment and the 5th Regiment, plus the 6th Machine Gun Battalion, to become the Fourth Brigade and part of the Second Division (Regulars).

After training, his regiment was sent to the Verdun Sector at which they remained between mid–March and mid–May 1918. Upon release the 2d Division was sent to refit just north and west of Paris. Within two weeks they were on the road east to stop the German advance, which was overwhelming all the French formations in their path. The brigade fought at Belleau Wood and there Cates earned a reputation as a brave and resourceful officer. He was awarded a Distinguished Service Cross for his part in taking a key position on 6 June, the town of Bouresches. One week later he was awarded an Oak Leaf Cluster for the DSC, though seriously gassed and wounded, for his refusal to leave his men. The French also awarded him two Croix de Guerre, a Palm and a Gold Star.

One month later, at Soissons, he was once again wounded, and noticed for his capable handling of a very bad situation on 19 July. At 1045 that morning he sent the following message to his battalion headquarters:

> I have only two men out of my company and 20 out of some other company. We need support, but it is almost suicide to try to get it here as we are swept by machine gun fire and a constant barrage is on us. I have no one on my left and only a few on my right. I will hold.

The message made history in the Marine Corps and Cates continued that kind of courageous action throughout his entire career.

On 28 August he received his first promotion, to first lieutenant. He served at St. Mihiel, Blanc Mont, and at the Meuse Argonne, where the war ended. His awards were numerous, including several Silver Star citations and later a Navy Cross. He, with his comrades, marched into Germany where they remained on occupation until the peace was signed in mid–1919. While there he also commanded the company composed of

Clifton Bledsoe Cates

Marines in the 3d Composite Regiment, sometimes known as "Pershing's Own." With his command he and they marched in several victory parades, in Paris and in London.

After the 2d Division returned home and the Marines were released from duty with the U.S. Army, Cates had a brief leave home and, deciding to make the Marines a career, returned to duty in Washington D.C. He was appointed as aide to the President during the first year. Following which he became the aide to MG Commandant (MGC) George Barnett. When MG Lejeune replaced Barnett as Commandant, the loyal Cates elected to remain with now BG Barnett who became CG, Department of the Pacific, until the latter's retirement in June 1923.

Capt. Cates (4 June 1920) was assigned to command the MD aboard the *California* where he remained until April 1925. One month later he was a company commander with the 4th Marines at San

Diego. One year later, 1 July 1926, he was sent to recruiting duty at Spokane, WA, then on 6 May 27 recruiting at Omaha, NB. On 6 March 1928 he was selected to be a part of the American Battlefields Monument Commission, in which he served in Washington D.C. In 1929 he received orders to report to the 4th Marines in Shanghai, China, arriving on 5 September. The Fourth had gone to China with the 3d Brigade in 1927 and when the brigade was recalled, the regiment remained behind to defend the American portion of the International Settlement in Shanghai. Cates remained until June 1932, then returned to the States.

Major Cates (29 October 1931) was assigned on 17 August 1932 as a student at the U.S. Army's Industrial College in Washington D.C. Completing his course of study in June 1933, Cates reported to Quantico and duty with the 7th Marines on 5 July. While there he also completed the Senior course at the MCS. With selection, Lt.Col. Cates (26 July 1935) was now pushing ahead of most of his contemporaries. In September he was assigned duty in Washington with War Plans Section, Division of Operations and Training at HQMC.

Trouble was once again brewing in China; the Japanese had landed troops, this time in Shanghai. Now a battalion commander and at San Diego, as of 30 July 1937, Cates was shipped to Shanghai with the 6th Marines. The disturbance in the Settlement was settled quite soon and the 6th departed China for home. Cates, however, remained once again with the 4th Marines until 1939. He was CO of the 2d Battalion between 1 February 1938 and 17 May 1939 and the period continued to be troublesome for everyone.

Upon his return to the U.S., Cates attended the AWC in July 1939 and graduated in June 1940, following which Col. Cates (11 April 1940) was transferred to the Philadelphia Navy Yard as Director of the Marine Corps' Basic School.

When war came, he was soon relieved of his position at the Basic School and in May 1942 Col. Cates assumed command of the 1st Marines, part of the 1stMarDiv. He brought the 1st Marines to New Zealand and then fought his regiment at Guadalcanal later that year, earning the Legion of Merit with a combat "V." With his experiences there he was brought back to the U.S. as Commandant of the MCS at Quantico. Brigadier General Cates (3 April 1943) remained at that post until June 1944. Major General Cates (23 June 1944) assumed the role of CG, 4thMarDiv. He fought the division at Tinian and later at Iwo Jima, bringing credit upon himself and the unit. He was awarded the Navy Distinguished Service Medal for Tinian, and a Gold Star in lieu of a second for Iwo Jima.

He was ordered back to the U.S. in December 1945 to become president of the Marine Corps' Equipment Board at Quantico. Six months later he was made CG of the MB at Quantico. This maneuvering put him in the appropriate location for the next move: Commandant of the Marines Corps on 1 January 1948. He and a long-time comrade, MG Lemuel Shepherd, were called to President Truman's office and the president selected Cates to be commandant because he was older than Shepherd. ("Your turn will come next," the president told Shepherd.) Cates had, in the meantime, been advanced to the rank of general.

During his "watch," his Corps was badly cut by the president and his minion, Secretary of Defense Louis Johnson. Having only about 9,000 Marines readily available, Cates managed, however, to collect together from reserves called to active duty a division (about 25,000 Marines) within several weeks. After preparing it, at the direction of the Joint Chiefs of Staff, on which there was no Marine representation, he sent it into action in Korea a few weeks later. General MacArthur had demanded a Marine division to make an amphibious landing on the west coast of the Korean peninsula. That division, the First, managed to stem the advancing hordes down the Korean peninsula, bringing about an eventual stalemate.

When Cates' term was up, he reverted to lieutenant general and the role of Commandant of MCS. On 30 June 1954 he retired, with promotion to the rank of general.

His decorations included the Navy Cross, two Distinguished Service Crosses, two Distinguished Service Medals, two Silver Stars, the Legion of Merit and two Purple Hearts, plus many campaign medals and foreign decorations.

General Clifton Bledsoe Cates died on 4 June 1970.

CAULDWELL, Major General Oscar Ray. "Speed" Cauldwell (sometimes spelled Caldwell) was born on 24 August 1892, in Nyesville, IN. He attended Wabash College, then graduated from the Naval Academy. He was commissioned a second lieutenant in the Marine Corps from Annapolis on 3 June 1916. After Marine Corps School, and now a first lieutenant, he was appointed "skipper" of the 80th Company, Second Battalion, Sixth Marine Regiment at Quantico. However, on 9 September he was detached for duty in France with 1/6 which was going to France first. On 6 October 1917 he was promoted to captain, later back dated to 26 March 1917.

While in France his duties included service as "skipper" of the 95th Company, 1/6, in which he served at Verdun and then later at Belleau Wood, where he was wounded in the leg on 2 June 1918. He was back in line for the Soissons bloodletting in which the 6th Marines were nearly destroyed on 19 July 1918. As Cpl. Warren R. Jackson later wrote, the 95th Company was "a thing of the past." Cauldwell, however, seems to have survived intact. Next came St. Mihiel, followed by another bloodletting at Blanc Mont in October. The final battle, the November drive along the Meuse River, was somewhat less destructive to the 6th Marines. Then into Germany and occupation, returning to the U.S. in July and August 1919.

After his return to the U.S. and leave, he was assigned to duty as Instructor at MCS, Quantico, where he remained from 9 August 1919 to June 1921. On 14 September 1921, he transferred to attend the Army Infantry School at Camp Benning, GA. A year later, having graduated the Advanced course, he was back at Quantico by 1 June 1922, and again assigned as an instructor.

On 2 July 1923 he went aboard the *Nevada* to command the MD. One year later, sea duty ended and on 6 September 1924 he joined the First Brigade of Marines in Haiti. In 1921 the Senate had held hearings on the occupation of Haiti as a result of numerous complaints about how the Marines were treating the native Haitians. The situation in that country had settled

Oscar Ray Cauldwell

down considerably since then, so while "Speed" was there, the situation was comparatively quiet. That duty concluded in February 1926 and on 14 May he was stationed at the MB, Quantico, and once again was teaching at MCS. Then, effective 10 August 1927, he was at the U.S. Army Command & General Staff School (C&GSS), at Fort Leavenworth, KS, from which he graduated in June 1928.

On 18 October 1928 he was again serving in Haiti, now with the *Garde d'Haiti*. Major Cauldwell (5 November 1929) served as Commandant of the *Ecole Militaire of the Garde d'Haiti* (the school for the *Garde*, a take-off on the famed school in Paris) from August 1930 to July 1933. After more than four years in Haiti, he returned to the States and on 15 August began the course at the AWC, in Washington D.C. Lt.Col. Cauldwell (29 May 1934) attended and graduated from the AWC and then attended the NWC in Newport, RI, graduating from the Advanced course. On 27 June 1935, he reported to Quantico once more and a few months later, 2 November 1935, he reported for duty at the MB, San Diego, CA.

Cauldwell, one of the best-educated Marine officers of his generation, was assigned to the War Plans Section, FMF, from November 1935 to May 1939. In May 1940 Col. Cauldwell (1 July 1939) became a member of the instructing staff at the NWC, remaining until March 1942.

After his stint at the NWC he was appointed the CO of the Third Marines, and remained with the regiment from 30 June to August 1942. From remarks made in one officer's memoir, "Speed" Cauldwell was very well-liked and admired by most officers and men of the regiment. He brought the regiment overseas and remained with it while they were at Samoa.

Brigadier General Cauldwell (26 August 1942) became Assistant Division Commander (ADC) of the 3d Division from 15 September 1943 to January 1944 and participated in the Bougainville campaign. During the Battle of Koromokina on 7 November 1943, he was recommended for, and later awarded, the Silver Star. From that point he was transferred back to the U.S. to become, from April 1944 to May 1946, the CG of Training Command, FMF.

Upon retirement in May 1946 he was promoted to major general. His decorations included the Silver Star and Purple Heart, Haitian expeditionary medals plus World War I and World War II area and campaign medals.

Major General Oscar Ray Cauldwell died on 8 September 1959.

CLEMENT, Lieutenant General William Tardy was born on 27 September 1894, in Lynchburg, VA. He was awarded a Bachelor of Science degree from Virginia Military Institute in 1914. Clement was appointed to the Marine Corps from West Virginia and commissioned a second lieutenant on 10 August 1917; however, the following day, like so many other war-time officers, he was promoted to first lieutenant. On 14 September 1917 he arrived in Haiti to join the 1st Provisional Brigade of Marines. Capt. Clement (1 July 1918) would remain in Haiti until May 1919 and after a brief leave on 17 July 1919 he reported for duty at the MB, Quantico. His confirmation as a permanent captain, like many others, changed to 4 June 1920.

His next duty was as Post Adjutant with the desirable and prestigious American Legation Guard in Peking, at which post he arrived on 24 August 1923. He left that post in October 1925 and in December arrived at MB, San Diego to become, in January 1926, adjutant of the 4th Marines. That October, and for three months, he assumed command of a Mail Guard Marine company out of Denver, CO, then rejoining his regiment. Returning to China with the 3d Brigade, he arrived in Shanghai on 24 February 1927, assuming the role of

Regimental Operations and Training Officer. Clement remained with the brigade in China until 15 March 1929 when it returned to the U.S. and he reported back to the MB, San Diego as EO of the Recruit Depot. On 23 June 1930 his next post was as CO of the MD aboard the *West Virginia*. There he remained on sea duty until he reported to the Naval Ammunition Depot at Puget Sound Navy Yard, WA, on 30 September 1932.

Major Clement (29 May 1932) reported on 22 June 1934 to MCS, Quantico as a student in the Senior course. Lt.Col. Clement (7 May 1938) would remain at Quantico as an instructor at MCS for the three following years. Between 12 July and 29 July 1939 he served as CO of the 5th Marines, then the final two years commanding a battalion of the regiment. He became FMO, Asiatic Fleet, on 14 July 1940, and served aboard the *Augusta* followed by transfer to the *Houston*.

On 13 December 1941 Clement visited headquarters of the U.S. Army Forces in the Far East and MacArthur asked him to have the recently arrived 4th Marines assigned to his command. Clement assured MacArthur that he believed Admiral Thomas Hart would relinquish his authority over the regiment and transfer it to the USAFFE, shortly after Hart agreed, with provisos. Hart ordered his fleet to vacate their untenable position in Manila Bay, Philippine Islands and Clement was assigned ashore on 27 January 1942 to the 4th Marines on Bataan. During his service with the 4th Marines, he advised USN Comm. Francis J. Bridget (an aviator without a plane) who was commanding the newly created Naval Battalion of the 4th Marines. The 5th Battalion, Naval, was engaged in fighting on Bataan and Clement was involved in that struggle.

Somehow, under orders (but it isn't clear whose), he would escape by submarine before the fall of Corregidor (details about

Willliam Tardy Clement

the reason for that escape are sparse). Upon arrival in the U.S., he provided MGC Holcomb with a report detailing the performance of the Marines, as he saw it, up until he left the Philippines on 22 April. (This part of his story has been very difficult to trace.)

For his actions on Bataan, Col. Clement (29 April 1942) was awarded a Navy Cross from 7 December 1941 until 22 April 1942. After a brief spell in the U.S., in November 1942 Col. Clement was on his way to London to become a staff officer with U.S. Naval Forces there. While there, Brigadier General (3 October 1942) would help prepare plans for the cross-channel invasion of France.

In 1943 he was returned to the U.S. and became Assistant Commandant, then Commandant of MCS from 1943 to 1944. Meanwhile, the war was heating up in the Pacific and Clement was assigned duty as ADC of the 6thMarDiv. He filled that post between 1944 and 1945 and with the division he fully participated in the Okinawa campaign.

Following that, on 11 August, he was assigned to be the Commander of Task Group Able, the Third Fleet landing force in Japan in 1945. The landing force was composed of the 4th Marines (reinforced), Marines from various ships' detachments, U.S. seamen plus assorted British seamen and Royal Marines. Clement was also present on the *Missouri* during the surrender ceremonies.

After the initial landing in Tokyo Bay at Yokosuka, he managed the balance of the occupation at and about that Japanese naval base. He was relieved on 20 September and rejoined the 6th Division on Guam which soon was in China. While the division was on "peace-keeping duty" in China, on 1 April 1946 Major General Clement (temporary 3 October 1942) relieved General Archie Franklin Howard in command of the Marines in and around Tsingtao. He, like many war-time temporary promotions, postwar reverted to the next lower rank.

In 1948 he was again promoted to temporary major general; it was made permanent in 1952. Lieutenant General William T. Clement reached that rank upon retirement in May 1952.

His personal decorations included the Navy Cross, three Legions of Merit, Navy, for 19 August to 18 September 1945, a Gold Star; one Army cluster for 1 October to 10 October 1945, and the Bronze Star. Other awards included a Presidential Unit Citation (Navy) with two Bronze Stars; another Presidential Unit Citation (Army) with Oak Leaf Cluster; Philippines Medal, 1942; World War I Victory Medal; Haitian Campaign Medal, 1919; Expeditionary Medal, Haiti, with two Bronze Stars, 1919; China 1924–25; Yangtze Service Medal, 1927; China Service Medal, 1940; various World War II campaign medals; plus several awards made by the Chinese government post–World War II.

Lieutenant General William T. Clement died on 17 October 1955.

CREESY, Major General Andrew Elliott was born on 7 November 1893, in Beverly, MA. A graduate of the Naval Academy, on 27 June 1917 Creesy was commissioned a second lieutenant of Marines from Annapolis. After a brief introduction to life as a Marine officer at the Marine Corps Officers' School, Quantico, VA, he was assigned to the 13th Regiment. Due to war-time promotions, Creesy became a temporary captain effective 1 July 1917 and served as CO of G Company beginning with the regiment's arrival in France in September 1918. He and his command served during the occupation of Germany through July 1919. Because his regiment was not selected for front-line combat duty, his responsibilities during this period were of a non-combat nature. Briefly, upon return home in August 1919, he and his regiment went to Quantico where the war-time officers and men were returned to civilian life. After a brief leave he elected to remain a Marine.

His next post was then from 10 October 1919 to the Second Provisional Brigade

Anrew Elliott Creesy

in the Dominican Republic. His permanent rank as captain was confirmed on 4 June 1920. Upon arrival back in the States 22 June 1922, after a brief leave he was assigned duty at the MB, Boston Navy Yard, Boston, MA. On 1 October 1923 he entered the U.S. Army Infantry School at Fort Benning, GA, for the one-year course for infantry officers. Upon graduation he was made instructor at MCS, from 31 July 1924 to September 1926.

On 26 September he became an aide to the American High Commissioner to Haiti, followed by a position in the *Gendarmerie d' Haiti* (now the *Garde d'Haiti*). He would remain in that post until June 1929. His next assignment, on 24 August 1929, was to the C&GSS at Fort Leavenworth, KS, and the two-year course from which he graduated in 1931. He was once again, from 17 July 1931 to June 1933, made an instructor at MCS at Quantico. On 13 July 1933 he was assigned to duty as the "skipper" of the MD, aboard the cruiser *Richmond*, remaining aboard for the usual two-year period.

Major Creesy (29 May 1934) was on 17 July 1935 delegated duty at HQMC. The following month, he went to Quantico and, a few months later, was back to HQMC where he remained for a few years in a quartermaster post. Lt.Col. Creesy (2 June 1938) reported for duty on 3 June 1939 at the Marine Base, San Diego. There he would serve from April 1939 until April 1941 as Supply officer and force quartermaster at FMF. Then between 20 April 1941 till January 1942 he was Division QM for the 1stMarDiv. Col. Creesy (1 January 1942) transferred as QM at Amphibious Corps, Atlantic Fleet, serving from 9 April 1942 to February 1943. His next move was to the Pacific where he became Corps QM of the IMAC from February to August 1943. Then he transferred to VAC in the same role, from August 1943 to January 1944. For his service during this period, 15 June to 18 July 1944, he was awarded a Legion of Merit.

His return to the States came when, beginning in January 1944 to August 1944, he became the Officer in Charge of the general supply section at HQMC. Brigadier General Creesy (4 May 1944) became Commander of Forward Echelon and First Field Service Command, FMF, Pacific, from August 1944 to May 1945. Then Director of Supply at FMF, Pacific between May and November 1945. Creesy was promoted to major general upon retirement in July 1951.

Creesy's decorations included the Legion of Merit and a Bronze Star plus the campaign medals from both World War I and World War II, and expeditionary medals awarded for service in Santo Domingo.

Major General Andrew E. Creesy died on 11 December 1974.

CUMMING, Major General Samuel Calvin was born in Kobe, Japan, on 14 October 1895. His parents were missionaries. He earned a Bachelor of Science from the Virginia Military Institute in 1917 and accepted a commission as a second lieutenant of Marines on 10 August 1917. His rank was upped to temporary first lieutenant the next day and as a temporary captain effective 1 July 1918. Capt. Cumming went overseas to France on 18 September 1917 as a member of Hiram Bearss' Base Detachment. There he joined the 5th Marine Regiment, serving until the regiment's return in July 1919. He earned a fine reputation while serving as a platoon leader with the 55th Company, 2d Battalion. He was wounded on 11 June 1918 at Belleau Wood and again at Soissons in mid–July. Later, after he had returned to his battalion, he led the 51st Company at Blanc Mont and again at the Meuse River campaign, fighting until after the Armistice hour. For his courage and abilities as a Marine officer he was awarded six Silver Star citations plus two French Croix de Guerres, both Silver.

Upon return to the U.S. he decided to

remain in the Corps and on 9 August 1919 began a tour at the MB, Quantico. During this period, Cumming was selected to accompany three other Marine captains, Charles Barrett, Lemuel Shepherd, and Lothar Long, to France and the now-named Bois de la Brigade de la Marine, to perform a survey of the "greatest battle the Marine Corps was ever in." The group returned to Quantico in early January 1920.

Cumming's permanent captaincy came through on 4 June 1920. On 16 August 1922 he began a tour of duty with the 1st Brigade of Marines in Haiti, which lasted until he was assigned during a troublesome period to constabulary duty with the *Gendarmerie d'Haiti*. Marines were angry with the guerrilla tactics being used by the Haitians and there were numerous cases of faulty discipline amongst them, officers as well as enlisted men. In fact, there was a serious investigation launched by the Congress into various allegations against Marines for mistreatment of the natives. Cumming seemed not to have been involved in any wrongdoing, and remained in Haiti until returning to the States in February 1926, a rather lengthy tour. He had a leave and then on 14 May 1926 reported to the MB, Quantico.

He was an officer selected to join with the 3d Brigade of Marines in China, serving from 2 May 1927 to 5 July 1928. He returned to the States and assumed duty at the MB, Navy Yard, Puget Sound, WA. On 4 November 1929 he was transferred to the MB, the Virgin Islands, remaining there until 24 June 1931 when he returned to MB, Quantico.

He arrived at Fort Leavenworth on 1 August 1932. Major Cumming (1 November 1932) graduated from C&GSS in spring 1933, then he attended the AWC in Washington D.C. During this period and later, he received a Silver Star and Purple Heart, both recently approved medals which had been earned while he was in France with the 5th Marines. Meanwhile, he graduated from

Samuel Calvin Cumming

both courses and returned to Quantico on 28 June 1935.

Lt.Col. Cumming (8 October 1935) served briefly as an Instructor at MCS, Quantico, between 1935 and 1936. Then Cumming became FMO in the Scouting Force from 14 June 1937 to 1939, his second tour of sea duty. After this, in July 1939, he was assigned to HQMC, remaining there between 1939 and 1943. While there he was promoted to full colonel on 1 March 1941.

Between July 1943 and April 1944 Col. Cumming was the CO of the 25th Marines, 4thMarDiv. He led the regiment at the Kawajalein Atoll in the Marshall Islands and, according to Holland Smith, "seized a number of small islands flanking Roi and Namur and we got our artillery ashore and brought it to bear on the two enemy islands." Their landing on three islands, then taking a fourth, was almost the first landing on Japanese soil of the war (the previous night the Division reconnaissance company had that honor). This landing of the "big" guns, however, made the task of the rest of the division that much easier.

Brigadier General Cumming (19 September 1942) served as ADC, 4th Division, at Saipan, and at Tinian, between April and September, 1944, for which service he was awarded a Legion of Merit medal.

He was CoS of MB, Quantico, between September 1944 and November 1946 upon which he was promoted to major general upon retirement that month.

His decorations included two Silver Star citations from the A.E.F., one of which was a medal, and four more citations from the 2d Division, and three Silver Star medals during World War II, plus two Purple Hearts from wounds received in France. He also was awarded several Expeditionary medal clasps for Haiti and China, and World War I and World War II campaign and Victory Medals.

Major General Samuel C. Cumming was a highly educated Marine officer. He had graduated from the AWC, the Command and General Staff School, and Army Transport School, completed the Junior and Senior courses at Quantico; and completed a NWC Correspondence course in International Law.

Major General Samuel C. Cumming died on 14 January 1983.

CURTIS, **Brigadier General Merritt Barton** was born on 31 August 1892, in San Bernardino, CA. Curtis received a B.A. from the University of California at Berkeley in 1916. On 10 August 1917 he accepted a commission as a second lieutenant of Marines and the following day was promoted to first lieutenant. Capt. Curtis (1 July 1918) remained at the MB, Quantico during World War I with his rank later made permanent on 4 June 1920.

On 1 June 1920 he reported for duty with the First Provisional Brigade of Marines in Haiti, and in January 1922 joined the *Gendarmerie d'Haiti*, remaining there until October 1923 when he arrived back in the States for a leave. On 19 November 1923 he was assigned to duty at the MB, Quantico. He reported on 5 April 1924 as the new CO of the MD at the MB, USN Submarine Base, New London, CT. Upon completion of this duty he was assigned to HQMC as a member of the Paymaster's Office where he remained for several years.

After earning an L.L.B. from George Washington University in June 1927, he was assigned to duty as Post Paymaster at the American Legation Guard in Peking, arriving on 23 October. He remained in that pleasant spot until November 1929 when he returned to serve as Officer in Charge at the Department of the Pacific, San Francisco. Curtis was soon sent to the U.S. Army Infantry School, Fort Benning, GA, arriving on 11 September 1930. Upon graduation he was assigned to duty at the MB, Philadelphia Navy Yard, Philadelphia, on 1 August 1931; he served as an Instructor at Basic School until June 1934.

Major Curtis (29 May 1934) then went to San Diego as Base Paymaster on 30 June 1934. In October 1935 he transferred to San

Merritt Barton Curtis

Francisco where he performed duties as Assistant CoS, Supply and Paymaster, Department of the Pacific, remaining there until he returned to China, arriving in Shanghai on 27 March 1936. He served as Paymaster with the Fourth Marine Regiment in Shanghai until July 1937. Although that was a month in which hell broke out in that part of China when the Japanese began the so-called incident, Curtis was on his way home. Upon arrival in the States he was briefly assigned to duty at the MB, Mare Island, CA, then to Quantico as Post Paymaster.

Promoted to lieutenant colonel and advanced one grade the following 29 June 1938, Curtis was back at the MB, Philadelphia, as Paymaster of the Northeastern Pay Area. On 7 July 1941 he became EO of the Paymaster Department at HQMC, in which post he would remain until December 1944. He was Col. Curtis (29 April 1942) then brigadier general on 7 May 1944, and assigned duty as Paymaster at FMF, Pacific, Pearl Harbor, from December 1944 to August 1946 when he was ordered back to HQMC. Promoted to Chief of the Disbursing Branch at HQMC, he was there from August 1946 until retirement in June 1949.

In addition to the Letter of Commendation for "Meritorious and efficient performance of duty" awarded by the CG, FMF, Pacific, his decorations and medals also included: the Haitian Campaign Medal, 1919–1920; Marine Corps Expeditionary Medal, Haiti; China, 1927, and a second for 1937; and various World War II campaign medals, including the World War II Victory Medal.

Brigadier General Merritt B. Curtis died at Bethesda Naval Hospital on 16 May 1966.

CUSHMAN, Lieutenant General Thomas Jackson was born on 27 June 1895, in St. Louis, Missouri. He attended the University of Washington between 1913 and 1917 and after graduation enlisted in the U.S. Marine Corps, serving about a year until he was commissioned a second lieutenant of reserves on 22 October 1918. He enrolled in Marine aviation and after completing flight training was designated Naval Aviator #2850 in June 1919. Like other officers commissioned after the war, on 15 July 1919 he was subsequently placed on the inactive list.

Like some others, Cushman managed to return to the Marine Corps. On 4 January 1922 he was given a temporary rank of first lieutenant and on 22 September as an aviator reached his first duty station at MB, Naval Station, Guam. His rank was finalized effective on 18 October 1921. By August 1924 he had returned to the U.S. and on 18 November was at Brown Field, Quantico. On 3 August 1925 he arrived at the Pensacola NAS in Florida as an instructor and the following year, on 2 November 1926, he was at the NAS, San Diego. Attached to Aircraft Squadrons, West Coast Expeditionary Force, he participated from March through June 1927 in temporary foreign service in Nicaragua.

Thomas Jackson Cushman

His next duty was in Haiti with the First Brigade of Marines as Communications and Aerological Officer with Observation Squadron 9-M from 2 May 1929 until August 1931. In December 1930 he became EO of the Squadron.

His next assignment was as an engineering student at the U.S. Army Air Corps School Technical School at Rantoul, IL, from which he graduated in June 1932. Then on 8 July 1932 to the MCS, Quantico, where he attended and graduated from the Company Officers' course in June 1933. Capt. Cushman's (1 July 1933) next assignment was in Washington with the Bureau of Aeronautics, Navy Department.

In August 1935 he was ordered to training at the Army's Tactical School, Maxwell Field, graduating from it in 1936. In July 1936 he joined Aircraft Two at San Diego, where he commanded Observation Squadron Eight and remained on aviation duty, as Operations Officer of Aircraft Two. The following year Major Cushman (1 July 1937) became CO of Fighter Squadron Two-M after which he returned to Brown Field, Quantico in June 1939, becoming Detachment Commander of the Base Air Detachment, remaining there until August 1941. Lt.Col. Cushman's (1 July 1941) next assignment was as CO of the Marine Corps Air Station, Cherry Point, NC, effective that month and promotion to colonel on 1 October 1942.

Col. Cushman later served as CoS to the CG MG Ross E. Rowell of Marine Aircraft Wings from September 1943 to May 1944. Brigadier General Cushman (7 December 1943) relieved General Lewie G. Merritt on 16 May 1943 as CG of Fourth Marine Base Defense Aircraft Wing and remained in that post until August 1944. In addition to his three USMC groups he also commanded Navy Fighter Squadron VF-39. At this post he directed his command in the saturation bombing of the bypassed Marshall Islands. In November 1944 he became Air Defense Commander of the Marianas Islands, remaining until April 1945. It was during this latter period that he was awarded a Legion of Merit and a Bronze Star.

In April he was ordered back to the States and in the following months he assumed duties as CG of Cherry Point, with additional duty as Deputy Commander, Marine Corps Air Bases. In September 1946 he assumed full responsibility, serving in that capacity until March 1947, then became CoS, Aircraft, FMF, Pacific, from May to July 1947. Followed by Deputy Commander of FMF, Pacific, August 1947 to May 1949, then Air, FMF Pacific and First MAW June 1949 to July 1950.

That month he was named Assistant Wing Commander, First MAW, then the CG from May until August 1951 serving in Korea. During this period he was retroactively promoted to major general dated back to 7 June 1944. Major General Cushman returned to the States where he commanded Aircraft, FMF, Atlantic, and then the Second MAW at Cherry Point, NC. Then he was Deputy Commander of FMF, Pacific 1953–1954. He was promoted to lieutenant general upon retirement in February 1954.

Decorations included the Distinguished Service Medal, two Legions of Merit (one with Combat V and a Gold Star for the second) and the Bronze Star. USA Distinguished Unit Emblem, Marine Corps Expeditionary Medal; World War I Victory Medal; Second Nicaraguan Campaign Medal; various World War I campaign medals; the Korean Service Medal and the United Nations Medal.

Lieutenant General Thomas J. Cushman died at Corona del Mar, CA in July 1972.

DeCarre, Major General Alphonse was born on 15 November 1892, in Washington D.C. He was, however, on 15 November 1913 appointed a second lieutenant of

Marines from Missouri. His first service, beginning on 29 November, was at the MOS, Norfolk, VA. DeCarre managed to be a member of a class that included a number of future World War II generals; among the group, Louis Larsen, Bill Rupertus, Hal Turnage, Matt Kingman, Sam Howard and Lyle Miller were some notables. Alphonse joined the 1st Brigade of Marines (ABF) at the Philadelphia Navy Yard on 30 June 1915 and on 15 August he began his first tour of overseas duty when the Brigade was transferred to Haiti. On 2 December 1916 he joined the MD aboard the *New York*, serving there briefly until he and his men were landed at Oriente, Cuba, in 1916, remaining there until early 1917.

As war approached, First Lieutenant DeCarre (29 August 1916) was, like so many other wartime officers, promoted quickly to captain, the latter rank being attained on 26 March 1917. It would be a permanent promotion, which was unusual for those times. He was transferred to Quantico in April 1917 and his next assignment was to command the Headquarters Company of the developing Fifth Regiment of Marines. The 5th was then gathering at the new Marine base and soon would be on its way to France. With it he served in France from July 1917 to March 1919.

At the Battle for Belleau Wood, on 11 June 1918, he led his company into the woods and captured two machine guns and crews practically single-handed, then with the rest of his company, captured an enemy machine gun company of 180 officers and men. For this achievement he earned a U.S. Army Distinguished Service Cross plus a Silver Star citation. Incidentally, he was the only officer to lead his company in the correct direction on that day.

Major DeCarre's (1 July 1918) other activities in France, especially at Blanc Mont, earned him the French Legion of Honor and a Croix de Guerre with Palm. He served in the Meuse River campaign, then with the Brigade in the occupation of Germany, and returned home in March 1919.

After a brief leave, beginning on 27 October 1919, his next assignment was with the MB, Philadelphia Navy Yard. He, like so many others at this time, was reduced to his permanent rank of captain. On 28 July 1920 he was transferred to HQMC and to Peking, China, on 25 January 1922 to serve with the Marine Legation Guard, a choice assignment for any Marine. In January 1924 he left China and on 24 February arrived at the Marine Corps Base, San Diego but was back at MB, Quantico, on 25 May 1925 and the following year, on 28 June 1926, he began a course at the NWC, Newport, RI. Having graduated, the following 5 June 1927 he was once again at the MB, Navy Yard, Philadelphia.

On 12 March 1928 he was promoted to major. In the interim period he had graduated from two courses at MCS, the Junior course, and the Field Officers' course at Quantico. He had also received the newly created Navy Cross as an adjunct award for

Alphonse DeCarre

his DSC. On 1 July DeCarre was transferred for duty with the 2d Brigade of Marines in Nicaragua but before he could take up those duties, was reassigned as FMO aboard the *Wyoming*, part of the Scouting Fleet. Two years later, on 23 June 1930, he was back at MB, San Diego and on 31 August 1931 at the MB, Quantico.

Arriving in Haiti on 23 May 1933 he spent exactly one year when he became Lt.Col. DeCarre on 29 May 1934. This was followed with the complete withdrawal of Marines from the unhappy land on 15 August. The following 8 February 1935 he was at MB, Norfolk Navy Yard and on 29 May 1936 was back at HQMC. In the meantime, he had picked up a newly created Purple Heart medal. One year later, as of 10 June 1937, he was again at MB, San Diego. In June 1939, Col. DeCarre (5 September 1938) assumed duties as CO, of the Naval Prison at Portsmouth, NH.

On 21 June 1941 he assumed command of the MB at Puget Sound, Washington State, remaining there until July 1942. Brigadier General DeCarre (retro to 22 March 1942) was assigned to the post of ADC of the 2dMarDiv which was in the process of being dispatched to Guadalcanal. DeCarre led the advanced guard as acting CG while MG John Marston remained in New Zealand. Marston was senior to the USA MG Alexander McC. Patch, who it was decided would command the balance of that island campaign. It was one of several times and situations when the Marines would defer to the U.S. Army to "sweeten" relationships. DeCarre, nonetheless, remained in command of all Marine ground units in the continuing campaign. This was his major contribution during World War II. He was quoted later as saying "I did my part in the last war." I have not been able to locate his assignments between 1943 and 1946. DeCarre was promoted to major general upon retirement in June 1946.

DeCarre's decorations included the Navy Cross and the U.S. Army DSC, a Distinguished Service Medal (I cannot locate a record for that), Silver Star and Purple Heart. He was also awarded a Croix de Guerre, Palm, from France. Other campaign medals included both World War I and World War II campaign and Victory medals, plus Haitian and Nicaraguan expeditionary medals.

Brigadier General Alphonse DeCarre died on 3 May 1977.

DEL VALLE, **Lieutenant General Pedro Augusto** was born on 28 August 1893, in San Jose, Puerto Rico. His father, a medical doctor and also mayor of the city, was a Spanish government official when the Spanish-American War was fought. He, however, accepted American supremacy and became a U.S. citizen. Pedro was also appointed, and graduated from the Naval Academy at Annapolis in 1915, accepting a commission as a second lieutenant of Marines on 5 June 1915. After MOS at Norfolk, VA, he served with the 1st Provisional

Pedro Augusto del Valle

Marine Brigade in Haiti. Upon arrival he was assigned to the 9th Artillery Company and served in command of a section of three-inch naval landing guns. Trouble was concurrently brewing in Santo Domingo and in May 1916, now First Lieutenant del Valle (4 January 1916) participated in the capture of Santo Domingo City. His knowledge of the Spanish language was of great assistance to Major General Pendleton, Pedro serving him briefly as his interpreter.

Capt. del Valle's (26 March 1917) next berth was as the "skipper" (CO) of the MD aboard the *Texas*, which served with the British Grand Fleet off the coast of Europe during World War I and participated in the surrender of the German Grand Fleet. In February 1919 he was at Quantico as adjutant of the 10th Marines, an artillery regiment. Next was a brief but, according to him, unhappy period at the Dover, NJ Naval Ordnance Depot in command of the MB. He was then assigned to sea duty aboard the *Wyoming* as CO of the MD. His work was cut out for him as he found the detachment and its senior noncom less than adequate, but he successfully brought the detachment back into "shape."

Still assigned to *Wyoming*, he served again as Aide-de-Camp to MG Joseph H. Pendleton between 1923 and 1924 in the general's tour of the West Indies. In 1924, at BG Paymaster George Richards' personal request, del Valle was transferred to his office. That training gave him a strong background in administrative details that would serve him well for the next two dozen years. During 1926 he was offered the opportunity to go to Peking as paymaster, or to the *Gendarmerie d'Haiti*. For personal reasons he selected the latter.

Pedro remained on this assignment until August 1928, after which he attended the Field Officers' course at MCS, Quantico. Upon graduation he became an instructor there. His next assignment was in Nicaragua. During service with the Second Brigade of Marines he helped to oversee the Electoral Mission in Nicaragua. Major del Valle (1 June 1929) remained in Nicaragua until November 1930 and then returned, with the same duties, between January 1931 to July 1933. In 1933 he was once again aboard ship, this time the cruiser *Richmond*, as part of the *Special Service Squadron* plying their trade off Latin America. Part of this time was spent in Cuba during a revolution; subsequent liquidation of the Platt Amendment; and the security of American lives, plus their property. The following year, 8 October 1934, Lt.Col. del Valle (29 May 1934) was back at HQMC.

At his own request, he was transferred to the Navy Department and assigned duty as Assistant Naval Attaché in Rome, October 1935 to June 1937. While on this duty he requested permission to march with and observe the Italian army invading Ethiopia. He later wrote a commercial book on the subject as well as writing his observations for the Navy. It became the background of serious problems for him in later years.

Back in the U.S. he graduated from AWC in June 1938. Between 23 June 1938 and 1941, he served in the operations and training division at HQMC. Meanwhile, he was promoted to colonel on 1 June 1939. Effective 19 April 1941 Col. del Valle he was with the newly forming 1stMarDiv in Cuba as a regimental commander. His command, the 11th Marines, the artillery regiment of that distinguished division, would be the beginning of his lengthy association with the same division, and eventually as CG.

In 1942, the division began its haul to the far western Pacific. They arrived in New Zealand and began training after the long stretch at sea. He was with the 11th when the landing on Guadalcanal took place on 7 August 1942, and remained all during that difficult campaign. The division returned for R & R to Australia but Pedro was soon after sent back as commander of all Marine units in the Solomon Islands. Brigadier General del Valle (15 September 1942) was badly hurt in an airplane accident and returned to the U.S. in 1943. After recovery, he was returned to the Pacific to train and lead the artillery of the newly formed III Amphibious Corps in the retaking of the island of Guam in July 1944.

Upon his return to the island of Pavuvu in the Russell Islands, Major General del Valle (10 January 1944) assumed command of the now badly beaten 1stMarDiv. At Peleliu, the previous CG and some regimental commanders had nearly destroyed its effectiveness. Pedro had the difficult job of turning it back into the first class unit it once had been. For various reasons, it wasn't an easy task.

The division's next trial was Okinawa. Under his command, the 1stMarDiv landed and in three days conquered what planners had allowed a month for. Nonetheless, the battle was long and proved what the Americans could expect would be their real danger when they landed in Japan proper. Fortunately, the war was over before that happened and del Valle went home.

His role after the war was to be the first Marine Corps Inspector-General and to ensure the smooth mustering out of all Marines. He did so well that for a brief time he became Personnel Director, and was slated to become Commander-in-Chief, FMF, Pacific in 1948. However, he instead selected retirement and promotion to lieutenant general on 1 January 1948.

His decorations included the Distinguished Service Medal, Legion of Merit (Guadalcanal), and a Gold Star Guam), and the Navy and Marine Corps Medal for his services in Ethiopia, plus numerous campaign medals; including World War I and World War II plus the expeditionary medal for Haiti, Dominican Republic, Nicaragua, and a number of foreign, especially Italian, decorations.

Lieutenant General Pedro A. del Valle died in Annapolis, MD, on 28 April 1978.

DENIG, Brigadier General Robert Livingston was born in Clinton, New York, on 29 September 1884. He attended the University of Pennsylvania between 1903 and 1905 and accepted his commission as a second lieutenant of Marines on 29 September 1905. His immediate assignment was to the MOS, but within the month that was interrupted by temporary duty with the First Provisional Regiment of Marines in Cuba. His CO was Capt. William C. Harllee and they landed at Nuevitas on 30 September 1906. Harllee and the majority of the company, two officers and 102 men, went by train to Camaguey, but 2dLt Denig and the balance of the detachment remained behind at Nuevitas. On or about 22 October, Harllee and Denig and about 598 other officers and enlisted Marines returned to the States.

Completing his education at the MOS, after graduation he began his first cruise with the MD aboard the *Missouri* on 17 November 1907, lasting until December 1909. While aboard he became First Lieutenant Denig on 14 May 1908. From 23 December 1909 he was on duty at the MB, Annapolis, MD but on 30 October 1911 he arrived for recruiting duty at St. Paul, MN.

His next service "beyond the seas" was to Olongapo, Philippine Islands, arriving at the MB on 19 July 1913 and at which post he remained until 14 January 1916. His first assignment upon arrival in the States, after a leave, was to the MB at Philadelphia on 3 May 1916, after which, on 29 August 1916, he was Capt. Denig.

Selected to join the newly forming 5th Marine Regiment for service in France with the AEF, Major Denig (22 May 1917) shipped out with the regiment in June 1917 to France, arriving on 27 June 1917. He remained with the regiment as it later joined with the 6th Marine Regiment and the 6th Machine Gun Battalion to become the 4th Brigade of Marines and as part of the 2d Infantry Division (Regulars). When the 3d Infantry Division arrived in France, it was short of senior officers with experience and five Marine majors, Denig included, were selected to join their ranks. He was assigned to command the 1st Battalion, 30th Infantry.

Army men with those field ranks, which had been in short supply, soon became available to the AEF and Denig was one of two Marines reassigned back to the 4th Brigade. He was briefly with the 5th Marines, and then for a short time commanded the 2d Battalion, 6th Marine Regiment at Soissons in July 1918. Though newly promoted to lieutenant colonel and assistant regimental commander, Thomas Holcomb, the former CO of 2/6 at his personal request, was reassigned to command 2/6. Denig remained as his assistant during that awful 19 July assault.

Following Soissons, Denig was then on 30 July 1918 assigned to command the 3d Battalion, 9th Infantry, part of the 2d Division. On 12 September he led his battalion forward at St. Mihiel on the extreme right flank of the 2d Division. With this regiment he made a name for himself on 3 October 1918 in the assault on Medeah Farm, at Blanc Mont. Though wounded, he refused to be evacuated and remained in command until the objective was taken. For that he was awarded a Distinguished Service Cross, and later a Navy Cross. He continued to command 3/9 until returning to the States just after the Armistice in November 1918. After a brief leave on 27 December 1918 he arrived at the MB, New York, NY.

Soon after, 24 January 1919, he was assigned to duty in Quartermaster's Department and relocated to the MB, Navy Yard, Philadelphia, PA, arriving on 7 February 1919. In the same capacity on 4 February 1920 he moved to the MB, Portsmouth Navy Yard, NH. On 16 October 1921 he was transferred to MB, New York City. On duty with the QM Department there, on 3 April 1922 he went to duty with the Second Brigade of Marines in Santo Domingo. In December 1923 he was reassigned to HQMC. This staff duty terminated in March 1924 and on 25 June he was transferred to the MB, Quantico. From there he graduated the Field Officers' course, MCS.

On 13 November 1929 he was assigned duty in Nicaragua with the *Guardia Nacional*. His rank with the GN was as a lieutenant colonel. He led at least one patrol of the *Guardia* and that was on 31 October 1930 when they met with "bandits" near Ciudad Antigua; no casualties were reported. During the earthquake in Managua on 31 March 1931, Denig's right leg was fractured. In April 1931 he returned to HQMC and was promoted to lieutenant colonel on 1 October. On 1 May 1933 he reported to Quantico for additional schooling.

Col. Denig (25 November 1934) assumed command of the Naval Prison, Portsmouth, NH, on 28 May 1936, remaining there until he was transferred to command the MB, Pearl Harbor, Hawaiian Islands in July 1939. The following year, June 1940, he was at Bremerton, Washington. On 30 June 1941 the Examining Board, at HQMC, allowed him to retire with the rank of brigadier general.

The coming war altered his status, however. He was retained at rank as Director of Marine Corps public relations. He is quoted as asking "What in Hell is public relations?" and was told by his friend, MGC Thomas Holcomb, "You had better learn about it because that is what you are going to be." The informal nickname his subordinates adopted for themselves was "Denig's Demons." It mainly pertained to the Combat Correspondents who served extremely well in the war zone between 1941 and 1945. They told the story of the Corps in action, writing and taking photos on the spot when the action was happening and Denig spread the good word around. After the war's end, Denig retired again in December 1945.

Denig's decorations included the Distinguished Service Cross, Navy Cross,

Legion of Merit and two Purple Hearts. His numerous campaign and expeditionary medals included those for service in Cuba, the Philippines, Santo Domingo, Nicaragua and of course France. He was the recipient of Victory Medals for World War I and World War II plus the latter campaign medals.

Brigadier General Robert L. Denig died on 25 July 1979.

EDSON, Major General Merritt Austin was born on 25 April 1897, in Rutland, VT, and raised in nearby Chester. He attended the University of Vermont from 1915 to 1916 and, as a member of the National Guard, was called to active duty on the Mexican border. Upon his return, he attended classes through the spring of 1917. When war was declared he applied for and was commissioned a temporary second lieutenant of Marines on 15 September 1917. His first posting was at the Parris Island MOS. In 1918 he was assigned to the newly formed 130th Company (later changed to "B" Company) of the 11th Marines as part of the 5th Marine Brigade. His company was an artillery unit, even though the balance of the regiment was then an infantry organization. First Lieutenant Edson (1 July 1918) and his regiment arrived in France on 13 October 1918. The 5th Brigade was too late to get into action against the German army and the officers and men were assigned various "housekeeping" tasks. Following the war he volunteered to serve in the newly created 15th Separate Battalion. Composed of various AEF organizations, it was tasked with maintaining the peace in Schleswig-Holstein during a plebiscite to be held in 1919. Trouble never came, and all members were returned to the United States in December 1919. Almost as his feet touched home soil he was assigned to the MB, Philadelphia Navy Yard; that, however, was modified to MB, Quantico, at which post he arrived on the 30th of December.

Upon his return there was a great shape-up going on (both the Russell, then the Neville, committees) and Edson had made a decision to terminate his commission and leave the Corps. Higher-ups, however, decided he was to remain and wrote letters of recommendation for him. Consequently he changed his mind and was assigned duty at Quantico and volunteered to teach math at the newly created Vocational School, a favorite of MGC John A. Lejeune. He also began shooting seriously, which made his future quite secure, since the Corps was heavy on marksmanship and looked kindly on officers and men who were good at it.

Another rather new innovation, aviation, took his fancy and he made efforts to succeed as a flyer. He went to the NAS at Pensacola, FL on 28 December 1921 and became a designated Naval Aviator on 12 June 1922. He went on expeditionary duty to Guam with Scouting Squadron 1 (VS-1M) on 3 January 1923, remaining there until July 1925. In the meantime, on 4 June 1920 the several committees finalized their differences and he, along with many other officers retained, were made permanent in their ranks. On 28 September he was at the MB, Quantico.

In a course at the U.S. Army's Advanced Flying School, Kelly Field, TX, in March 1926 he was discovered to have problems with depth perception. That effectively ended any career in aviation. Returning to Quantico, he was assigned to the Company Officers' course. Upon graduation he went sea-going in December 1927 aboard the cruiser *Denver* as detachment commander. Capt. Edson's (21 December 1927) ship was part of the *Special Service Squadron* and ruled the waves about Panama and Nicaragua. On 28 June 1928 he was serving aboard the cruiser *Rochester*, the flagship of the squadron.

At this time, Nicaragua was in a constant state of upset with what the Marines called "bandits," and Marines were doing their best to flatten the foe. Edson was selected, at his own urging, to create a river patrol to block any guerrilla adventures in eastern Nicaragua. The Coco River ran from the western mountains to the east coast and was an excellent highway for travelers in Nicaragua, east to west or vice versa. During many boat trips, Edson and his men used the waterway to interfere with "General" Augusto Sandino's depredations and the lessons learned became the bible for jungle-type warfare. Edson wrote a series of articles for the *Marine Corps Gazette* about his experiences and was awarded a Navy Cross for his services during those river patrols.

He returned to the U.S. in August 1929 and on 3 September assumed duties at the MB, Philadelphia Navy Yard. Once again he took up shooting in earnest. On 15 June 1931 he transferred to the Depot of Supplies, also based at Philadelphia. Major Edson (9 February 1936) was jumped over numerous officers with seniority and was assigned duty at HQMC on 30 April 1936.

Soon after he was assigned to attend the Senior course at MCS, Quantico.

Upon graduation his next tour of duty was with the 4th Marines at Shanghai, at which post he arrived on 19 June 1937. He was assigned as plans and training officer. The regimental commander was his old friend and battalion commander in France, Col. Charles F.B. Price. He experienced the turmoil of 1937 when the Japanese Navy and Army invaded China and fought the Chinese forces in Shanghai. He was also there when the Japanese sank the *Panay*, a period when the U.S. and Japan came very close to war. He and his family left China in May 1939 and he arrived at HQMC in June that year. His first assignment was to write a new *Small Wars Manual*. He also went back to shooting.

Lt.Col. Edson (1 April 1940) received a visitor, Capt. Victor Krulak, an aide to BG Holland McT. Smith, the new CG of the 1stMarDiv, on 27 May 1941. Smith (under pressure from President Franklin D. Roosevelt, who was under pressure from Prime Minister Winston Churchill) wanted him to form the 1st Raider Battalion out of the 1st Battalion, 5th Marines. This was to be an American "commando" unit. Edson accepted, then formed, trained and commanded the battalion from 7 June 1941 to September 1942 on Guadalcanal. He earned the Medal of Honor for his leadership of the defense of the Henderson airfield on the night of 13–14 September 1942. He was also awarded a second Navy Cross for his successes on Tulagi (the first earned by his work in Nicaragua).

Col. Edson (21 May 1942), again retroactively, was promoted to full colonel and on 1 December 1943 pushed ahead of officers with seniority when he became a brigadier general. He was transferred to the 2dMarDiv as ADC to MG Julian Smith and fought with it at Tarawa. Smith hurt himself and was replaced by MG Thomas E. Watson, which displeased Edson and

Merritt Austin Edson

prompted him to request a transfer. He was selected as the new CoS in Hawaii and the person to be between Holland Smith and Admiral Chester Nimitz in planning for the Okinawa invasion.

He was one of the first senior Marine officers to return after the war and landed in Washington just as the senior officers of the U.S. Army were trying to force amalgamation of the Corps with the Army. Although Edson jumped in feet first, he quickly realized that he was probably not going to be promoted and decided that he would retire and be able to speak his mind in any collisions between the two services and Congress. He retired as major general on 1 August 1947 and soon after was selected to appear before the Congress where he was well received.

His awards were numerous and included, besides the Medal of Honor and two Navy Crosses, the Silver Star and two Legions of Merit with Gold Star. General Edson also earned numerous campaign medals including those from Nicaragua and China, Victory medals from both World War I and World War II, various World War II campaign medals with six bronze stars, and the Distinguished Service Order from Great Britain, for his part in the retaking of the Tarawa atoll.

After retiring, he held several Vermont state positions. Most importantly he was the first Commissioner of the State Police, creating that new body of police along military lines. His final role was that as Executive Director of the National Rifle Association and his part as Navy representative on the Defense Advisory Committee on Prisoner of War Problems.

He died at home in Vermont on 14 August 1955 of carbon monoxide poisoning. Major General Edson was truly a splendid Marine and has been greatly missed.

ERSKINE, General Graves Blanchard, born on 28 June 1897 in Columbia, Louisiana, attended Louisiana State University. When war with Germany broke out in April 1917 he was an enlisted man in the Louisiana National Guard and had seen service on the Mexican border. Erskine applied for and was commissioned a second lieutenant of Marines on 21 May 1917 but actually dated effective on 15 August 1917. However, the following day, 16 August, he was promoted to first lieutenant. He spent a brief period at a MOS, Parris Island, SC. Then he transferred to Quantico where he was assigned to the newly formed 6th Marine Regiment.

In January 1918 he sailed for France as a platoon leader in the 79th Company, 2d Battalion, 6th Marines. He saw service at Verdun and Belleau Wood, where he was wounded leading his platoon to Bouresches on the 6th of June. Back in harness in late June, he next saw war as a captain at Soissons, somehow managing to survive the 19

Graves Blanchard Erskine

July bloodbath. Then in mid–September he fought at St. Mihiel where he had been leading a conglomerate of headquarters and intelligence men when he was once again wounded and hauled out of the battle over Pvt. Archie Vale's shoulder. For St. Mihiel he received two Silver Star citations, which later became a Silver Star medal. Because of the second wound, in October 1918 he was evacuated back to the United States where he continued to be briefly hospitalized. On 12 November 1918 he was transferred to the MB, Norfolk, Navy Yard. During that period he, like so many other temporary promotions, was reduced to first lieutenant.

On 25 August 1920, he went to recruiting duty at Kansas City, MO. On 4 June that year Erskine was one of numerous promotions to captain and was briefly assigned duty with the First Provisional Brigade in Haiti, returning to the States in July 1921. On 27 September 1921 he began his first seagoing cruise in command of the MD aboard the cruiser *Olympia*. This duty required him to organize the Honor Guard that returned the body of the Unknown Soldier, directly up the Potomac River to Washington D.C.

On 19 October 1922 he was assigned duty with the Quartermaster's Department and on 7 November was sent to the Second Brigade of Marines in Santo Domingo. This was followed by duty as Depot QM at the MB, Quantico, beginning in September 1924. On 6 September 1926 he attended the Army Infantry School, Fort Benning, GA and after graduation on 23 June 1927 was assigned teaching duties at MCS, Quantico, as Instructor in the Department of Tactics.

His next overseas assignment was to Nicaragua, where he joined the Second Marine Brigade in March 1928. Three months later he was assigned to the *Guardia Nacional* in which he led small bands of *Guardia* searching for guerrillas belonging to Sandino's army. He was returned to the U.S. on 23 June 1930 to teach at the Basic School, MB, Philadelphia. On 13 August 1932 he arrived at Fort Leavenworth to begin a course of study and was promoted to Major Erskine (31 March 1934) as he was preparing to graduate the C&GSS. He taught in the 1 and 2 Sections, MCS, Quantico, following which came the choice appointment to the MD, Legation Guard, Peiping, China, arriving on 1 January 1935.

He served as EO of the embassy guard at Peking until 21 June 1937 and while there became lieutenant colonel on 1 March 1936. "Bobby" Erskine returned to Quantico to begin a three-year assignment as section chief at MCS and on 1 March 1941 was promoted to full colonel. In the interim he had briefly served as EO of the 5th Marines, and before the U.S. entered World War II, he was CoS, Amphibious Force, Atlantic Fleet. In September 1942 he joined the Amphibious Corps, Pacific Fleet, in San Diego as CoS and performed duty in Alaska in July and August 1943.

Erskine assumed duties as CoS of the 5th Amphibious Corps and in November 1943 was retroactively Brigadier General Erskine (19 September 1942), the youngest in the Marine Corps. He was also assigned as Deputy Commander of V Amphibious Corps. For meritorious service at Kwajalein, Saipan, and Tinian, he received two Legion of Merit awards, both with combat "V." Major General Erskine (September 1944) assumed command of the 3dMarDiv in October, leading it in the invasion of Iwo Jima. For this he was awarded the Distinguished Service Medal. After the battle, and when the division was back in a rest zone, he also started vocational training schools for his Marines in order to facilitate those going back to civilian life.

At war's end, he received an unusual appointment in October 1945; as a "civilian" Administrator of the newly formed Retraining and Re-employment Administration. This was based upon his pro-active services for his Marines going back into civilian life. In June 1947 he requested return to the Marine Corps and assumed command of Camp Pendleton, CA; when the 1stMarDiv returned from China, he became their new CG. In 1949 an added task was as Deputy Commander of FMF, Pacific, with headquarters in Hawaii. For a time he went back and forth between the islands and California.

Following this, for a three-month period, he was on special duty in Southeast Asia as Chief, Military Group, in a State Department exercise. Then he was CG, Department of the Pacific in 1950. In 1951 now Lieutenant General Erskine became CG, FMF Atlantic and by a special act of Congress he was authorized to retire as general in June 1953 and to accept a civilian post as assistant to the Secretary of Defense.

In addition to the awards mentioned above, he also received two awards of the Legion of Merit, both with combat "V." They were issued for exceptionally meritorious service during the assault and capture of Kwajalein; and the second for the same reasons while taking Saipan and Tinian. He was also awarded both Victory Medals, World War I and World War II, plus the campaign medals with bronze stars. His role in Haiti, in Santo Domingo and in Nicaragua brought forth those expeditionary medals and a China service medal.

General Graves B. Erskine died on 21 May 1973.

FARRELL, Major General Walter Greatsinger was born on 4 June 1897, in San Francisco, CA and raised in Chicago. He attended the University of Illinois, and while there served as an enlisted man in the Illinois National Guard. Later he joined the Marine Corps as an enlisted man and was in the Marine Corps Reserve between 1916 and 1917. He accepted a commission as a second lieutenant of Marines effective on 15 September 1917 and was promoted to first lieutenant on 1 July 1918. He went overseas to France on 26 August 1918 and arrived at the tail end of the St. Mihiel campaign when he was assigned as a platoon leader in the 51st Company, 2/5.

Farrell's first combat was at the assault upon the heights at Blanc Mont in early October 1918. He had been appointed EO of the Company and remained so through the campaign along the Meuse River. He served on Occupation Duty in Germany and was returned to the States in April 1919. After a leave, Farrell decided to make the Marine Corps his career.

First responsibility was as CO of the 53d Company, First Provisional Brigade of Marines in Haiti, arriving there on 24 August 1919. He was immediately put to active duty as a platoon leader going after Cacos. After the assassination of Charlemagne Peralte by Hanneken and Button, Farrell led one of the trail-blocking patrols to engage and destroy the fleeing Cacos. His activities in Haiti kept him and his Marines quite busy for many months afterward. During this tour he became interested in, and applied for aviation training.

His next move was in November 1920 when he was assigned as a student flyer at Pensacola NAS, FL. Having successfully completed his training in 1921 he was designated a naval aviator and then assigned to what became known as Brown Field at Quantico, arriving on 16 September 1921. On 1 March 1923 he was back in Haiti, serving a year until transferred to HQMC, arriving on 11 April 1924.

On 15 September 1926 Farrell attended the U.S. Army Tactical School, Langley Field, VA. Upon graduation, Capt. Farrell (14 April 1927) arrived for duty at the NAS, San Diego, for further flying duties in November. One year and one month later he arrived at the MB, Guam and in December 1929 he went back to the States and began serving with the Department of the Pacific. In February he took some leave and reported for duty at HQMC. On 10 May 1930 he was detached for duty with the Bureau of Aeronautics, USN. On 27 June 1933 he attended the NWC, Newport, RI, graduating the following year. He saw some foreign duty aboard the *Lexington* as commanding officer of VS-14M from 3 July 1934 until 15 November when he transferred to the NAS, San Diego.

Major Farrell (1 October 1935) was an instructor from 27 March 1937 at MCS at Quantico, and on 14 August 1939 he received another promotion: to lieutenant colonel. In June 1940 he assumed duty with the Second MAG in San Diego. From there he next became the Assistant Naval Attaché in London on 16 July 1941, remaining in that post until 18 September 1941. Farrell, along with six other Marine officers, had been sent to study RAF operations. He served in the Mideast, based out of Cairo, like so many other American officers had, and then went back to the U.S.

Col. Farrell (20 May 1942) was again promoted, following which he was made CoS of the Second Aircraft Wing in July 1942. When the wing went to Guadalcanal in February 1943, he accompanied them and stayed as CoS until November 1943 and was decorated with the Silver Star for "conspicuous gallantry and intrepidity" while there. Farrell was returned to the U.S. that month, following which in 1944 he became Commander of MAG 32, Hawaiian Area. Brigadier General Farrell (25 November 1943) was then Deputy Commander of the 1st MAW based in Tientsin in early 1946, followed by deputy commander of Naval Air Bases in the Eleventh Naval District, then CG of the Third MAW from 8 May to January 1946. He requested retirement and was promoted to major general in November 1946.

His decorations included the Silver Star and Bronze Star plus the World War I and World War II Victory and campaign medals and several expeditionary medals including those for Haiti.

At age 93, Major General Walter G. Farrell died in San Diego on 11 October 1990 and was buried at Fort Rosecrans Memorial Cemetery.

Walter Greatsinger Farrell

FEGAN, Major General Joseph Charles was born on 6 November 1886, in Dallas, TX. He accepted a commission as a second lieutenant of Marines on 6 January 1909 and was assigned to the MOS, Port Royal, SC on 8 February 1909. He was quickly diverted to Nicaragua to gain an education and to "help" during another revolution against Zelaya, the president. Fegan also served with Butler's battalion in Panama between 1909 and 1910, and upon return in April 1910 was assigned duty at the Naval Prison, Portsmouth, NH. From there, on 15 September 1911, he went aboard the *Florida* to serve with the MD, which posting terminated on 7 January 1913. First Lieutenant Fegan's (3 January 1913) next station was at the MB, Washington D.C. following which he spent a brief period "pacifying" Cuba during 1913. He went with the 2d Provisional Brigade, under the command of Col. "Uncle Joe" Pendleton, from Philadelphia on 20 February to forestall another revolution in Guantánamo City, returning on 30 April. On 25 June 1913, he was assigned to duty at the Naval Disciplinary Barracks, Puget Sound, Washington State and the following 14 April 1914 he was on duty at the Receiving Ship, same station.

His next post was overseas at the MB, Olongapo, the Philippines, on 6 January 1916. Capt. Fegan (29 August 1916) was back in the U.S. in September 1918. Soon Major Fegan (1 July 1918) was at the MB, Navy Yard, Boston, MA, from 5 December 1918. On 11 August 1919, he was transferred to the Recruiting Office, Los Angeles, CA, and his majority was made permanent on 4 June 1920. On 14 September 1921 he was back at the MB, Quantico.

Next overseas duty, on 16 April 1923, was with the Second Marine Brigade in Santo Domingo. The newly elected provisional government had taken power and the Marines were greatly restricted in their activities. The newly created 1st Regiment's (from the 3d Marine Regiment) job was to serve as back-up to the Marine organized and trained *Policia Nacional Dominicana*. On 30 August 1924 Fegan assumed a brief role at the MB, Mare Island, CA, followed by lengthy service at HQMC, beginning on 3 September 1924.

On 21 April 1929 he arrived in Haiti and took service with the Constabulary Detachment, *Garde d'Haiti*. He was there when the student strikes broke out in October and spread nationwide in early December. The constabulary was, of course, very busy during this period. What his role (if any) might have been in the "infamous" U.S. Marine massacre of civilians on 6 December, isn't known. What is known is that the members of the *Garde* were definitely siding with the students against the Marines and government. The revolt became very violent with students seriously threatening Dr. George F. Freeman, American head of the school *Service Technique* after he recommended cuts in student aid.

In June 1932 Fegan arrived back in the States and took leave. On the following 14 July he was at Quantico, and one year later at HQMC in Washington. In the meantime, Lt.Col. Fegan (29 May 1934) had graduated from the MCS Field Officers' Senior course. Now Col. Fegan (30 June 1936) attended and graduated from the NWC Senior course in Newport, RI. On 20 May 1937 he returned to HQMC, remaining there until his next foreign service.

He arrived at Shanghai on 23 September 1938 to command the 4th Marines. This was a time when this regiment was undergoing severe reductions in personnel. Relations with the Japanese invaders of China became a series of provocations for all occidentals and the U.S. Marines were no exception. Like his predecessors and successors, Fegan managed to avoid any serious

Joseph Charles Fegan

altercations with the constantly pushing Japanese. He did, however, continue to write letters of detailed information regarding the situation, which MGC Thomas Holcomb later said were the best he'd ever gotten. Col. Fegan left China in December 1939 and returned to duty at HQMC, arriving on 15 January 1940.

He was next assigned duty as the Director of Marine Corps Reserve from 16 June 1940 to 6 January 1941. It was during this tour that the Reserves were called up and integrated within the Marine Corps and his part in the process was highly commended. Brigadier General Fegan (7 November 1941, permanent on 1 February 1942) became the first CG of the newly created Camp Pendleton on 1 February 1941. Upon arrival, instead of occupying the CG's house, the old Ranch House, he turned it over to be used as a Marine Officers' Club and ensconced himself in an old bunkhouse in which he remained for the entire period he was there.

President Franklin D. Roosevelt came out to Camp Pendleton for the official dedication in September 1942. Fegan, who had served at Warms Springs, was quite friendly with FDR, and took the president around the camp and later introduced him to a number of retired generals living in the area. Major General Fegan (26 August 1942) regretfully hauled down his two-star flag in May 1944 after twenty months commanding at Pendleton. Next, he was the CG of the Marine Corps Department of the Pacific from May 1944 until his retirement in August 1945. His son, Lt.Gen. Joseph C. Fegan, Jr., was also a Marine.

General Fegan's decorations included (according to the records though I can't locate the citation) the Distinguished Service Medal. Additionally he also received the various expeditionary medals for service in Cuba, Panama, the Philippines, Haiti, Santo Domingo, and China, plus the World War II Victory medal.

Major General Joseph C. Fegan died on 26 May 1949 from injuries suffered in an automobile accident five days earlier.

FELLOWS, Brigadier General Joseph Howard was born on 16 April 1897 in Washington D.C., later attending George Washington University in that city. Fellows enlisted in the Marine Corps Reserve in August 1917 and, appointed from Pennsylvania, he accepted a commission as second lieutenant of Marines dated 15 September 1917. After a brief bit of schooling, his first assignment was as a replacement officer in the 5th Regiment of Marines, arriving in France in March 1918. On 4 May he became a platoon leader in the 20th Company, 3/5, and was seriously wounded in action at Belleau Wood on 11 June. After First Lieutenant Fellows (1 July 1918) was detached from the hospital, he returned to the States in December 1918.

After his return from France, his first foreign duty was in Santo Domingo with the Second Brigade of Marines; he arrived on 2 November 1920. In April 1923 he returned to the States, took leave and on 27 June attended the MCS, Quantico, graduating from the Company Officers' course. Fellows then served as an instructor at MCS from June 1925 to May 1927. His first sea duty was when he went aboard the *Procyon* to serve with the MD on 25 May 1927. This was followed on 12 March 1928 by his promotion to captain.

Capt. Fellows (12 March 1928) joined the 2d Brigade of Marines in Nicaragua on 14 July 1928. This was an intense period during the Marine attempts to bring the guerrilla war to an end. He had spent nearly a year there when he returned to the States in June 1929; on 3 September 1929 he assumed duties at HQMC. On 20 June 1930 he transferred to the Office of the Chief Coordinator, also in D.C., but in the meantime had graduated from the U.S. Army Industrial College that month. On 1

November 1933 he went aboard the cruiser *Indianapolis* where he assumed command of the MD. The Purple Heart medal was issued at that time and he was awarded his. In June 1935 he went ashore and on 3 August assumed duties at Quantico. While there he became Major Fellows on 29 May 1936.

In June 1938 he went for schooling at the NWC, in Newport, graduating from the Senior course in May 1939. On 26 June 1939 he was assigned to the Quartermaster Department at HQMC and on 8 July 1940 was promoted to lieutenant colonel. On 5 May 1942 Col. Fellows (21 May) became Plans Officer for Commander, Service Squadron, South Pacific Area and South Pacific Force. In December 1943 he became executive assistant to the assistant CoS for logistics at Commander in Chief, Pacific Fleet, until December 1945.

During this period, Brigadier General Fellows (9 November 1944) was one of eight Marine officers on board the Battleship *Missouri* present at the signing of the Peace Treaty on 2 September 1945, he representing CinCPAC–CinCPOA. Following the war's end, however, he was reduced to colonel, which rank he retained though his permanent rank was lieutenant colonel and became permanent retroactive to 21 May 1942. He next served as CO of the MB, Charleston Navy Yard, and was retired in June 1949, a 32-year veteran, and promoted to brigadier general retroactive to 11 September 1944.

His decorations included the Legion of Merit, Bronze Star and Purple Heart. Additionally, expeditionary medals for Santo Domingo and Nicaragua, and Victory Medal for World War II.

Brigadier General Joseph H. Fellows died in Martinsburg, WV, on 26 February 1980.

GEIGER, General Roy Stanley was born on 25 January 1885 in Middleburg, FL. He graduated from Florida State Normal and obtained an LL.B. from John B. Stetson University in 1907. Not sure what he wanted to do with his life, he tried practicing law for a couple of months but soon decided that wasn't the life he wanted. For unknown reasons, he enlisted as a private in the Marine Corps on 2 November 1907. After spending a year and three months as an enlisted Marine, on 4 February 1909 he was discharged as a corporal and the following day accepted a commission as a second lieutenant of Marines with rank from 20 January.

He was a member of the first class to attend MOS at Port Royal, SC and at graduation he took a leave for Christmas and then reported to the MD aboard the *Wisconsin*. His ship immediately went into drydock and he was transferred to the *Delaware* which participated in the British Coronation Review in June 1911. On 15 May 1912 he briefly served on recruiting duty in New York City but the Nicaraguan revolution of 1912 "required" services of Marines and he participated with 2d Battalion, Artillery Company E, of the 1st Provisional

Joseph Howard Fellows

Regiment. With it, and their two three-inch guns, on 3 October he helped support the assault up the slopes of Coyotepe Hill. Subsequently, he was one of the Marines selected to remain in Nicaragua as a member of the new Legation Guard under skipper, Capt. Robert O. Underwood.

This duty lasted but a few months: He was transferred to Camp Elliott in Panama and on 20 March 1913 he was aboard the *Buffalo* headed for the MB at Mare Island, CA. But that too was brief, just about a month. His next assignment was with the 2d Regiment, 1st Marine Brigade at the Cavite Navy Yard in the Philippine Islands. For some reason, that detail only lasted a few months; next, beginning on 19 July 1913, he was with the Marine Legation Guard, Peking, China. That lasted a bit longer with him remaining there until January 1916.

First Lieutenant Geiger (16 May 1916) decided to try a new adventure: His next assignment was as an aviator trainee at Pensacola NAS, arriving there on 31 March 1916. Capt. Geiger (29 August 1916) was designated Naval Aviator #49, (USMC Aviator # 5) in June 1917 and on 15 December 1917 was designated CO of the Aeronautic Detachment at the Philadelphia Navy Yard but that command was transferred to the Marine Flying Field at Miami. The unit was now designated the First Marine Aviation Force which Major Geiger (1 July 1918) next led to Brest, France, arriving on 12 July 1918.

Soon after arrival in France, Marine air units were altered in name and scope. His next command was of Squadron A, 1st Marine Aviation Force in France. It was soon known as the Marine Day Wing of the Northern Bombing Group, with a relationship with the U.S. Navy flying units and the British R.A.F. His squadron soon became Number Seven and flew bombing runs over German positions, mainly in northern France and Belgium. Soon after the war, he and his flyers were returned to the U.S. on 12 January 1919, and for his meritorious service while "over there," Geiger was awarded a Navy Cross.

After a brief leave he was, like so many other officers, reduced to his permanent rank of captain. Upon return from France, his first foreign duty was on 27 November 1919 as CO, 4th Squadron, attached to the 1st Provisional Brigade in Haiti. The squadron assisted in breaking up the rebellion led by Peralte. On 22 September 1920, dated back to 5 June, he returned to his rank of major. He was ordered back to the U.S., arriving in early January 1921. After a leave, on 19 February 1921 he was on duty at the MB, Quantico. His next assignment: the Office of the Judge Advocate General of the U.S. Navy as of 21 April 1921.

His next command was entitled the 1st Aviation Group, based at Brown Field, Quantico. This was when the base commander, BG Smedley D. Butler, was using the Marines to "re-fight" Civil War battles. Butler, pre-dating most military men, also utilized air to support the campaigns and

Roy Stanley Geiger

Geiger's pilots were getting training in ground-air support services. At this time Geiger's unit consisted of half of the entire Marine Corps aviation section.

He managed to renew his flight duty in July 1922, avoiding the then usual USMC policy of airmen returning to the ground troops. During this extended period he organized a flight of four bombers from San Diego, CA, to Brown Field, VA, a major feat for the time. Following this, on 28 August 1924 he was sent to the C&GSS, Fort Leavenworth. After graduation in June 1925, he was back in Haiti from 13 November 1925, with the First Brigade of Marines. His command: the observation squadron, VO-2M. This was a relatively dull period and on 7 July 1927 he was on his way back to the States and to Quantico (arriving on 10 August) where he assumed command of a squadron and became an instructor in MCS. In May 1928 he was assigned to duty in the Aviation Section, Division of Operations and Training at HQMC.

Following this, on 10 August 1928, he began studies at the AWC, Washington D.C., graduating in June 1929. Returning to Quantico on 1 August, he was assigned command of Marine Corps aviation, East Coast Expeditionary Forces. On 6 November 1931 he replaced the recently deceased Col. Thomas Turner at HQMC as head of Marine Aviation. Geiger was selected over Major Ross E. Rowell because he had more administrative experience. Lt.Col. Geiger (29 May 1934) returned to Quantico on 5 June 1935 as CO of Aircraft One, FMF. Col. Geiger's (1 December 1936) next schooling was at the NWC, entering on 30 June 1939; he took both the senior and advanced courses graduating in March 1941.

He next went to London as a Naval Attaché for Air. This trip was a stop-off for a journey to Gibraltar where he flew with RAF groups over the Mediterranean. He returned on 20 August 1941 with a critical report on the performance of the RAF in general. That month he became the CG of the 1st MAW, FMF with a promotion to brigadier general on 1 October. His next overseas assignment was as the leader of the venerable "Cactus Air Force," from 3 September to 4 November 1942, during the Solomon's campaign. For his courage and efficiency, Major General Geiger (8 September 1942) was awarded a Gold Star in lieu of a second Navy Cross. He was recalled to HQMC in May 1943 to become Director of Marine Aviation.

The following November, at the express request of General Vandegrift who had just recently returned to again command IMAC (upon the death of Gen. Barrett), Geiger returned to the field to be Vandegrift's deputy. When Vandegrift returned to the U.S. to become the 18th Commandant, Geiger, now CG, led the I Marine Amphibious Corps (IMAC) during the Bougainville operation, from 9 November to 15 December 1943. For this he was awarded a Distinguished Service Medal. His Corps was redesignated in April 1944, III Amphibious Corps (IIIMAC) and Geiger led this organization in the recapture of Guam between July and August 1944. In September and October 1944, he led IIIMAC in taking Peleliu. For the two operations he was awarded two Gold Stars in lieu of two Distinguished Service Medals.

His final campaign at Okinawa saw Lieutenant General Geiger (9 June 1945) leading IIIMAC once more. He also assumed the role of Assistant 10th Army Commander and, upon the death of the 10th Army CO, Lt.Gen. Buckner, he briefly commanded 10th Army. As such, he was the first and only Marine CG of an Army. In July 1945 he was CG of the FMF, Pacific. While in that position, on 2 September 1945 he was the primary Marine Corps representative at the surrender aboard the *Missouri*. That November he was back at HQMC but still commanding the FMF. In the summer of 1946, Lt.Gen. Geiger attended the atomic tests at the Marshall Islands but that fall his health began to decline. On 15 November he turned his command over to Gen. Turnage and returned to the U.S., arriving at HQMC on the 17th. A few physical exams found nothing serious. Then after the holidays, still not feeling well, he returned to the Naval Medical Center in Bethesda on 16 January 1947 but soon lapsed into semi-consciousness and never awoke, dying on 23 January 1947. His autopsy showed that he suffered from cancer of the lungs. General Geiger was buried at Arlington National Cemetery and was promoted to general posthumously in January 1947 by the 80th Congress.

His decorations included two Navy Crosses, three Distinguished Service Medals, the Distinguished Flying Cross and Air Medal, plus campaign medals from both World Wars and expeditionary medals for service in Nicaragua, Haiti, and China.

GREGORY, Brigadier General Maurice Clinton was born on 9 October 1881, in Cresco, IA, and enlisted in U.S. Marine Corps in February 1905, serving as an enlisted Marine for a period of twelve years and eight months. During this period, on 5 June 1917, he had been promoted to Quartermaster Clerk, then equivalent to a Marine Gunner's rank. When the U.S. went to war, the Marine Corps required numerous officers, many that were service-oriented, and he was appointed a temporary second lieutenant on 16 June 1917. On 12 July he arrived at Parris Island, SC, and was appointed as QM Capt. on 15 September 1917. As far as the records indicate, Gregory remained there for the following three years.

His rank was reduced to second lieutenant effective 19 August 1919 and on 1 October 1920 he arrived at Managua, Nicaragua, to begin service as the Post QM with the MD, Legation Guard. Capt. Gregory (4 June 1920) returned to the States in June 1922 and on the 22d to duty at the MB, Quantico. It appears (according to the registers) as though he was no longer attached to the QM Department. He remained at Quantico until being sent to recruiting duty at Omaha, NB on 1 September 1925. On 19 August of the following year, he arrived at the Army Quartermaster Subsistence School in Chicago. After graduation, he arrived at the Marine Corps Base, San Diego on 30 June 1927 and again listed as a member of the QM Department.

He was assigned as Brigade QM to the 2d Brigade in Managua, Nicaragua, on 7 December 1928, and then on 20 May 1930 was re-assigned as QM to the *Guardia Nacional de Nicaragua* until 31 May 1931. He served in Managua during the March 1931 earthquake. On 1 June 1931 he was one of nineteen Marine officers upon whom the president of Nicaragua pinned the Presidential Gold Medal of Merit for services rendered during that disaster. He returned to the U.S. in June 1931.

Maurice Clinton Gregory

After a brief leave, on 12 August 1931 he went to Quantico as Post QM and attended MCS at Quantico. By 1933 he had completed three service schools: the Army QM school and the Marine Corps' Company Officers' and Field Officers' courses. He was serving at the time as Post QM. During that period, he became Major Gregory (29 May 1934) and Post QM at San Diego, between 29 June 1937 and June 1940. He became Lt.Col. Gregory (2 June 1938) and that was followed his transfer in August 1940 to Philadelphia in the Depot QM, for the Depot of Supplies, remaining there until September 1945. He was, in the meantime, promoted to colonel, on 1 January 1942, and then to brigadier general on 7 May 1944. Brigadier General Gregory retired in September 1945, effective in April 1946.

He was the recipient of several Victory Medals from both World Wars, plus expeditionary medals for Nicaragua.

Brigadier General Maurice C. Gregory died on 27 October 1949.

HALL, Brigadier General Elmer Edwards was born in Rocky Bar, Idaho, on 20 April 1890, attended local schools and then the University of Oregon from 1910 until 1913. Hall enlisted in the U.S. Marine Corps as a private in May 1917 and accepted a commission as second lieutenant on 15 August 1918. He became First Lieutenant Hall (16 August 1918) and the next month was in France.

The 13th Regiment, of the 5th Marine Brigade, both being too late for combat service, served wherever A.E.F. Headquarters assigned them to duty. He served in Germany on occupation duty, which lasted until July 1919 when most Marines were returned to the States.

Deciding to remain in the Marine Corps, on 1 October 1919 he was reassigned to the MB, Mare Island Navy Yard. There he played football for the Mare Island Marines in the 1919 Rose Bowl. Football was then, and for many years after, an important element in the Marine Corps; the Corps utilized fine college players to promote its image. Hall was head coach of the Quantico Marines numerous times in the '20s and '30s, helping it to become a great team while playing many colleges and universities as well as other service teams.

On 24 June 1920 he went to the recruiting office in Salt Lake City and on 9 November 1921 he was at Quantico, playing for the Quantico Marines' football team. Like other officers, his reserve commission became permanent effective 4 April 1921, which set him back in the lineal list and seniority.

On 28 February 1922 he was once again on foreign service, this time, with the Legation Guard, Managua, Nicaragua, from which he returned to Quantico on 16 September 1923. On 3 March 1924 he was at MB, San Diego, CA, remaining there until his reassignment to Quantico, arriving on 6

Elmer Edwards Hall

September 1927; he was still involved in playing and/or coaching football for Marine teams. This governed his dispersal as an officer of Marines for many years and probably retarded his promotions as well.

On 20 January 1928 he reported for duty with the 2d Brigade of Marines, Managua, Nicaragua, then returned to Quantico on 13 May 1929. Capt. Hall (16 May 1929) was still busy with football and one of his "jobs" still included managing the football team. His next duty as a Marine officer began when on 25 June 1931, he went aboard the *California* to command the MD. Two years later, on 1 July 1933, he arrived at the MB, San Diego, and there he completed the Marine Officers' class for company officers. He reported to HQMC on 4 June 1934 and two years later was Major Hall (30 June 1936).

In June 1938 he returned to Quantico; one of his tasks was as head coach of the football team, the other was to graduate from the Field Officers' course. The following year, on 9 July 1939, he was back at the MB, San Diego. He became Lt.Col. Hall (8 July 1940) and full colonel on 21 May 1942. During this period he went from being CO of the Second Engineer Battalion at Pearl Harbor, to CO of the 18th Engineers, of the 2dMarDiv.

From that command he went to being CoS of the division, then regimental commander of the 8th Marines at Tarawa. He and 1/8 of the regiment was afloat, but were "lost" in the confusion. Supposedly he had received orders to land on the afternoon of 20 November, but they never arrived. Then on the early morning of 21 November he received several different messages from various sources ordering him to land 1/8 on Beach Red 2. At 0615 the first wave of 1/8 climbed out of their boats at the reef and began wading in. Casualties were very heavy. The remnants fought as Marines always do; they won.

Following Tarawa, Hall's combat days were over when, in early 1944, he was assigned duty as liaison officer of Personnel, at HQMC. Then he was promoted to brigadier general, effective 1 August 1944. On that same date his retirement was for incapacity based on service injuries.

His awards included the Legion of Merit for events, including Tarawa, between 1 May and 15 December 1943. Another award was a Navy Commendation Medal. He also was awarded several medals for service in World War I and others for World War II, plus expeditionary medals for service in Nicaragua.

Brigadier General Elmer E. Hall died on 22 September 1958.

HARRINGTON, Brigadier General Samuel Milby was born on 13 November 1882 in Annapolis, MD, the son of Navy officer Purnell F. Harrington. He attended and later earned a B.A. from Yale University in 1909. Appointed from Delaware, he accepted a commission as a second lieutenant of Marines on 6 January 1909, then attended MOS at Port Royal, SC. His first tour beginning on 29 December 1909 was with the MD aboard the *Idaho*.

First Lt. Harrington (23 May 1911) transferred ashore on 28 June 1911 to the MB at Norfolk Navy Yard. His first foreign service with the 1st Brigade of Marines in the Philippines was brief, then on 2 September 1913 he arrived for duty with the Marine Legation Guard, Peking, China. In February 1916 he returned to the States and a brief leave. Then on 12 June, he packed up and joined the 2d Provisional Brigade of Marines in Santo Domingo. Capt. Harrington (29 August 1916) was back in the States in February 1918.

Major Harrington (1 July 1918) was assigned 30 September 1918 to duty with the Adjutant and Inspectors office, beginning with a tour at the MB, Quantico on 20 November. Like so many other officers, after the war he reverted to permanent captain but on 4 June 1920 was back to major.

He was, as of 17 July 1920, back with the troops at MB, Quantico. On 16 August 1922 he joined the First Brigade of Marines in Haiti and soon assumed duty with their constabulary force, as Department Commander of the *Gendarmerie d'Haiti*. In August 1925, he returned to the States and on 15 September joined the next class at the U.S. Army Infantry School at Fort Benning, GA. Upon graduating the Advanced course, he returned to Quantico on 8 June 1926 to serve as an instructor at Marine Corps schools.

His stay in the U.S. was brief. On 10 July 1927 he arrived in Managua, Nicaragua, to serve as Assistant Chief of the *Guardia Nacional* until March 1929 when he returned to the States. After a leave on 13 July he then reported to HQMC. Next Harrington was in Newport and the following year graduation from the NWC, Senior's course in 1935. It was time for sea duty and on 27 April 1935 he became the FMO (ship unknown) and on 30 June 1935 he was promoted to full colonel. (I cannot locate a promotion to lieutenant colonel in the records.) In the mid–30s he was the prime mover and author of the *Small Wars Manual*, produced in 1935. Harrington was detached from the fleet in March 1936 and after leave joined the MB, Boston, MA, on 16 May 1936. One year later, 25 May 1937, he was back at Quantico. On 25 May 1937 until 20 October and then again from 28 October until 31 October, and finally, on 11 November he once again assumed command of the 5th Marines and retained command until 25 June 1938.

He served as EO of the First Marine Brigade (1938–39), the precursor to the 1stMarDiv. Between December 1939 and July 1941 Brigadier General Harrington (1 January 1940) became president of the Naval Examining Board following which, 2 July 1941 until January 1943, he became Commandant of Marine Corps Schools. General Harrington retired 1 January 1943 but continued to serve on active duty. Between April and July 1943 he was president of the Marine Corps Equipment Board and then on the Permanent General Court Martial Board from July 1943 to February 1945.

His decorations included the Distinguished Service Medal and Victory Medals from both World Wars, plus several expeditionary medals for service in China, Santo Domingo, Haiti, and Nicaragua.

Brigadier General Samuel M. Harrington died on 31 March 1948.

HARRIS, Lieutenant General (Thomas) Field was born on 18 September 1895 in Versailles, Kentucky. He was a Naval Academy graduate and accepted a commission as a second lieutenant of Marines from Annapolis on 30 March 1917. (Early records show his first name as "Thomas.") As was usual in those days, he was temporarily promoted to first lieutenant and, effective on 23 May 1917, to captain. He spent his first six months at sea, terminating in November 1917. His next tour was with the Third Provisional Marine Brigade at Guantanamo Bay, Cuba, and then, on 6 August 1918, he was assigned to the 9th Marines stationed in Galveston, TX, facing the border with Mexico. In the early spring of 1919 the Brigade was disbanded as were both regiments.

He next served at the MB, Naval Station Cavite, the Philippine Islands from 26 December 1919; he was still a "temporary" captain and permanent second lieutenant but his permanent captaincy was approved on 4 June 1920. He returned to the States in January 1922 and on 14 June he was transferred to the Office of the Judge Advocate General, Navy Department, Washington D.C. He earned an LL.B. from George Washington University in 1925 and then went to sea with the MD aboard the *Wyoming*. His sea duty terminated in August 1927 and on the 22d of that month he reported for duty at the MB, Quantico.

He applied for and was accepted as an aviator trainee, obtaining his wings and recorded as Naval Aviator on 15 May 1928. Upon graduation he was assigned to the NAS, Pensacola, FL on 5 July 1928. The following year, 8 June 1929, he was transferred to the NAS, San Diego, CA and on 10 August 1930 he was sent to the U.S. Army Air Tactical School at Langley Field, VA for additional training.

As of 13 August 1931, he was flying for the 1st Brigade of Marines in Haiti. In December 1932 he went to sea again with Scout Squadron 15-M aboard the carrier *Lexington*. Major Harris' (29 May 1934) next assignment was at HQMC on 15 June 1935. He made Lt.Col. Harris (30 June 1937) while there. It was a period with a large increase in the influx of new officers and enlisted Marines; consequently increases in rank followed.

In June 1938 he arrived at the NWC and graduated on 29 May 1939, returning to duty at Quantico. Observing the RAF in the Mideast, Col. Harris (1 February 1942) was on detached duty as an Assistant Naval Attaché in Cairo, Egypt. Brigadier General Harris (30 September 1942) became CoS to the Commander of Aircraft, Guadalcanal, between April and July 1943. Following which he became Commander of Aircraft, Northern Solomons 1943–1944 then Commander of Air in the Green Island Operation, February–April 1944. He was made commander of AirSoPac on 20 April 1944 and was commanding all planes flying in the Bougainville area. He was soon after made Director of Marine Aviation from 18 July 1944, following which he was promoted to major general on 10 September. He would remain in command until 24 February 1948.

In August 1950, as Marines were preparing to launch an invasion in Korea, Harris commanded the 1st MAW. He was one of the three members of the "Special Board" which also included the Commandant, MG Lemuel Shepherd, and BG Oliver Smith. The board was formed to investigate amphibious problems the Navy and Corps might have in a future dominated by nuclear weapons.

Upon arrival in Korea the 1st MAW took control of Kimpo Airfield and mainly operated from there, while several squadrons operated from nearby carriers. Under his general direction, Marine Air close support of U.S. Army ground units earned them many plaudits from soldiers. One especially prized was from the general commanding the 77th Infantry Division's artillery. Oliver Smith was also elated by Marine support and said so to Harris in a letter. However, directions from the 5th AF Command made the hands-on direction of close support more than difficult.

Among his many contributions was his planning for and removal of wounded around the Chosin Reservoir area. He was also the first CO of a Marine jet squadron, VMF-311, operating in Korea. Harris was relieved on 29 May 1951 by his deputy, Major General Thomas J. Cushman, and returned to the States.

According to one source he was promoted to lieutenant general upon retirement in July 1953, but rosters show only that his rank was major general. He was, however, promoted to lieutenant general some time during this period.

His decorations included two Distinguished Service Medals, four Legions of Merit, the Bronze Star, Air Medal and Commendation Ribbon plus World War II Campaign medals including a Victory Medal.

Lieutenant General Field Harris died on 21 December 1967 in Versailles, KY.

HART, General Franklin Augustus was born on 16 September 1894, in Cuthbert, GA. He was awarded a B.S. from Alabama Polytechnic Institute in the class of 1915 where he had been very active in sports.

Hart served in the Alabama National Guard during the Punitive Expedition against Mexico in 1916. Appointed from Alabama, he accepted a commission as a second lieutenant of Marines on 6 February 1917. Four days later he was promoted to first lieutenant and, like so many other Marine officers of that time, on 23 May 1917 he was promoted to temporary captain. After completing a course of instruction at the Marine Officers' School, Norfolk, he was ordered to sea and on 16 August he joined the MD, aboard the *Vermont* in the Atlantic Fleet. While aboard, his captaincy was affirmed in October 1917.

Hart was detached in September 1918 and detailed as the "skipper" of Company B, 5th Machine Gun Battalion. On 10 November 1918 the battalion joined the 5th Marine Brigade in France. The brigade, recently arrived in France, was not to see any combat but he and many of his fellow officers remained on occupation duty in Germany. They left Europe in early July and returned to Quantico in mid–August 1919.

After a very brief leave he was assigned to the Second Brigade of Marines in Santo Domingo, arriving there on 23 October 1919. He became the District Commander of Santo Domingo City, and assigned to the *Policia Nacional Dominicana* until November 1921; he then returned to Quantico. On 5 December 1921 he became the skipper of the 77th Machine Gun Company, 2/5, remaining at that post until his transfer to the MB, Washington D.C., on 18 October 1922. There he served as adjutant, plus other related duties.

On 1 October 1923, he was assigned as a student to the U.S. Army Infantry school, Fort Benning, GA. Hart graduated the following May and on 19 July 1924 was delegated as an instructor to the Basic School at the Philadelphia MB, remaining there until June 1926. Later that same month he assumed command of the MD aboard the *Seattle*. The following 22 January 1927 he went aboard the *Rochester* to assume the same duties. One month later he transferred to command the MD aboard the *Milwaukee*. That detachment served ashore in Nicaragua for the following five months. In June 1927 he returned to the *Rochester* to again command that MD until July when he and his men went ashore to once again serve as a landing force in Nicaragua at a time of electoral problems in that region. That sojourn lasted for six months; in August 1928 he returned to the United States.

On 14 September 1928 he assumed duties as EO at the MB, Norfolk Navy Yard and on 16 August 1929 Hart was once again assigned to duty as an instructor at the Company Officers course at the MCS, Quantico. That tenure lasted a year. On 6 August 1930 he was made District Commander of the constabulary detachment, *Garde d'Haiti*. He held that post until May 1933 when he began serving as the Assistant CoS of the Haitian *Garde* (May 1933 to July 1934).

Major Hart (29 May 1934) returned to

Franklin Augustus Hart

the U.S. in July 1934 to attend the Senior course at MCS, graduating in May 1935. On 5 June 1935 Major Hart was assigned duty at HQMC at the War Plans Section, Division of Operations and Training, the beginning of his securing major roles in the future. Lt.Col. Hart (30 June 1936) jumped several numbers on the lineal list in advance of his colleagues and in October 1937 he was made Officer-in-Charge, War Plans Section. Hart then attended the AWC at Fort Humphrey in July 1938 graduating in June 1939.

Next he was Chief of the Planning Section at Marine Corps Base, San Diego, June 1939–July 1940. In July 1940 he was appointed CO of the First Battalion, Eighth Marines, which post he held from July 1940 until June 1941. Hart was one of the Marine officers selected to observe the British in action; consequently he was made Assistant Naval Attaché in London from June 1941 until September 1941. Next he was Special Naval Observer from September 1941 until October 1942. While so engaged, he had additional duty on the staff of the Chief, Combined Operations (British) as an instructor in amphibious warfare.

Col. Hart (1 December 1941) participated in the unsuccessful July 1942 Dieppe Operation, at which he was specially commended for outstanding conduct by the British commander, Lord Louis Mountbatten, Chief of Combined Operations. He remained in England until October 1942, then returned to the United States. Upon his return he was assigned duty on the staff of the Commander-in-Chief, U.S. Navy, as Chief of the Future Plans Section. He held that position from October 1942 to June 1943.

Next Col. Hart was made CO of the 24th Marine Regiment, Fourth Marine Division, holding that position from June 1943 to August 1944. During his incumbency he led the Combat Team 24 during the Marshalls' Campaign and was awarded the Navy Cross for leading his regiment in the Roi-Namur attack. Brigadier General Hart (August 1944) became ADC of the 4thMarDiv from August 1944 to September 1945. During the assaults upon Saipan and Tinian islands, and also in the Marianas, he was awarded a Legion of Merit. While participating in the assault upon Iwo Jima he was awarded the Bronze Star with Combat V.

Assignments after the war (from September 1945) included being Director of Reserves at HQMC. In January 1946 he became Director, Division of Public Information, and that July, Director of Personnel. The following October he was sent to Parris Island, SC, as CG of that post. Major General Hart (December 1946) remained at the recruit depot until made CG of the 2dMarDiv, with additional duties as the Commanding Officer, Camp Lejeune, NC, on 31 January 1948. In July 1950, he was made Commandant of Marine Corps Schools at Quantico. Lieutenant General Hart (February 1951) was made CG, FMF, Pacific in January 1952.

General Hart retired in August 1954 after 37 years as a Marine and at that time was advanced to general.

His decorations include the Navy Cross, Legion of Merit and Bronze Star, a Presidential Unit Citation with a Bronze Star for Saipan and Tinian; Navy Unit Commendation, Iwo Jima 1945; Mexican Border Service, 1916; Victory Medal with Atlantic Fleet Clasp and Maltese Cross, 1917–1918; Marine Corps Expeditionary Medal with two bronze stars, for the Dominican Republic, 1919–1921; Nicaragua, 1927; Haiti 1930–1934; Second Nicaraguan Campaign, 1927–1928; American Defense Service Medal with one Bronze Star; Asiatic-Pacific Campaign Medal with three Bronze Stars; Haitian Diploma for the Order of Honor and Merit; Haitian Distinguished Service Medal with Diploma; and the Haitian Brevet of Merit with Diploma.

General Franklin A. Hart died on 22

June 1967 at the U.S. Naval Hospital, Bethesda, MD.

HERMLE, **Lieutenant General Leo David** was born on 30 June 1890, in Hastings, NE and attended the University of California in 1914, receiving a B.A. and J.D. degree in 1917. Hermle was appointed a second lieutenant of Marines on 27 August 1917 and assigned to serve with the 6th Marines, then at Quantico prepared for service in France with the 2d Division. Upon landing in France on 25 February 1918, he was assigned duty as a platoon leader with the 74th Company, 1st Battalion, 6th Marines.

A bit of training for the Marines, then the 4th Brigade, of which the 6th Marines was an integral part, served near Verdun from mid–March to mid–May 1918. After spending ten days in the trenches at the Toulon Sector, near Verdun, his company went into reserve at Camp Fontaine Saint Robert. On 13 April 1918 a surprise bombardment of gas hit the company, practically wiping it out. Most of the officers and men were out of action for months or even longer; a number died from the effects. Several months later now Capt. Hermle (1 July 1918) rejoined his platoon before Blanc Mont and went up the hill on 3 October 1918. Within minutes, his "skipper," Capt. Robert H. Sheil, was down, with Capt. Harold D. Shannon replacing him. In ten minutes Shannon was also down and Hermle assumed command of the 74th Company. Leading his company, he fought the battle for that height, and it was bloody for many Marines, but he managed to survive it.

After Blanc Mont came the first day of the Meuse River campaign on 11 November. Hermle's company went forward and in the course of action he and his company surrounded a large number of Germans, capturing 115 plus 17 machine guns. For this he was awarded a DSC, later a Navy DSM and two Silver Star citations, plus the French Legion of Honor (Chevalier) and the Croix de Guerre, Palm. For some reason, as was usual, the DSC was not later supported by the Navy Cross. Hermle was wounded that day and, even though he refused to be evacuated, several days later he was ordered to leave for hospitalization. He later managed to rejoin his company and served during the occupation of Germany, returning with his brigade to the U.S. in August 1919. Hermle soon after decided to remain a Marine.

His rank was now 1stLt, reduced as with so many other war-time promotions. After a brief leave, on 1 October 1919 he reported for duty at the MB, Mare Island Navy Yard, CA. Effective 4 June 1920 he was back up to permanent captain and on 27 December 1921 he was reassigned to the office of the Judge Advocate General, U.S. Navy. This was followed on 10 July 1924 by his assignment to command the MD aboard the cruiser *Seattle*. On 5 August 1926 he was with the MB, Quantico. During this period he obtained numerous educational attainments, among which was graduating from the MCS, Field Officers' course; Company Officers' course, and a post-graduate degree in law. Beginning in June 1928 he served as an instructor at the MCS, Quantico and remained in that post until 28 May 1930, when he was assigned to constabulary duty with the *Garde d'Haiti*, which lasted until the Marines evacuated that nation in August 1934.

Upon Major Hermle's (29 October 1931) return, his first assignment was as Assistant Adjutant and Inspector at HQMC, beginning on 15 September 1934. There he remained until August 1938, a rather lengthy tour. On July 1938 Lt.Col. Hermle (27 July 1935) attended the U.S. AWC at Fort Humphrey, Washington D.C., graduating in June 1939.

His next assignment was back with the troops when at San Diego he became EO of the 6th Marines from 9 August 1939 until June 1941, and part of the 2d Brigade. Now colonel (1 April 1940) he became the CO of the regiment in May 1941, now part of the 2dMarDiv. On the 24th he received orders to prepare his regiment "for temporary shore duty beyond the seas." In six days he had everything loaded and on 31 May they sailed. Its proposed duty was with the Atlantic Fleet, which really meant the occupation of Iceland. He remained in command until 31 December 1941, then, briefly, until 25 March 1942, was replaced by Lt.Col. William Marshall. He remained in Iceland when he became CoS of the 2d Division, but soon after returned to the States.

When MG Julian Smith replaced MG John Marston as CG, Brigadier General Hermle (16 September 1942) became ADC. He participated in the assault upon the island of Tarawa, 20 November to 24 November 1943, being ashore most of that time. From January to April 1944 he was Administrative Deputy at VAC followed by ADC, 5thMarDiv, April 1944 to June 1945. At Iwo Jima on D-Day, he and BG Franklin Hart were both observing their respective divisions, 4th for Hart, 5th for Hermle, as they prepared to go ashore in the landing exercise. Hermle was the first American general officer to land on Iwo when he went ashore and established an advanced command post at 1430 hours on D-Day. General Keller Rocky entrusted Hermle with the final clean-up of the island, which he led in person.

Between June 1945 and February 1946 Major General Hermle (16 September 1942) served as Deputy Island Commander of Guam and the Marianas. He then returned to the States and served in various posts until he retired in September 1949 after thirty-two years service as a Marine. Upon retirement he was promoted to lieutenant general.

In addition to the numerous meritorious decorations from the first World War mentioned above, he was also awarded the Legion of Merit for services during the Tarawa campaign; the Bronze Star, with Combat V, plus a Commendation Ribbon and two Purple Hearts were also part of his collection. His DSM during World War I was the only one issued to a platoon leader, all else were to senior officers, most of whom went to commanding generals.

Lieutenant General Leo D. Hermle died on 21 January 1976.

HILL, **Brigadier General Walter Newell** was born in Haverhill, MA, on 29 September 1882. After local schools he attended Harvard University from 1900 to 1904, graduating with a B.A. degree. He decided to join the military and selected the U.S. Marine Corps, accepting a commission as a second lieutenant of Marines on 16 January 1904. His first duty was when he attended the School of Application at the Naval Academy, Annapolis, MD, and on 28 December 1904 went aboard the *Massachusetts* to join the MD. While aboard, he was promoted to first lieutenant on 26 June 1906.

Expeditionary duty with the 1st Provisional Regiment of Marines in Cuba followed (October-November 1906) under the requirements of the Platt Amendment to the Cuban Constitution. The government was pressed by rebel forces and by September 1906 large detachments of Marines and a few sailors had been landed in response. By October the Marines on the ground totaled about 1,000 officers and men with another 6,000 USA soldiers being assembled at Norfolk for transportation south. Hill served there for a couple of months, went back aboard ship, and then, when the situation heated up anew, landed in Cuba once again on 21 December 1907, remaining until January 1909.

Following this period he was briefly reassigned to the U.S., and then was transferred to the 1st Brigade of Marines in the Philippines on 14 July 1909. During this period of political unrest, he, with nine other

Marines and seamen, landed from the *Helena* at Hankow, China, to protect Standard Oil Company property. They remained in China from October 1911 to January 1912. He returned to the States in May 1912. After a leave, his next assignment, on 6 November 1912, was at the MB, Portsmouth, NH. Capt. Hill (5 February 1913) remained there until transferred to the MB, Boston, MA on 1 October 1913.

During this sojourn, he was part of the expeditionary brigade that went aboard warships to participate in the Mexican Intervention of April 1914. He was awarded a Medal of Honor for his part in the landing and subjugation of the Mexican defenders of Vera Cruz. Leading his company during the street fighting on 21 and 22 April 1914, he "was eminent and conspicuous in his conduct, leading his men with skill and courage."

Upon his return to the States, he was posted to the 1st Brigade of Marines at the Philadelphia Navy Yard on 2 January 1915. This was the home base of the new Advanced Base Force (ABF), parent organization of the later Fleet Marine Force. With this unit he was sent to participate in the intervention of Haiti, "to protect American interests," from August 1915 to December 1916 when his unit returned to Philadelphia.

On 16 November 1917 Major Hill (22 May 1917) arrived in France. However, instead of the anticipated duty with the 4th Marine Brigade, he was assigned to duty with the 7th Field Artillery of the 1st Division (Regular) of the AEF. Hill was later also assigned to duty with the 91st Battery, the British army's Royal Garrison Artillery in Belgium. (As far as I have been able to deduce, he is the only Marine officer of the AEF who served with a foreign organization.) Soon after the armistice, he arrived back in the U.S. in November 1918, enjoying a brief leave.

On 16 December 1918, he was back to the 1st Provisional Brigade in Haiti, remaining there until August 1921 when he left the island. On the 18th he arrived for duty at the MB, Quantico. He would later be awarded the Haitian Medaille Militaire for his services to that republic.

After graduation from the MCS, Field Officers course, his next assignment was a transfer from Quantico on 21 August 1924 as Officer in Charge of the Central Recruiting Division in Chicago, IL. Lt.Col. Hill (24 February 1926) on the following 13 April assumed command of the MB at the Naval Station, the Virgin Islands. He returned to the U.S. and next entered the AWC, Washington D.C., on 20 August 1928, graduating in June 1929 and was back at HQMC, effective on 1 July 1929.

On 20 May 1931, he was commanding the MB, at Charleston Navy Yard in SC. After his rather pleasant post, Col. Hill's (24 December 1933) next assignment, beginning on 15 June 1935, was on the island of Guam. That only lasted until May 1936 when he returned Stateside and in July reported once again to Quantico. The

Walter Newell Hill

following July he was "home awaiting orders." After 30 years' service and at age 56, effective 1 September 1938, he voluntarily retired as a brigadier general and took up residence in St. Paul, MN.

That retirement did not last long, however. When war came to the U.S. he was recalled to active duty in January 1942 and continued to serve at HQMC throughout the war. His final service terminated at war's end.

He was awarded a Medal of Honor for his services at Vera Cruz, Mexico in April 1914. Although no record of his many campaign medals is available, presumably he would have received the following: Cuba, Philippines, China, Vera Cruz, World War I Victory Medal and possibly British medals for that period (unknown), plus other medals from Haiti.

Brigadier General Walter N. Hill died at age 72 on 29 June 1955 in the St. Albans Naval Hospital, in New York City.

HILL, **Major General William Pendleton Thompson** was born on 22 February 1895, in Vinita, OK. "Pete" Hill attended the Kemper Military School in Boonville, MO, and later graduated from the Western Military Academy in Norman, OK. After matriculation, he was awarded a B.S. from the University of Oklahoma in June 1917. At New Orleans, LA, Hill accepted a commission as a second lieutenant of Marines on 21 May 1917. His first posting was to the MOS at Port Royal, SC, then to Quantico on 18 September of that year. In October he was assigned to the 1st Aeronautic Company at Philadelphia. Hill attended the Naval Air School at Cape May, NJ, and in October 1917 was designated naval aviator #853, USMC #00429, then returned to the MB at Philadelphia.

On 9 January 1918 he sailed with the aero company for Naval Base #13 in the Azores. Upon arrival he was designated a Heavier Than Air (balloon) officer and, like the other flyers, flew over the ocean looking for German submarines. It was a boring existence, according to several memoirs of that period. However, it was over sooner than most of the other European duty and in August 1918 the Company returned to Miami, FL where, First Lieutenant Hill (1 July 1918) would serve as an instructor in aviation. On 24 April 1919, Hill was transferred to HQMC and subjected to the Marine Corps regulation that all air officers had to return to ground service after a certain period of time. He did not, however, ever go back to flying.

Capt. Hill (4 June 1920) was assigned duty as a geologist with the Bureau of Mines 26 May 1920 and assigned to the Naval Alaskan Coal Commission in Chickaloon, Alaska. Hill was more than satisfactory, earning a commendation from the Secretaries of War and Interior. According to the register, he was also back to first lieutenant (obviously an error). In September 1923 he served at the Department of the Pacific in San Francisco, and on 16 October he was back at Quantico and again captain (now obviously correct). He graduated from the Company Officers' course and served there as Operations and Training Officer with the 10th Regiment, and then the 5th Engineer Company until June 1926.

Capt. Hill was due for foreign duty and he lucked out: He was sent to the MD at the American Legation in Peking, China, as company commander and Post QM, arriving on 18 June 1926. Hill had an additional, unusual and highly prestigious duty, as a member of the Roy Chapman Andrews exploration expedition, searching for dinosaur remains in the Gobi Desert of Mongolia. He remained in China until November 1928 when he returned to HQMC on the 19th. His next assignment was quartermaster duties while serving as a member of the Federal Specification Board and as Officer in Charge of the Utilities Division of the Quartermaster Department. These positions lasted from 1929 until May 1933.

On 12 June 1933 he reported for duty as quartermaster and paymaster director with the *Garde d'Haiti* and the 1st Brigade at Port-au-Prince, Haiti. Major Hill (29 May 1934) returned to Quantico the following 1 October as a senior instructor after graduation from the Senior course, until being transferred to the MB, Washington, as Post QM in June 1938. The following July 1939 Lt.Col. Hill (29 June 1938) transferred to the Depot of Supply at Philadelphia.

During the construction of Camp Lejeune (April 1941 to May 1943) he was named Liaison Officer. Next he was Officer in Charge of the Supply Division in the Quartermaster Department from June 1943 to January 1944. Brigadier General Hill (January 1944) became Quartermaster General of the Marine Corps, a position he held until retirement in January 1955. He was promoted to major general in April 1945, but effective back to 30 June 1942.

"Pete" Hill became well-established at HQMC, and was a strong personality. He was later described by "Brute" Krulak as "the classic representative of the Quartermaster's tradition of fierce frugality ... part Indian, World War I aviator, competent geologist, world authority on coral, writer, Gobi Desert explorer, and anthropologist ... insisting on each occasion of each promotion being administered the oath of office on his Indian bible. Hill was no ordinary man. He was proud, intelligent, eloquent, stubborn, and possessed of an immense memory. *Thrift* was his watchword..." Hill fought many battles, most with fellow Marines.

His decorations included the Distinguished Service Medal; World War I Victory medal with aviation clasp and one bronze star; World War II American Campaign medal; Asiatic-Pacific Campaign medal with one bronze star; Victory medal; plus the Haitian Distinguished Service medal and Diploma; and Commander in

William Pendleton Thompson Hill

the Order of Orange Nassau with Swords from the Netherlands.

Major General William "Pete" P.T. Hill, died on 6 December 1965 at the Naval Hospital in Bethesda, MD, and was buried in Arlington National Cemetery.

HOLCOMB, General and 17th Commandant Thomas was born on 5 August 1879, in New Castle, DE. His schooling ended upon graduation from Western High School in New Castle after which he spent a two-year period engaged in business at Bethlehem Steel Corporation at Sparrows Point, MD. He then decided to accept a commission as a Marine second lieutenant on 13 April 1900. The School of Application (later Basic School), where all new officers of Marines had been matriculating, had been deactivated in April 1898 and was not to be reopened until July 1903; therefore he lacked even that basic training. Although he was not a graduate of the Naval Academy and did not have a college background,

"Tommy" was to attain the highest position in the Corps, the 17th Commandant and first general officer. His was a true success story.

His first assignment was to the MB at Newport, RI (beginning on 13 June 1900) and next to the MB, Annapolis, on 8 August 1901. From there, between September 1902 and April 1903, he was detached to serve with the First Marine Battalion in the North Atlantic Fleet. This was a time when Marines were landed in Panama to maintain that newly created nation's ability to remain free from Columbia, and insure that the State Department's "men" remained in power. When not in Panama, he and the battalion participated in maneuvers at Culebra, Puerto Rico.

During this same time, he made a name for himself by winning the long-distance rifle championship at the International Matches, Ottawa, Canada in 1902. He would continue with the various Marine Corps' marksmanship programs for many years to come. First Lieutenant Holcomb (3 March 1903) was placed in charge of the fledgling Marine rifle team that summer and served on that team in 1901, 1902, 1903, 1907 and 1908, and led the team to victory in 1911.

On 8 December 1902 he was assigned to the MB, Washington D.C., following which he was transferred to the Philippines to join the 2d Regiment of the 1st Marine Brigade at Olongapo in April 1904 where he served as adjutant. Following the Boxer Rebellion, the U.S. Army remained and provided protection for the American Legation at Peking, China. That would create a stir between the two services since Marines were the usual organization to perform those functions. That would change on 12 September 1905, however, when Capt. Harry Lee, assisted by 1stLt Tommy Holcomb, brought a detachment of 100 enlisted Marines to Peking, to replace the U.S. Army. The Marines would remain there on post until December 1941.

Although he only remained in Peking for a little over a year, he would have a continued interest in that nation for many years to come. He was ordered to HQMC in September 1906 and exactly one year later to the MB, at Washington D.C. The next year Capt. Holcomb (13 May 1908) was posted as military aide at the White House. He also managed to take some time off to coach the rifle team that year.

His tenure and relationship in the Far East was to continue. He left for China on 15 December 1908 to command the guard at the legation in Peking until July 1910. While there, he would be promoted to an attaché to the American Minister in order to allow him to study the Chinese language. The only interruption was when he returned to the States to lead the Marine Rifle Team to a winning season at the Camp Perry matches in 1911. This was, I believe, the first time the Marines had been the victors in inter-service competition, but it would not

Thomas Holcomb

be the last. Back he went to China in December 1911 to continue to learn as much as he could about the culture, habits and language of that land and it was his fortune to remain there until May 1914.

After leave, he joined a select group of fellow young Marine officers as an aide to the MGC George Barnett. The others were John A. Lejeune and Ralph S. Keyser with the former to be Barnett's successor as MGC, and the latter to become a general officer and serve in World War II. As an aide, Holcomb had several duties but he retained his association with marksmanship improvement, with the official title of "Inspector of Target Practice." As the war in Europe deepened and eventual U.S. involvement was becoming very evident, the military services, including the Marine Corps, were expanding. With expansion came promotions and Holcomb was soon to become a major effective on 29 August 1916.

When the U.S. declared war on 6 April 1917, Holcomb was selected to command the newly formed 2d Battalion of the 6th Marine Regiment. His battalion was delayed in going to France, being the final primary formation of the 4th Marine Brigade to arrive. They would debark on February 1918 and upon arrival would immediately go into training with the balance of the regiment as well as the 5th Regiment and the 6th Machine Gun Battalion. From mid–March to mid–May the entire brigade, now part of the 2d Division (Regulars), served in the Toulon Sector, near Verdun. Upon relief, the 2d Division went to a location west of Paris for rest and recuperation. A couple of weeks later, the 2d Division, was shipped pell-mell toward Chateau Thierry to help stop the rapidly advancing German troops. The men in his battalion were the first Marines to arrive and occupied the front line until the balance of the 4th Brigade showed up.

The battle for Belleau Wood was lengthy, more than a month, and very bloody. Holcomb's men played an essential part, being the most badly hurt battalion of Marines at that battle. Holcomb was advanced to second in command of the 6th, to his old comrade, Col. Harry Lee. He continued to participate in the war and the resultant occupation of Germany, as a temporary lieutenant colonel. During his tenure in France he was awarded three Silver Star citations, in later years followed by the medal and three oak leaf clusters. The French awarded him a Legion of Honor, Chevalier, plus three Croix de Guerre, with Palm, and Gen. Pershing issued him a Meritorious Service Citation. After the war, the Corps awarded him a Navy Cross and a Purple Heart for his part in the war.

Upon his return to Quantico he became BG Smedley D. Butler's CoS until the summer of 1922. His war-time promotion to lieutenant colonel in France was made permanent on 4 June 1920. On 3 September 1922 he was posted to the MB, Guantanamo Bay, Cuba. The following 27 August 1924 he attended the C&GSS at Fort Leavenworth, KS, from which he was listed as a "Distinguished Graduate" in June 1925. His next duty assignment was at HQMC in the Division of Operations and Training where he remained until June 1927.

It was back to Peking, China, on 1 August 1927, to again practice his language and to command the legation detachment. Col. Holcomb (22 December 1928) would continue at this post until February 1930. That spring he attended the Senior course at the NWC, and following his graduation in the spring of 1931 he was assigned to the AWC at Carlisle, PA, graduating in the spring of 1932.

His following two years were spent in the Office of the Chief of Naval Operations, serving on several contract boards, and on special duties performed for the CNO. In January 1935 he returned to head up the MCS at Quantico and he at once put into the curriculum theoretical exercises relating to amphibious warfare. While there, Holcomb utilized his many talents to push forward a grand building program, replacing many of the antiquated World War I temporary buildings. Brigadier General Holcomb (March 1935) remained at Quantico until he was appointed Major General and Commandant on 1 December 1936.

He served nearly eight years in the post, one of the longest in Marine Corps history, and, arguably, was the most important man to fill that position, at least up until that time period. Certainly, in the twentieth century, only John Archer Lejeune might have a claim for similar recognition. Holcomb may not have created the amphibious program which was to make the Marine Corps an outstanding success during the forthcoming war in the Pacific, but he definitely made sure that the Corps would be prepared to fight it.

Tommy Holcomb became a lieutenant general in 1942 and, in retirement, a full general in 1944, both latter ranks being the first in USMC history. When it became his time to step aside after serving in that demanding role for the first four years, President Franklin Delano Roosevelt extended him in that post. Even in 1943 when he had reached the mandatory retirement age of 64, there were serious efforts to keep him in harness. However, he was finally allowed to step down on 1 January 1944, with the award of a Distinguished Service Medal and four stars to take into retirement.

But full retirement was not yet to come to this man who had labored for so many years. He was appointed Ambassador to the Republic of South Africa in May 1944 and would reside in Pretoria, serving the U.S. in that demanding role until May 1948. Then he was allowed to retire to his farm in southern Maryland to be a farmer, later moving to Chevy Chase, MD, then to Washington D.C.

His decorations, besides the Distinguished Service Medal, included the Navy Cross, four Silver Stars and the Purple Heart from his contributions to the 4th Brigade in France in 1918. Additional decorations included: the China Expeditionary Medal; World War I Victory Medal with the Aisne, Aisne-Marne, St. Mihiel, and Meuse-Argonne Clasps; Army of Occupation of Germany Medal; American Defense Service Medal with Base Clasp; Asiatic-Pacific Campaign Medal with a bronze star, for Guadalcanal; the World War II Victory Medal; the Naval Order of Merit, First Class (Cuban award) in 1943; and the Knight Grand Cross, 1944 (The Netherlands).

Following a serious illness in 1964, he returned to his home town, New Castle, DE, and died there at age 85 on 24 May 1965. General Thomas Holcomb was interred in Arlington National Cemetery.

HOWARD, Major General Archie Franklin was born on 29 January 1892, in Clay Center, KS. Howard was appointed to the Naval Academy and graduated in 1915. He accepted an appointment as a second lieutenant of Marines on 5 June 1915 and after schooling at the MOS, MB, Norfolk, VA, on 22 December 1915 he arrived at the MB, Mare Island, CA. First Lieutenant Howard (29 August 1916) boarded the cruiser *Brooklyn* on 5 December to join the MD. His ship would make history when, in early 1918, it went to Vladivostok, Siberia, which was being torn apart between the Czech Legion and Bolsheviks, each fighting for control, and landed ship's detachment of Marines to protect Allied interests in that town. The Czechs were victorious but the Marines remained ashore for at least six weeks to protect the American consulate and assist a largely Japanese force in maintaining order. Capt. Howard (26 March 1917) became Major Howard on 1 July 1918 in another Corps-wide increase in rank but this was reduced postwar to captain.

Howard transferred to the MB at Quantico in November 1918. On 6 November 1919

Capt. Howard was stationed at the recruiting office in Houston, TX. That detail ended when on 23 February 1922 he was shipped to Santo Domingo to serve with the Second Brigade of Marines. Col. Harry Lee, commanding the Marines in the country, began a series of anti-bandit campaigns which effectively put a stop to serious guerrilla activity. Howard joined several other officers in directing the *Policia Nacional Dominicana* which was taking over the task of restoring order from the Marines. Though the guerrillas were still causing some problems, for the most part, the military government was not as affected and the Marines were being prepared for withdrawal.

Back from Santo Domingo in October 1923, Howard, on 8 November took up duties with the Paymaster's Department. His first assignment was in the Assistant Paymaster's Office, Philadelphia, in December of that year. A year later, effective 24 October 1924, he was attending the Field Officers' course at the MCS, Quantico, from which he graduated the following spring. His next post was at the MB, USN Submarine base, Coco Solo, Panama Canal Zone. He arrived on 3 August 1927 and left for HQMC on 10 December 1928 and while there he regained his majority on 12 May 1929.

On 26 August 1931 possibly the most important educational opportunity opened up for him when he was appointed to the C&GSS, at Fort Leavenworth, KS. Upon graduating in May 1933, he returned to Quantico to serve as an instructor at the MCS. He had been on the grade list just one "signal" following DeWitt Peck. Both went to Newport, RI to attend the NWC Senior course in June 1935 and both had been promoted to lieutenant colonel on 29 May 1934. In fact, Howard was in the same group of 1915 Naval Academy graduates, which included such later luminaries as Pedro del Valle, Oscar Ray Cauldwell, and Raymond Race Wright; all would become World War II Marine flag officers.

Upon graduating the NWC he returned to HQMC, arriving in June 1936. He was immediately appointed to a newly created board with Alfred Noble and headed by Keller Rockey to revise the *Tentative Landing Operations Manual*. The "final" report was sent through the Commandant's office to the Chief of Naval Operations and subsequently was printed as *Landing Operations Doctrine, 1937*.

On 27 May 1937 he reported as Senior Marine Officer, for the naval training squadron, the summer training sessions for the Naval Academy, then back to Quantico as Assistant Commandant of MCS on 7 December 1938. Col. Howard (1 April 1939) became Commandant of MCS that July and would remain in that post until 6 May 1941 when he became CoS for the newly formed 1st Marine Amphibious Corps.

This was an administrative organization situated in Noumea and then under the command of Major General Clayton B. Vogel and during this period he would be promoted to brigadier general effective 30 March 1942. His later posts during the war included command over the island of Guadalcanal, New Georgia, and the Solomon Islands, from July 1943 to June 1944, and Inspector General, FMF, Pac. He assumed command of the 6thMarDiv from General Lemuel Shepherd on 24 December 1945, when the former returned to the United States for new duties. On 5 January 1944 he was promoted to major general and to the command of the base at San Diego until he retired in November 1946.

His decorations, in addition to the usual campaign medals, included the Distinguished Service Medal for command of Guadalcanal and New Georgia.

Major General Archie Franklin Howard died on 24 June 1964.

HOWARD, Lieutenant General Samuel Lutz was born on 8 March 1891 at Washington D.C., and was graduated from the Virginia Military Institute in 1912. He was commissioned a second lieutenant in the Marine Corps on 13 April 1914, and on 11 May he reported for duty at the MOS (Basic School), MB, Norfolk, VA. His classmates included such later luminaries as Henry Larsen, James Underhill, Keller Rockey, Allen H. Turnage, George W. Hamilton, Matthew Kingman, Alphonse DeCarre, and Lyle H. Miller. Following completion of his studies, he joined the First Brigade of Marines at the Philadelphia Navy Yard before embarking for duty at Port-au-Prince, Haiti, on 31 July 1915.

First Lieutenant Howard (29 August 1916) went to sea on 2 December as a member of the MD aboard the *Wyoming* and remained on sea duty for almost three years. Capt. Howard (26 March 1917) assumed command of the MD aboard the *Georgia* on 1 September 1917, and then Major Howard (1 July 1917) the MD on the *New Mexico* on 20 May 1918. His term at sea was over in July 1919.

With the end of the war, he, like so many others, was reduced one grade to captain effective on 26 March 1917. Beginning on 1 August 1919 next came two years of recruiting duty in Richmond, VA. Then on 19 October 1921 he was at the MB, Washington Navy Yard and two years later, in November 1923, he was with the Second Brigade of Marines in Santo Domingo. Returning to the United States in August 1924 when the Marines left that island, he served at the Marine Corps Base, San Diego, CA, with the Fourth Marine Regiment until on 25 September 1925 he was assigned to the Field Officers' course, MCS, Quantico. Upon graduation in May 1926 on 4 June 1926 he was assigned to duty at HQMC, where he was a member of the War Plans Section, and later Major Howard (16 July 1928) became a member of the Major General Commandant's Department.

On 24 July 1929, Howard joined the *Garde d'Haiti* where his duties for the next years included being Chief of Police and Department Commander, Port-au-Prince, Haiti. He was returned to the U.S. and on 7 June 1933 assumed duties with the First Battalion, Seventh Marines, based at Quantico. On 29 May 1934, along with numerous others, he was selected and promoted, this time to lieutenant colonel. On 6 August 1934 he was again transferred to HQMC. The following four years found Howard performing the duties of EO, Division of Operations and Training at HQMC.

In June 1938, he was ordered to the NWC, Newport, RI, as a student in the Senior course. Following graduation in June 1939, Col. Howard (1 October 1938) on 21 June joined the Second Brigade, FMF, as CO of the Sixth Marine Regiment at San Diego, later becoming Brigade EO, and finally Division CoS.

As luck would have it, eight months prior to Pearl Harbor, General Howard

Samuel Lutz Howard

went to China to assume command of the Fourth Marines at Shanghai. In late November 1941, the Regiment was withdrawn from China, arriving at Olongapo in the Philippines on 2 December. Five days later, Howard and the Regiment began the fight that lasted until the fall of Corregidor in May 1942. The regiment had been offered by Admiral Hart to General MacArthur and, instead of being used as infantry in the ensuing campaign (the 4th Marines was considered to be the best fighting regiment in the islands), was instead used as guards over MacArthur's Army headquarters, soon after being transferred to Corregidor where they sat out the war until too late to make a major contribution. When General Wainwright surrendered, he was forced by his Japanese captors to surrender all units, including the 4th Marines.

The Marines destroyed their weapons and as Col. Howard, shaken by tears, ordered the 4th Marine's colors burned, he turned to his EO, Col. Donald Curtis, and blurted out, "My God ... and I had to be the first Marine officer ever to surrender a regiment." He was, however awarded a Navy Cross for his courage and service to the nation as the leader of the 4th Marines at Corregidor. His citation reads in part, "Col. Howard successfully and efficiently employed his force in the defense of Olongapo until ordered to withdraw. The Regiment was then shifted to Corregidor where it rendered outstandingly courageous service in the defense of the beaches of that island fortress.... During the prolonged siege, Col. Howard commanded all beach defenses ... though exposed to many and repeated bombing and strafing attacks, and terrific artillery bombardments, Col. Howard displayed outstanding qualities of courage, leadership and efficiency under most difficult and hazardous conditions."

Col. Howard remained a prisoner of war until liberated in August 1945. He was retroactively promoted to permanent major general effective on 30 March 1942, which put him at the top of the lineal list for that rank. He was returned to the United States, and, after several months recuperation from his prisoner of war hardships, was ordered to the MB, Parris Island, SC, as Deputy Commanding General.

Returning to China in September 1946, General Howard assumed command of the First Marine Division (Reinforced) with headquarters in Tientsin. Upon withdrawal of the Division from China in June 1947, he was transferred to Pearl Harbor to become CG, Marine Garrison Forces, Pacific, which post he held until 1 September 1948, when he returned to the United States once again. On 10 September 1948, he was ordered to HQMC as President of the Naval Examining Board and of the Marine Corps Reserve Examining Board. He remained at that post until assuming his final duties as Inspector General of the Marine Corps on 6 June 1950. He retired from the Marine Corps on 31 March 1953 and was advanced to the grade of lieutenant general.

In addition to the Navy Cross, his decorations and medals included the Purple Heart, Philippines, 1942; Army Distinguished Unit Badge with Oak Leaf Cluster, Philippines 1941–42; Haitian Campaign Medal, Haiti 1915; Expeditionary Medal with two Bronze Stars, Haiti 1915–16 and 1929–31, Dominican Republic 1922–24; Victory Medal with Atlantic Fleet Clasp, 1918; American Defense Service Medal with Bronze Star; Asiatic-Pacific Campaign Medal with one Bronze Star; Philippine Defense Ribbon with one Bronze Star; World War II Victory Medal; Haitian Medal of Honor and Merit; Haitian Distinguished Service Medal and Diploma; and the Grand Gordon of the Cloud and Banner, China.

Lieutenant General Samuel L. Howard, who in 38 years of Marine Corps service amassed a record of distinguished and outstanding military achievement, died on 12 October 1960 and was buried with full honors at Arlington National Cemetery.

HUNT, General Leroy Philip was born on 17 March 1892 in Newark NJ. His parents moved to Berkeley CA where he attended the local schools and then matriculated at the University of California from 1911 to 1913. He applied for and accepted a commission as a second lieutenant in the Marine Corps on 6 February 1917. Like all the other novices, he was sent to the newly named Marine Officers Training Camp at Quantico where he received a rapid introduction to the Corps. He was, however, one of the early recruits to be promoted from 2d lieutenant (permanent rank) to first lieutenant and then captain effective on 23 May 1917.

Capt. Hunt was shipped overseas to France with Lt.Col. Hiram I. Bearss, and the 5th Regiment's Base Detachment (Marine replacements which included Hunt's 17th Company), arriving on 22 August 1917. There they later joined the 5th Regiment in various responsibilities including guard duty and ship unloading tasks. In the meantime the 2d Division (Regulars) was forming and the regiment was to be joined by the 6th Regiment and the 6th Machine Gun Battalion to form the division's 4th Brigade. Late that year the Marines finally began training and in mid–March 1918 went into French trenches in the Verdun Sector. In the middle of May they were pulled out of the lines and sent to recuperate northwest of Paris. That lasted a brief two weeks when the Germans broke through French lines and headed for Paris.

The 2d Division was called upon and hastened to stop the onrushing Germans. They met just northwest of Chateau Thierry and, after a month's brutal fighting, stopped them cold and began a retreat which didn't end until November 1918. Huge losses occurred and numerous replacements joined the brigade in early July. Like so many other Marines, Hunt was gassed. He was back in action at Soissons when the next action occurred. There, on 18 July 1918, he was wounded as he led his company across the wheat fields and swerving northward to get at the Boche. As John W. Thomason so eloquently said it, "The 17th Company went in [Chaudun] and stamped the Maxims flat."

He was out of action for Marbache and St. Mihiel but back in at Blanc Mont, another bloody affair. There he earned a Distinguished Service Cross plus three Silver Star citations and later a Navy Cross for his efforts at Blanc Mont on 4 October 1918. As the CO of his battalion, 1/5, at the bloody Meuse River crossing on the night of 10–11 November he earned a Silver Star citation and a Croix de Guerre with Palm. He served with occupation forces in Germany and returned to the U.S. in July-August 1919. He elected to remain a Marine.

After a brief leave he arrived on 1 October 1919 at his next duty post, the recruiting station in Portland, OR. A few months later, on 12 February 1920, he was back at Quantico, as part of the staff of the MCS. This was followed by his assignment as a member of the 5th Marine Regiment at Quantico. His captaincy was affirmed on 4 June 1920. On 20 June 1924, Hunt went aboard the *Maryland* to command the MD. He remained aboard until 15 July 1926 when he transferred ashore to the MB, San Diego. During his stay at San Diego, he also spent some time as CO of the Western Mail Guard unit.

Hunt was then assigned to temporary duty on 24 February 1927 with Smedley D. Butler's 3d Marine Brigade, which was going to China. Upset among the various warlords meant that American citizens required protection, so in the Marines went. Hunt was acting as battalion commander of 3/4 when the 4th Marines remained in Shanghai between 1 April to 2 August 1927. Matters settled down a bit and many

Marines, Hunt among them, were returned to the U.S. in September 1928. His next duty station became the MB, Quantico, on 5 December 1928; he acted in the capacity of Post Adjutant while he attended as a student in the Field Officers' course.

Matters in Nicaragua demanded continual replacement of officers and men to lead and instruct the U.S.–created *Guardia Nacional*. He arrived there on 3 August 1930 and, as a major in the Guard, he led several successful patrols, some in which his assistant was a fellow 4th Brigade officer, Capt. William B. Croka. While there, Major Hunt (1 September 1931) also acted as the CO, Northern Area and Intelligence and Operations Officer.

He returned to the U. S. in December 1932 and was assigned to duty at the Naval Station, Great Lakes; the following 6 October 1933 he was reassigned to HQMC. On 23 July 1934 he was again at Quantico where he rejoined the 5th Marines. Next, on 30 June 1935, came promotion to lieutenant colonel and award of two Purple Heart Medals and two Silver Star Medals, for wounds and courage during his service in France. For a period, during 1935, he served in Alaska with the Matanuska Colonization project and was duly commended by Harry Hopkins, head of the WPA. In July 1936 he returned to HQMC and while there he was Registrar of the Marine Corps Institute, also serving as EO and then CO of the MB at Eighth and Eye. His next assignment, beginning in June 1938, was attendance at the Senior course, NWC, Newport, RI. The following 24 June 1939 Lt.Col. Hunt was FMO, Battle Force, aboard the *California*, remaining in that position until transferred to the forming Second Marine Division in February 1941.

Col. Hunt (1 January 1940) saw duty with the division as CO of Special and Service Troops and went with elements of the Division to Iceland on 6 June 1941, for a brief period until he was transferred to the First Marine Division where on 9 April 1942 he assumed command of the 5th Marines. After more training on New Zealand, the 1stMarDiv landed on Guadalcanal with Hunt leading his regiment ashore. After the battle of Bloody Ridge, on 22 September 1942 Col. Hunt was replaced by another Marine hero, Col. Merritt Edson. Col. Hunt was returned to the U.S. and was promoted to brigadier general in June 1943, effective on 16 September 1942.

Soon he was reassigned as ADC to the 2dMarDiv between September 1942 and September 1944, and was active in the clean-up at Tinian. Later he would continue at Okinawa and was assigned the leadership role for the division's planned landing on the southeast coast. That never came about, based upon the Tenth Army command decision "No more Marines needed ashore." Then, as major general effective on 1 February 1944, he became CG of the 2dMarDiv. In that role, on 23 September 1945, he led the division in the occupation of the island

Leroy Phillip Hunt

of Kyushu, Japan. On 15 June 1946 he turned over responsibility to the CG, 24th Infantry Division, USA. While in that post he was, however, briefly CG of the I Army Corps.

In February 1946 Hunt returned to the U.S. and assumed command of the Troop Training Unit, Training Command, Amphibious Forces, Pacific Fleet. In January 1947 he became CG of the Department of the Pacific, at San Francisco. Two years later, on 1 July 1949, he became CG, FMF, Atlantic, based at Norfolk, VA, and was promoted to lieutenant general. Two years later, on 1 July 1951, he was promoted to general upon retirement from the Corps.

His decorations were many. Besides his World War I awards; the NC, DSC, SS with 2 Oak Leaf Clusters, Purple Heart with an Oak Leaf Cluster, foreign medals, Victory Medal with five clasps, and numerous assorted campaign medals, he also was the recipient of two Legion of Merit awards; U.S. Navy award, for the period May 1943 through 22 August 1944, a U.S. Army award, for the occupation of Japan; and a Bronze Star Medal while on duty in Japan.

General Leroy P. Hunt died of a (presumed) heart attack in San Francisco, CA, on 8 February 1968.

JACOBSEN, Major General Arnold Windom was born on 9 May 1892, in Walnut, IA. Upon graduation from the Naval Academy, he accepted a commission as a second lieutenant of Marines on 3 June 1916. At this time the Corps was beginning an expansion program; like so many other recent "recruits," Jacobsen was promoted to first lieutenant on 29 August 1916. Capt. Jacobsen came next on 26 March 1917. In the meantime he was assigned to the newly developing 6th Regiment of Marines, but when that regiment went overseas he was retained at Quantico. It wouldn't be until 26 August 1918 that he would arrive in France. After the major fighting at Blanc Mont, on 11 October 1918 Jacobsen was given command of the 84th Company, 3d Battalion, 6th Marines. With his company he would participate in the final Meuse River campaign which began on 1 November for the 2d Division.

Upon taking the town of Bayonville, Jacobsen was especially noted as effectively organizing a hospital using captured German medical personnel. To quote Major George Shuler, battalion commander, "the efforts of Capt. Jacobsen in this town which was constantly under fire were most commendable." For those efforts he was awarded a Silver Star citation. Jacobsen went with the division into the occupation of Germany and then on the return trip to the U.S. in May 1919.

After a brief leave he was sent to join the MD in Camaguey, Cuba, on 27 October 1919; Marines had been sent there in 1917 to protect sugar production from "enemy activities." He was returned to the U.S. in May 1920 and to duty at the Navy Yard, Washington D.C. on 16 July 1920.

On 9 July 1921 Jacobsen reported to the Judge Advocate General, Navy Department, Washington D.C. While there, he would receive an L.L.H. degree from George Washington University School of Law in 1924. Upon graduation, on 26 August 1924, he went aboard the *West Virginia* to command the MD for about two years. Then Jacobsen was sent to the U.S. Army Infantry School at Fort Benning, GA, arriving on 6 September 1926. The following year, after graduation from the Senior course, he returned to Quantico on 6 June. Major Jacobsen's (6 November 1929) next post was the MB at the New York Navy Yard, at which he arrived on 25 July 1930.

His next posting was to the 1st Brigade at Port-au-Prince, Haiti, arriving there on 11 July 1932. There was still a measure of unrest among the natives, but essentially it was near the end of the U.S. occupation and very little unpleasantness was continuing; it wouldn't be long before the Marines were completely withdrawn. Soon after final agreements were signed, on 19 August 1934 the 1st Marine Brigade was back at Quantico. Soon after his return, Lt.Col. Jacobsen (29 May 1934) was made an instructor at MCS at Quantico, remaining in that post for two tours, until assignment at Philadelphia on 3 June 1938. There he assumed duties as an assistant to the quartermaster, Depot of Supply.

Col. Jacobsen (1 July 1939) was at HQMC, Washington D.C. on 5 July 1940, and had advanced one number and received the newly created Silver Star medal for heroics in France. As Assistant to the Quartermaster, he would remain in Washington until sent in December 1942 as Commander to the Depot of Supplies in San Francisco where he would remain until after the war in 1946. On 30 April 1944 he would be promoted to the temporary rank of brigadier general.

He would retire a brigadier general in July 1946. Long afterward, in the 1950 roster, he would be retroactively elevated to major general effective on 30 April 1944. His decorations included the Silver Star and the usual campaign medals from Haiti; World War I and World War II Victory Medals, plus a Legion of Merit for directing Depot of Supplies, San Francisco, plus the Depot of Supplies, Barstow, CA and the Forwarding Depot, U.S. Naval Station, Seattle, WA.

Major General Arnold W. Jacobsen died at age 77 on 22 March 1970.

JAMES, **Brigadier General William Capers** was born on 22 June 1896, in Florence, SC, and attended the local schools before graduating from the Citadel in 1916. He accepted a commission as a second lieutenant of Marines on 18 November 1916. In barely six months' time he was one of the officers promoted to first lieutenant, then captain. His first foreign service was with the Second Provisional Brigade of Marines at Santo Domingo beginning on 19 April 1917. This was a time when the fighting between the "bandits" and Marines was at its height. Two regiments of Marines, the 3d and 4th, were kept very busy during that period and the following several years. James left the islands in February 1919 and his next assignment was at Quantico, arriving on 21 June 1919. He is listed in the 1920 roster as a permanent captain, effective 23 May 1917.

On 27 March 1922 he arrived for duty at the MB, Naval Base, Guantanamo, Cuba, remaining until June 1924 when he returned to the States and took a brief leave. Afterward he reported to the MB, Philadelphia Navy Yard on 22 July 1924. For some reason, at this time, his acceptance date of commission was advanced two months to 3 February 1917. On 13 September 1926 he arrived for duty at the MB, Charleston Navy Yard, SC. Next he briefly served, between 22 October and 21 November 1927, in the Department of Chinandega, Nicaragua, as CO of the *Guardia Nacional* detachment. Then he returned to the States and was posted to the MB, Parris Island, 20 March 1928 followed by becoming skipper of the MD aboard the *Tennessee* on 27 July 1929. James returned to the MB, Quantico, on 25 August 1931 and Major James (1 September 1931) also completed at that time the Field Officers' course at the MCS. His next assignment: back to Parris Island effective 30 June 1932.

James was back at Quantico 6 October 1934 and the following 14 May 1935 was promoted to lieutenant colonel. In June 1936 he attended the NWC at Newport, RI, and graduated the Senior course in May 1937. His next duty, with the American Embassy in Peking, was every Marine's highlight, arriving on 18 June 1937. While he was stationed there, the *Panay* was sunk by the Japanese and, to avoid further provocations, and the possible loss of a regiment, the president had the 15th Infantry (stationed in

Tientsin) returned home. On 21 February 1938, James and 230 Marines under his command occupied the 15th Infantry's post in Tientsin. That post was there to protect any potential withdrawal of Americans from North China. Apparently Marines weren't provoking the Japanese, or their possible loss wasn't considered significant. At any rate, the Marine Legation Guard remained long enough to be captured in December 1941.

Col. James (21 August 1939) was reassigned to HQMC in August 1939 as secretary to the Commandant of the Marine Corps, serving MGC Holcomb until early 1942. His next posting was as CoS with MG A.A. Vandegrift and the 1stMarDiv, serving from June 1942 until being relieved on Guadalcanal in September 1942. He was not the appropriate man to fill that position under the pressure and was returned to the U.S. The next assignment was at Camp Lejeune between January and April 1943. Then he was CO of the Marine Corps Base at San Diego from May 1943 until 1944. General Watson brought him to HQMC as assistant director of personnel, U.S. Marine Corps, and he was promoted to brigadier general, effective in July 1944. This was followed by him becoming deputy chief, civil affairs officer, on Tinian 1944–45. Then Commander of the forward echelon, FMF from January to June 1945. Next he was Assistant Director of Personnel at HQMC, remaining in that post from July 1945 until retirement in November 1946.

I cannot locate any medals awarded to him during his 30 years of service but he was the recipient of various campaign and expeditionary medals including Santo Domingo, Nicaragua, China, and Victory medals for both World War I and World War II.

Capers James, as he was most commonly known, was a very good friend of the CG A.A. Vandegrift, and it was a difficult decision for the latter to make when he relieved his "pal" as CoS on Guadalcanal in the middle of that campaign. He did make sure, however, that his friend was found suitable employment.

Brigadier General William Capers James died on 30 September 1974.

JOHNSON, Major General Byron Fillmore was born on 15 November 1894, in Elk Falls, KS. He had some enlisted service as a Marine between 1917 and 1918 and, because he had experienced some college training, he was commissioned a second lieutenant on 15 August 1918; then to first lieutenant on 16 August. On 13 September he served as an instructor at the Officer Training Camp, Quantico, until discharged a first lieutenant on 10 September 1919.

He went back to college and received his B.S. degree from the University of Minnesota in 1920 and decided to return to the Marine Corps in 1921, and was accepted, date of rank, 4 June 1920. First duty station was at the MB, Washington D.C. on 10 June 1921. On 18 June 1923 he joined the MD on board the *Utah*. In August 1925 he went ashore and on 29 September returned again to the MB, Quantico.

On 5 May 1927 he joined the 3d Brigade of Marines in China. He remained there until returning to the U.S. in January 1928. While on duty in China he became interested in the air service and applied for and was accepted for training on 5 December 1927. He became a naval aviator in January 1929 and assigned to duty at the San Diego, NAS on the 10th of that month.

Capt. Johnson (9 April 1929) was assigned duty with the 2d Brigade of Marines in Nicaragua, serving from 20 April 1930 until 1931. At the time, guerrilla activity had slowed down a bit and the air service had little to do but he did earn a couple of awards, the Distinguished Flying Cross and a Silver Life Saving Medal from the Treasury Department. By 28 November 1931 he had returned to the MB at Quantico. On 22 August 1932 he was assigned to training at the U.S. Army Air Service school at Maxwell, AL, completing the course at the tactical school. The following 21 August 1933 he was a student at the two-year course, C&GSS, Fort Leavenworth, KS, graduating in June 1935, and then back to Quantico on the 28th. Major Johnson (30 June 1935) on 5 July 1937 was at HQMC on 5 July 1937 where he remained for nearly five years.

On 28 February 1941 Lt.Col. Johnson (8 July 1940) was assigned duty as Naval Attaché at the American Embassy in Bogota, Columbia, remaining in that post until March 1944. Upon his return to the U.S., Col. Johnson (21 May 1942) served at the Marine Air Station, Cherry Point, NC, between March and November 1944, then as Commander of Third MAW with headquarters on Ewa, from 8 January 1945. Brigadier General Johnson (January 1945) became deputy commander of the First MAW in August 1945. On 22 September he landed on Okinawa and remained at the Command Post while his CG, MG Claude Larkin, conferred aboard ship with the 1stMarDiv CG.

The IIIMAW was scheduled for duty in North China and all Marines to be sent there were in preparation for that event. In China, Johnson commanded the busiest airfield at Tsangkou, not very distant from Tientsin. MAG 25 and MAG 32 were constantly flying supplies in and out of China for the Marines and to enhance the Chinese Nationalist forces nearby. On 17 February 1946 Johnson was relieved by BG Walter G. Farrell, from back in the '20s another China Marine.

Upon return to the U.S., BG Johnson had leave and then prepared for retirement after 28 years' service. A former enlisted Marine, he became a major general (retroactive to 27 January 1945) upon retirement in November 1946.

His decorations included the Distinguished Flying Cross plus the Treasury life-saving award and various campaign medals including China, and the World War II medals for service in the Asiatic Theater.

Major General Byron F. Johnson died on 8 April 1980.

JONES, Major General Louis Reeder was born on 29 June 1895, in Philadelphia, PA. He enlisted in the Marines in 1914 and served until 1917 when he accepted a commission as a second lieutenant of Marines on 15 August of that year. The following day he was promoted to first lieutenant. After a modest period of training at the MOS, Port Royal, SC, he was assigned to the 75th Company, 1st Battalion, 6th Regiment of Marines, then forming at Quantico, VA. They would be the first battalion of the 6th to be shipped to France, arriving on 6 October 1917. There they joined the members of the 5th Regiment in non-hazardous duty.

By the end of January 1918 upon the arrival of all Marines of the 6th Regiment and the 6th Machine Gun Battalion, their training period finally began. The Marines, as members of the 4th Brigade, 2d Division, entered the French lines in the Toulon Subsector near Verdun in mid–March 1918. He was wounded during this period. The regiment remained active until mid–May when the entire division was pulled out of the lines and sent west, beyond Paris, for refitting and more training.

At the end of May, a call from French army headquarters went out to General Pershing at AEF Headquarters, requesting help to stem the tide of Germans that were descending upon Paris. The division rushed out, arriving on 1 June 1918 at a place that would later become famous: Belleau Wood. The wounded Jones was to miss this affair but, when recovered, was back with his regiment for Soissons. Capt. Jones (1 July 1918) was now a platoon leader with the 83d Company, 3d Battalion, 6th Regiment, and with his men participated in the disastrous advance on 19 July 1918 for which the regiment was to lose about half their manpower as casualties. His heroics earned him three Silver Star citations that day, one of which was from the AEF. At the battle for St. Mihiel he was again cited, this time by the French with the Croix de Guerre with Palm.

In the latter stages of the war, he was skipper of the 83d and a thorough professional in his chosen career. In early October he and his company served during the assault upon Blanc Mont, then during the Meuse River campaign in early November. After the Armistice, he led his company on the march into Germany and then served during the occupation. That ended in April 1919 when, because of his wounds, he was sent home for leave and to duty, briefly, at the MB, Quantico. Then on 17 August he was sent to the Naval Proving Ground at Indian Head, MD. On 4 June 1920 his commission as captain was affirmed. He returned to Quantico on 26 September 1921 and there he attended the MCS and graduated the Company Officers' course.

His next foreign assignment was with the 2d Brigade in Santo Domingo, where he arrived on 6 November 1922. That was at a time when guerrilla attacks were slowing and the Marines were preparing to remove themselves from that nation, and did so in August 1924. That month he arrived at the Marine Base, San Diego, CA and on 4 October was assigned duty in the QM department at that base, remaining there until deployed as an assistant QM with the 3d Brigade to China on 25 March 1927. He remained with the 4th Marines in Shanghai until returning to the U.S. in November 1929. After leave he was placed with the Department of the Pacific on 30 December 1929. This was followed by his transfer to the MB, Quantico, on 25 August 1930. The following year, after graduating from the Field Officers' course on 21 September 1931, he arrived back at the MB, San Diego.

His next assignment was to command the MD aboard the *Texas*, which he assumed on 30 July 1932. In the meantime he received a Purple Heart medal and two Silver Star medals for his services in France. Major Jones (1 March 1934) was assigned in July 1935 to command the Marine Air Station at Sunnyvale, CA. However, by 30 October, he was once again at Quantico as an instructor at MCS and, subject to confirmation, a lieutenant colonel effective the following 29 May 1936. He remained there until assigned as the Director, MCI, at Eighth and Eye, between May 1938 and May 1939. That 19th of June he was posted to the Parris Island Recruit Depot at which Col. Jones (1 March 1941) remained until assigned to command the newly formed 23d Marines of the 4thMarDiv.

When his regiment went ashore for the first time at Roi (the 24th Marines went on to Namur) on 1 February 1944, he was up front as they landed at Beaches Red 2 and 3. The same thing happened on 15 June 1944 when his regiment landed at Beaches Blue 1 and 2, Afetna Point, on Saipan. Although few of his men managed to make the 0–1 Line that day, they did get far enough inboard to insure their stay was permanent. Despite the fact that their fight was constantly challenged by the enemy, Col. Jones' maneuvering skill and his troops' tenacity, finally helped to make the island secure. His part was honored by the award of the Navy Cross for the period of the Saipan campaign, 15 June to 2 August 1944.

In August, Brigadier General (retroactive to 4 October 1942) relinquished his command of the 23d Marines in preparation for assuming a post as ADC of the intrepid 1stMarDiv in October 1944. He served at Okinawa and remained in that post until after the war was over and his men had landed in North China. He went in with the assault group from the 7th Marines at Tangku on 30 September 1945.

Brigadier General Louis R. Jones participated in the occupation of North China from September 1945 to 1946. While there he was assigned the task of ensuring tranquility in the capital Peiping with two battalions from the 5th Marines. The following spring, while heavy reductions in manpower were in progress, he lost 3/5 and was down to one battalion only. General officers were also being reduced in the Pacific and in China and Jones was among them.

His next post, upon return to the U.S., was as President of the Marine Corps Equipment Board, from June 1946 until June 1949. That month he retired and was promoted to major general.

His decorations included the Navy Cross, two Silver Stars, the Purple Heart for services in France, and three Legions of Merit, for 1 and 2 February 1944, capture of Roi; 7 November 1944 through 22 June 1945; 1 October to 10 November 1945; plus a U.S. Army Oak Leaf Cluster for services rendered in October–November 1945 in China.

Major General Louis R. Jones died on 2 February 1973.

KEYSER, Major General Ralph Stover was born on 10 May 1883, in Thoroughfare, VA. It does not appear in the records that his schooling went beyond public education and probably just through high school. After he had enlisted service in the U.S. Army from 1902 to 1905, Keyser applied for and was awarded a commission as a second lieutenant of Marines on 10 March 1905. Beginning on 13 April 1905, he attended the new MOS then located at the MB, Annapolis, MD. His first duty posting was with the MD aboard the *Louisiana* which he boarded on 2 June 1906. This lasted until April 1909, when he was transferred to shore duty.

First Lieutenant Keyser (13 May 1909) on 20 November 1909 (later changed to 3 December 1910) assumed command of the MB, Pensacola, FL. On 1 January 1912 he was assigned duty as an attaché at the American Embassy in Tokyo, remaining there until detached in February 1915. Following the usual leave he was then assigned on 29 November 1915 to the newly created 1st Brigade of Marines, part of the ABF, located at the Philadelphia Navy Yard. His next stage of advancement came when he was promoted to captain on 29 August 1916 and assigned on 21 September 1916 as an aide to the MGC George Barnett at HQMC. He was bright and quickly made friends with his fellow aides as well as the Commandant. Among his fellow officers at the Commandant's office, also promoted that date, was BG John A. Lejeune.

Like most Marine officers, Major Keyser (22 May 1917) knew he had to get to France if his career was to advance. Like Lejeune, he also managed to get back with the troops when he arrived in France on 25 February 1918. His first assignment was as Chief Intelligence Officer for the 2d Division. However, when the serious fighting began at Belleau Wood in June, he managed to get there and was assigned as assistant to Lt.Col. "Fritz" Wise in the 2d Battalion, 5th Regiment. During this period he was involved in the intense fighting within the woods. Wise had some personality problems and, when the 4th Brigade was finally relieved briefly in mid-month, so was Wise; Keyser replaced him in command, effective on 23 June. He and his battalion were in close support to 3/5 which eventually took Belleau Woods. Major Keyser continued in command until the end of that battle and into the next at Soissons.

The next battle fought by the 5th Regiment was at Soissons on 18 July 1918. Keyser was leading 2/5 and was commended by the 3d Brigade for his support of their advance. In August he was needed back at 2d Division headquarters and returned as Intelligence Officer. He went through the war and the occupation of Germany remaining in that position. In France he was awarded a Navy Cross, an Army

Distinguished Service Medal and three Silver Star citations. Foreign decorations included a Belgian Croix de Guerre and two French, Croix de Guerre, with a Palm and a Gilt star.

Keyser returned home with the rest of the 4th Brigade in July-August 1919 and managed to retain his majority. After a brief leave, on 19 October 1919 he arrived at the recruiting office in Atlanta, GA and that posting lasted until he arrived at Quantico on 1 March 1920. On 15 March 1924 he was awarded the desirable post as CO of the Marine Legation Guard in Managua, Nicaragua. This was a very delicate post and it was very important to have an understanding and intelligent officer there. After discerning what was going on in that nation, he determined that what they lacked was an effective police force beholden to the government. Keyser set about making plans for the implementation of the future *Guardia Nacional*. His plans were adopted and he received a written commendation from the Secretary of State, Charles Evans Hughes. Unfortunately, another American officer was hired to create that unit but failed to complete the task.

In August 1925 Keyser left Nicaragua and arrived at HQMC on 30 September 1925, remaining there until 3 April 1930 when he was transferred to the MB, Navy Yard, Pearl Harbor. Lt.Col. Keyser (1 September 1930) with no military schooling was, however, listed as an interpreter in the Japanese language. (It was a skill he must have picked up during three years in Tokyo, a dozen years before.) On 9 May 1931 he was back at HQMC. Col. Keyser (29 May 1934) was listed in July 1936 as being on duty at "Washington."

Keyser retired on 1 February 1937 at age 54 and was promoted to brigadier general. He lived in Falls Church, VA until recalled to active duty in April 1941. During the war years he served as director of the Marine Corps research division, then assistant to the commandant between 1941–1942. During that period, on 20 March 1942, he was promoted to major general. Keyser retired once again on 26 September 1942 as major general.

Among his many contributions to the Marine Corps was his record as a distinguished rifleman. He managed various rifle ranges or led the Marine team in 1911, 1915 and 1917, and he was Team Capt. in 1922.

His decorations included the Navy Cross, Distinguished Service Medal, two Silver Stars and the Purple Heart, plus several expeditionary medals, and both Victory medals for World War I and World War II.

Major General Ralph S. Keyser died at the Bethesda Naval Hospital on 19 April 1955.

Ralph Stover Keyser

KINGMAN, **Brigadier General Matthew Henry** was born on 1 March 1890, in Humestown, IA. "Matt" Kingman was awarded a B.S. from the Virginia Military Institute in 1913 and accepted a commission as a second lieutenant of Marines on 20 August 1913, taking his basic training at the MB, Navy Base, Norfolk, VA. He was in splendid company. His fellow 2dLts at the time were such stalwarts as George Wallis Hamilton, George Stowell, Allen Hal Turnage, Keller Rockey, Henry Larsen and Alphonse DeCarre. His first posting was with the MD aboard the *Delaware,* which he boarded on 5 June 1915. He was promoted to first lieutenant on 29 August 1916 and to captain on 26 March 1917. Wartime promotions were coming fast and furious.

He joined the 15th Company, 5th Marine Regiment as its "skipper" at Quantico and went to France with it, landing at St. Nazaire on 27 June 1917. When the 6th Machine Battalion was created from the 1st Machine Gun Battalion, the 15th and 23d Companies in the 5th Marines were transferred to that battalion to join with 77th and 81st Companies. He fought his company at Verdun and then at Belleau Wood. He, like so many other Marines, was wounded on 6 June, and earned a Silver Star citation that day. Major Kingman (1 July 1918) returned from the hospital to his company in September 1918 and was just in time for the blood bath at Blanc Mont in early October. There he earned another Silver Star citation and two French Croix de Guerre, both with Palm. On 24 October Major Littleton T.L. Waller, Jr., CO of the battalion, was moved up to Division Machine Gun Officer and Kingman replaced him in command of the 6th MG Bn.

He continued in that role through the Meuse Argonne campaign and into the occupation of Germany and returned to the States with the rest of the brigade in July-August 1919. Upon arrival, he, like many other officers, was reduced to their permanent rank, he to captain. After a brief leave, he arrived for duty at the Recruiting Office, New Orleans, LA, on 24 September 1919. On 27 September 1921 returning to the MB, Quantico, and there graduated from the Field Officers' Senior course and then became an instructor in MCS.

Events were heating up again in Haiti and he arrived there for duty with the First Brigade of Marines on 10 April 1923. The following 30 August he was assigned as a major to the developing *Gendarmerie d'Haiti*. Haiti had been a duty station for Marines ever since the first landings in that republic in 1915. Since then there had been constant upset, with natives engaged in guerrilla warfare against their government and especially against the occupying U.S. Marines.

His stay until 1926 was, for some reason, unusually lengthy but finally left Haiti in May and arrived back at Quantico on 5 June 1926. During the following year, in May 1927 and for a few months longer, he landed at Corinto, Nicaragua, with the rejuvenated 11th Marines as a member of the 1st Battalion. Although the regiment was destined for a more lengthy stay, Kingman for some reason was one of those selected to return to the U.S. in July 1927. On 16 July 1927 Capt. then Major Kingman (7 September 1927) was at HQMC.

His next foreign duty station was as SMO, with the Special Service Squadron aboard the cruiser *Memphis* on 18 June 1931 and stationed off Latin America until July 1933 when he headed back to the States. He arrived at HQMC on 14 August.

He was Lt.Col. Kingman, effective 29 May 1934, and transferred to Quantico as an instructor at MCS on 21 May 1935. Matt Kingman was detailed to duty in the Adjutant and Inspector's Department on 1 June 1936. In the meantime, he had received the Purple Heart Medal and two Silver Star Medals for his services in France.

Kingman arrived at his new duty station in San Francisco, CA, on 1 April 1937, probably inspecting Marine installations on the West Coast including at the Department of the Pacific. Next he was assigned to duty as EO of the 2d Brigade, FMF, San

Diego, from 12 August 1938 to January 1939. While in that post he was promoted to colonel on 1 September 1938.

Kingman retired after 27 years as a Marine on 1 April 1940 and returned to live in Collins, IA. He was, however, recalled to active duty in February 1942 and stationed at the training center, San Diego. Brigadier General Kingman (March 1942) was made tactical instructor with 2dMarDiv from 1942 to 1944 but his next assignment was rather unusual. He served with the Office of Strategic Services from 1944 until retiring a second time in October 1944.

His decorations included the Silver Star with cluster and Purple Heart plus both World War I and World War II Victory and campaign medals.

Brigadier General Matthew H. Kingman died on 16 November 1946.

LARKIN, Lieutenant General Claude Arthur was born on 21 June 1891 in Garfield, Washington. "Sheriff" Larkin attended the local schools and the University of Washington. When the war commenced in Europe, Larkin was riding as a cowboy and, as part of his duties, in 1915, was to take a load of cattle to Chicago. While there he enlisted as a Marine on 21 December, and his first service was as part of the MD, aboard the newly commissioned *Oklahoma*. In service for a year and a half, he was selected to apply for a commission. On 6 July 1917 Larkin accepted a commission as a second lieutenant of Marines. On 16 August he was promoted to first lieutenant and on 12 September 1917 he arrived for duty with the 6th Provisional Brigade in Cuba, sent there to protect sugar resources against any possible enemy efforts to interrupt supplies. Effective on 1 July 1918 he was promoted to captain, which was re-affirmed postwar on 4 June 1920.

In June 1919 he transferred back to the U.S. and on 6 December 1919 arrived for duty at the MB, Navy Yard, Puget Sound, WA. On 23 May 1922 he was assigned to duty at the MB, Naval Station, Guam, but changes made that the MB, Pearl Harbor in the Hawaiian Islands instead. In May 1924 he went to the recruiting station in Portland, OR, and remained there until reassigned on 20 September 1926 to the MB, Quantico.

On 4 May 1927 Larkin was assigned duty with the 3d Brigade in China then returned to the U.S. in February 1929 and on 10 September that year went to the NAS, Pensacola, FL, to train as an aviator; the following 6 April 1930 he was designated a naval aviator. His first assignment as an aviator was to the NAS, San Diego, arriving on 27 June 1930. On 29 August 1933 he reported for further training to the U.S. Army Air Force Tactical School at Montgomery, AL. After graduating, Major Larkin (29 May 1934) returned to Brown Field, Quantico, on 28 June 1935.

Larkin attended the NWC in Newport, RI, in September 1935 and graduated

Claude Arthur Larkin

from the Junior course the following June, after which his next assignment was to the air unit at St. Thomas, the Virgin Islands, arriving in July 1936. After two years flying in that area he returned to Brown Field in June 1938. Lt.Col. Larkin (29 June 1938) reported to the NAS, San Diego in July 1939.

He next became Assistant Naval Attaché for Air in London, arriving on 20 May 1941, spending some time there then in Cairo, observing the RAF methods in fighting the German *Luftwaffe* in the Middle East. He returned to the U.S. and soon was made commander of MAG 21 on Ewa where he would remain from 23 October 1941 until late 1943. When war came to the U.S. with the attack upon Pearl Harbor, his command was severely struck and although he was wounded, Larkin continued to direct his men against the enemy. At this time, Larkin was the Senior Naval Aviator Present for Marines (SNAP) in the war zone. That meant that he also technically commanded the air forces at Wake Island and at Midway. For his outstanding service he was awarded the Legion of Merit. Col. on 30 June 1942, effective on 1 January 1942 and brigadier general on 5 October but effective back to 30 June 1942.

He became CG of the Third MAW in December 1943 and would remain so until April 1944. Later he became Deputy Commander of air operations in the Northern Solomons between April and August 1944, then Commander of Third MAW again from August until December 1944. Major General Larkin (April 1945) was CG of MarFairWest, March 1945 to March 1946. Upon retirement, on 1 March 1946, he was promoted to lieutenant general.

His decorations included the Legion of Merit and Purple Heart and Victory Medal, World War I and World War II, plus various campaign medals. Those included the Victory Medal, World War I with West Indies clasp for the Cuban intervention, the Yangtze Medal and Expeditionary Medal for service in China, American Defense with clasp for Egypt and the Asiatic-Pacific Campaign Medal.

Lieutenant General Claude A. Larkin died at the Air Force Base Hospital, Riverside, CA, on 2 November 1969.

LARSEN, Lieutenant General Henry Louis was born on 10 December 1890, in Chicago, Illinois. He was appointed from Colorado and accepted a commission as a second lieutenant of Marines on 20 August 1913. His first assignment was at the MOS, Norfolk, VA, from 29 November 1913. Like most of his contemporaries, he served at Vera Cruz in April 1914. His next appointment was with the 4th Regiment based at San Diego, at which he arrived on 6 November 1915. Following was expeditionary duty in Santo Domingo, and there he commanded a bevy of 12 newly purchased Ford Model T touring cars. They were utilized as both reconnaissance vehicles and to carry wounded, and other similar missions. First Lieutenant Larsen (29 August 1916) joined the MD aboard the *Pennsylvania* on 2 December 1916.

Capt. Larsen's (26 March 1917) next service was with the 5th Regiment in the AEF, which arrived in France on 27 June 1917. Larsen's regiment was assigned duty with the 4th Brigade. This was followed by his assignment to 3/5 as adjutant while at the Battle of Belleau Wood. Now a major (retroactive to 1 July 1918), he had temporarily assumed command of the battalion when Major Benjamin Berry had been badly wounded. Larsen was relieved by Major Maurice "Mud" Shearer and on 25 June 3/5 took control of the entire woods.

Re-assuming full command of 3/5 following the St. Mihiel campaign, he led them through the next two battles, Blanc Mont and the Meuse River campaign, and then into Germany for the occupation. He had managed to pick up a Navy Cross and a Navy Distinguished Service Medal plus three Silver Star citations and a Croix de Guerre with Palm for his heroics and leadership skills on 4 October 1918, the bloodiest day of the war for the 5th Marines.

Upon return to the States in July-August 1919, and after a brief leave on 10 September 1919, he began recruiting duty at Cleveland, OH. Like most wartime promotions, his rank was reduced one grade. Capt. Larsen spent several years at Cleveland and did not move until 24 September 1922 when he went aboard the *New Mexico* to command the MD. On 5 September 1924 he attended the Infantry School at Fort Benning, GA, graduating from the Senior course in May 1925. He was back at MB, Quantico on 2 June where he was promoted back to major on 24 February 1926.

Larsen was detailed to the Adjutant and Inspector's Department on 27 March and further assigned to the 2d Brigade of Marines in Nicaragua on 31 March 1928. He returned to the U.S. in November 1930 and after leave arrived for duty at HQMC in December. While in Nicaragua he had earned a gold star in lieu of a second Navy Cross. After this experience Larsen requested and was approved for detached schooling for the years 1932–1934, at the Ecole Superieure de Guerre in France, arriving at Paris on 3 November 1932. He successfully completed that rigorous course and returned to Quantico on 30 August 1934. Meanwhile, on 29 May 1934, he had been promoted to lieutenant colonel. On 4 April 1938 he reported to HQMC and the following 29 June was again promoted, this time to full colonel, to rank from 2 June 1938.

On 22 July 1940 he was transferred to San Diego. Brigadier General Larsen (22 December 1941) and the rank was made permanent the following 29 April 1942. That was while he commanded the 2d Marine Brigade, which included the 8th Marines, 2/10 and the 2d Defense Battalion, and he was also island governor on Samoa. Upon arrival on 3 January 1942 the Samoan Marine Reserve Battalion was activated and also became part of his command. Not long after arrival, an agreement was reached whereupon he was also made commander of the New Zealand portion of the islands as well as the French possession of Wallis Island. Major General Larsen's (28 September 1942) Samoan duty lasted until June 1943 and, during this time, he was awarded a Legion of Merit. He was returned to the U.S. and was Commander of Camp Lejeune between June 1943 and July 1944.

Larsen's next major assignment was again overseas as military governor of Guam; however he had to wait until the island was assaulted and taken before he could assume command. That was on 15 August 1944, and would be his major contribution to the war in the Pacific. Development of the former American base as a secure anchorage for the U.S. Navy ships as well as a primary air base would earn him a second Legion of Merit award. Following the war he decided to retire and did so in November 1946, as a lieutenant general, effective 28 September 1942.

He had earned numerous awards for courage, the most notable being a Navy Cross in France, another (Oak Leaf cluster) in Nicaragua, Navy Distinguished Service Medal in France, plus three Silver Stars, also in France. He was also the recipient of numerous campaign and expeditionary medals among which were those from the Mexican intervention at Vera Cruz in April 1914, Santo Domingo, and Nicaragua; Victory medals from both World War I and World War II, plus the assorted campaign medals from each.

Lieutenant General Henry L. Larsen died on 2 October 1962.

LITTLE, **Major General Louis McCarty** was born on 16 January 1878 in New York City. He attended the *St. Gregorie de Lycee* in Tours, France, and Rogers High School in

Newport, RI. Little received a B.S. from, Rensselaer Polytechnic Institute as a Civil Engineer in June 1899, then accepted a commission as a second lieutenant of Marines on 1 July 1899. His first foreign duty was in 1900, during the Chinese Boxer Rebellion, where he served under Col. Robert L. Meade as part of the 1st Marine Brigade. There First Lieutenant Little (23 July 1900) commanded the artillery company of the 1st Regiment of Marines. Following the Battle at Tientsin, then the drive through to, and capture of Peking, the Marines were returned to the Philippine Islands, arriving there on 28 September 1900. There he participated with U.S. Army forces during the Philippine Insurrection until May 1902.

He was returned to the U.S. and briefly served with a potential intervention force in Panama. But, instead of Panama, he participated in winter maneuvers in West Indian waters. This was followed by assignment on 30 June 1902 to the MB, Newport. The following October 2 he was assigned duty with the North Atlantic Fleet. He became Capt. Little (3 March 1903) and that summer he was aboard both the *Panther* and the *Dixie* plowing the waters about the West Indies as CO of both MDs. On 16 December he was stationed at Camp Elliott in Panama. In December 1904 he was relieved and on the 22d of that month was headed back to the U.S. His next duty was at the MB, Boston, arriving on 5 January 1905. The following 27 July he was on recruiting duty in Buffalo, NY.

On 19 February 1906 he joined the MB, Newport, and in December 1907 he joined the MD aboard the *Rhode Island*. Little would circle the globe aboard his ship as part of the "Great White Fleet," President Theodore Roosevelt's effort to make the world look at what a strong and virile young nation was developing in North America. In those times Marines didn't vegetate long at any one place, they seemed always on the move.

Upon return to the U.S., his next assignment, on 12 October 1909, was at the MB, Washington Navy Yard. But while there, between December to April 1910, he was part of a group assigned to temporary duty in Nicaragua as part of the 1st Provisional Regiment of Marines. This was a gathering of Marines from most stations and ships along the eastern seaboard. Its objective was to deliver tranquility where there was revolutionary activity. After some off and on shipboard duty aboard the *Panther*, activity in Nicaragua settled down and the Marines went home; Little returned to the Navy Yard at Washington.

Little was next assigned to duty with the Advanced Base School then in New London, CT, arriving on 5 July 1910. On 15 March 1911 the ABF, now subtitled the First Provisional Brigade, were on temporary duty at Guantánamo, Cuba, under the command of Major George C. Thorpe. Marines assigned to duty with the ABF could, when called upon, expect to relocate almost in

Louis McCarty Little

minutes. During the first ten years of the century, Marines landed nearly forty times in the Caribbean area alone. In July 1911 Little was an instructor at the MOS (Basic School), Philadelphia, and then back to New London which was the home of the ABF.

His next duty was with the MD, American Legation in Peking as a student of the Chinese language. He arrived on 21 August 1913 and remained at this desirable post until July 1917. In the meantime Major Little had been promoted on 29 August 1916. In July Lt.Col. Little (26 March 1917) went as FMO, serving with the Asiatic Fleet until reassigned back to the U.S. Upon return Col. Little (temporary 1 July 1918) was assigned to the naval planning section at headquarters of U.S. Naval Forces in London, arriving on 14 September 1918 and relieving Col. Robert H. Dunlap, who went on to serve as the CO, 17th FA, 2d Division in France. Little remained in Europe until February 1919 when he returned to the U.S. with the Victory Medal with overseas clasp and a Letter of Commendation from the Secretary of the Navy.

That summer, on 1 July 1919, he was sent to command the 8th Marines in Haiti, remaining there until assigned to the NWC, Newport, RI, on 30 June 1921. His rank as colonel was confirmed on 14 July that same year. Following this successful graduation, he next attended the AWC in Washington, and graduated in May 1923. On 5 July 1923 he was immediately returned to Newport, this time as an instructor at the NWC and would remain there until 31 May 1924.

The next month he was ordered back to China to command the American Legation Guard, arriving on 18 July 1924. During that period he managed to develop plans and procedures to defend the Legation in the event of further disorders and armed efforts against the Legation. This was always in the minds of foreigners as represented by the Boxer Rebellion of 25 years earlier. On 4 August 1927, he returned to the U.S., where he was ordered to HQMC as Director of Operations and Training. He was to retain that billet until assigned as CO, First Marine Brigade in Haiti on 3 June 1931. Among additional duties during this period, Little also edited the *Marine Corps Gazette* from 1928 until 1931.

Returning from duty in Haiti with the withdrawal of Marines from that nation on 15 August 1934, Brigadier General Little (1 January 1934) was back, briefly, at Quantico. From there he was appointed Assistant to the Commandant, Major General John Russell, in June 1935. He was next promoted to major general on 27 July 1935, holding that same post with the new Commandant, Thomas Holcomb. From that position he went to being the CG of the FMF, and the Marine Corps Base at San Diego, from June 1937 to September 1939. From 25 September 1939 until his retirement in February 1942, he was CG of the MB, Quantico, whereupon he and his wife resided in Washington D.C. When she died in 1949, he returned to his old home in Newport, RI.

During his years of service he was awarded numerous campaign medals, from China, 1900, 1913 to 1914, and 1924 to 1927; the Philippines; Panama, 1903 and 1909; Haiti 1920 to 1921; and many in between, plus both the World War I and the World War II Victory Medal and several foreign decorations including a Haitian Medal of Honor.

Major General Louis McCarty Little died at his home on 16 July 1960 at age 82, and was buried alongside his wife, the former Elsie Cobb, in the Arlington National Cemetery.

LONG, Major General Earl Cecil was born on 4 November 1883 in Clayton, NJ. He attended the University of California from 1901 and graduated in 1905. He accepted a commission as a second lieutenant of Marines on 5 August 1909. On 15 September he arrived at the MOS, Port Royal, SC, for an education as a Marine officer. Upon graduation he was ordered to the MB, Mare Island, CA, arriving on 17 January 1911. On 16 July 1912 he boarded the *Denver* to join the MD. While aboard, in August 1912 the cruiser's Marines and bluejackets were sent ashore at Corinto, Nicaragua, to support the activities of Major Smedley D. Butler.

Later, Long's ship was part of the fleet assembled off Mexico which landed Marines at Vera Cruz in April 1914. Not long after, the U.S. Army assumed responsibility for the intervention and most of the shipboard Marines returned to their "homes." He disembarked from *Denver* in December 1914 and after a brief leave on 10 January 1915, was assigned to the newly created 4th Marine Regiment at San Diego.

On 18 June the 4th Marines landed at Santo Domingo City and their first task was to go north to the town of Santiago. It was decided, however, that the best method of arriving there was by sea and the 4th Marines boarded, landed at Monte Cristo, further east on the coast, and then had the walk of their lives. Down they went from Monte Cristo, fighting most of the way, toward their original target, Santiago. At times, the fighting was fierce, and several Medals of Honor were earned during this period.

First Lieutenant Long (16 June 1916) was promoted to captain on 29 August 1916. Promotions were coming fast, mainly because the war in Europe was affecting the "peaceful" United States, which was just beginning to prepare to engage Germany.

He was assigned duty (according to some sources) with the Marines already in France (however, I cannot locate his record there). He supposedly arrived in France on 11 October 1917 but returned to the U.S. in June 1918 and on the 14th of that month was posted to the MB, San Diego, still as a captain. In the 1919 Register he is listed as a major as of 1 July 1918 but, like many of his compatriots, reverted back to captain in 1920.

On 22 January 1920 he was detailed to the Quartermaster's Department as a captain and the following 4 May arrived for duty at the MB, Cavite, Philippine Islands. By 1 November 1922 he was back in the States and serving with the 5th Brigade of Marines at San Diego. Subject to confirmation, on 11 February 1923 he was major once again and on 1 October 1924 he was at the MB, Quantico.

His next overseas assignment was with the 3d Brigade in China, arriving on 2 May 1927. That was mostly an occasion to "show the flag" and nothing of serious consequence occurred during the period. When that duty terminated in January 1929, he was back in the U.S., this time at HQMC on 16 March.

He graduated from the MCS, Field Officers' course in 1934 then Lt.Col. Long (5 September 1934) arrived for duty at San Diego 7 November. On 25 June 1936 he transferred to San Francisco, probably to the Department of the Pacific. Col. Long (7 May 1938) remained in San Francisco and assumed responsibilities as the Marine Corps representative to the city's Golden Gate International Exposition 1938–1940. (As a person who was there in 1940 at the artificial island known ever since as "Treasure Island," I can tell you it was an exciting "World's" Fair.)

Long was made Assistant CoS for Supply at headquarters of Department of the Pacific 1940–1943 and during that period was promoted to brigadier general on 10 September 1942. He became CG of Supply Service for IMAC and VAC in 1943 and through much of 1944. Major General Long (7 January 1944) was then promoted to the Service Command, FMF, Pacific, 1944–1945 then was CG of the Marine Base, San Diego, 1945–1946. In August 1946 General Long retired from the Marine Corps after 37 years of service.

His decorations included the Legion

of Merit for 3 January 1943 to 6 April 1944 (CG Supply, IMAC) and a Gold Star in place of a second, for 6 April 1944 to 30 June 1945 (Service Command, FMF). Additionally, his many campaign and expeditionary medals included those from Nicaragua, Mexico, China, and of course for Victory Medals for his service in France during World War I and in the Pacific in World War II.

Major General Earl C. Long died on 6 August 1983.

MCKITTRICK, Major General William Lake was born on 30 June 1897, in Petzer, SC. Awarded a Bachelor of Science from the Citadel in June 1918, he briefly served as an enlisted Marine from 10 March 1918 and then accepted a commission as a second lieutenant in the reserves on 16 December 1918 and was assigned to the 15th Marines stationed at the MB, Quantico. On 2 January 1919, he was promoted to first lieutenant, reserves, which was reduced to second lieutenant, permanent, on 4 June 1920. On 26 February 1919 McKittrick arrived in Santo Domingo to serve with the 2d Provisional Brigade of Marines.

At this time, most of the activity on the island was made up of patrols of Marines, often mounted on local horses, and numbering 20 to 30 officers and men. They engaged "bandit" units of between 50 to 150 and relied upon training and marksmanship to carry the day. McKittrick left there on 21 August 1921 and on 1 October, having requested service in aviation, arrived for pilot training at Pensacola, FL.

McKittrick qualified as a student naval aviator on 1 July 1922 and was awarded his wings in February 1923. On 25 July 1923, First Lieutenant McKittrick (10 April 1923) arrived for duty with Observation Squadron Two, which was attached to the 1st Brigade in Haiti. At the time there were four squadrons of Marine air. The 4th Squadron, Flights G and H, were in Haiti supporting the 1st. Prov. Brig. McKittrick's tour in Haiti concluded upon his return to the States in January 1925. The following August 4 he was serving in Fighter Squadron Two, based at Brown Field, Quantico, remaining there until 1 August 1927 when he was transferred as an instructor to the NAS, Pensacola, FL. On 22 July 1929 he was reassigned to the NAS, San Diego, CA.

On 9 May 1931 he was shifted to Nicaragua to serve with the 2d Brigade of Marines. At this late date Marines were still involved with leading *Guardia Nacional* patrols on the ground and Marine air was still supporting them, dropping supplies and/or observing native patrol activities. He returned to the U.S. in June 1932 and, after a brief leave, on 6 July was back at Quantico. There he attended and graduated from the MCS Junior Officers' course.

Capt. McKittrick (29 May 1934) was transferred in June 1935 to the Army Advanced Flying School in the Air Tactical course at Maxwell Field, Montgomery, AL. The following 4 June 1936, after completing the course, he was back at Brown Field where he performed duties as Officer in Charge, Aerial Operations and Training, as well as serving as squadron commander.

Major McKittrick (2 June 1938) was assigned duties on 1 July 1939 to HQMC as Aviation Officer in the War Plans Section of the Division of Plans and Policies. He remained in that post until December 1941. In the meantime, however, he was sent to Cairo, Egypt, to observe the Royal Air Force in action. In November 1941 he rejoined his office at HQMC and on 4 December he was en route to his new post in the Pacific. On 8 December he was promoted to lieutenant colonel.

On 24 February 1942 Lt.Col. McKittrick arrived at the island of Ewa and assumed command of the newly formed MAG 24, a partial dive bombing unit, which later became an all SBD squadron. In mid–March the squadron left Ewa for

Efate to prepare an airstrip there, then the squadron returned to Santa Barbara, CA, on 24 May 1942. Col. McKittrick's (5 October 1942) command departed San Diego for Ewa on 20 January 1943. In March 1943 he brought his unit to Bougainville, where he also assumed additional duties as CO, Air Operations, Northern Solomons. He was later in command of the squadron in the Russells in November 1943 and on 19 February 1944 Col. McKittrick was detached in order to serve as officer in charge of air operations upon Emirau in March 1944. In the Marianas in June 1944, McKittrick was made CO, Air Defense Command. Meanwhile he was Brigadier General McKittrick in January 1945, but effective back to 5 June 1944.

With that rank he became Assistant Director of Marine Corps Aviation from January 1945 through June 1947. In 1949 McKittrick was transferred to Cherry Point where he assumed command of that air station. He was promoted to major general upon his retirement from the Marine Corps in October 1951.

His decorations included the Legion of Merit for his service in the Marianas and a Bronze Star. He was also the recipient of numerous expeditionary medals for service in Santo Domingo, Haiti, and Nicaragua as well as the Victory Medal for World War I and World War II, plus all the campaign medals for the later service.

Major General William L. McKittrick died at age 87 on 27 March 1984.

MARSTON, Major General John, III, was born on 3 August 1884, in Somerset County, PA. He attended the University of Pennsylvania from September 1901 to June 1904, then accepted a commission as a second lieutenant of Marines on 25 May 1908. Marine Officers' School had been discontinued in June 1907 so his service education really began on 10 January 1909 when he went abroad to the MB, Honolulu, HI. The following 30 October he was at the Naval Prison, Portsmouth, NH, where he was to remain a considerable period. During this tenure he was promoted to first lieutenant on 25 March 1911.

His next post, effective on 10 May 1912, was with the MD aboard the *Michigan*. That terminated when on 23 June 1913 he was transferred to the MB, Philadelphia Navy Yard. This assignment was with the ABF, 1st Brigade of Marines, with which he landed at Vera Cruz in April 1914. On 1 May the Marines were assigned to duty with the newly arrived U.S. Army occupation force. He was shipped off to the intervention in Haiti and eventually became a civil administrator, joining the newly formed *Gendarmerie d'Haiti* on 10 August 1915. On 17 November 1915 he was with Major Smedley D. Butler at Fort Rivière, where he commanded the Benet-Mercie machine guns covering the Marines advance. Capt. Marston (29 August 1916) remained in Haiti until 1918 and was promoted to major on 22 May 1917.

On 31 August 1918, back in the U.S., Major Marston was CO of the MD, Naval Academy, Annapolis, MD. On 22 July 1920 he was made a permanent major, effective 4 June 1920, and was now at the MB, Quantico. On 28 February 1922 he became the CO of the MD, American Legation in Managua, Nicaragua, and remained in that post until February 1924. On 1 March 1924 Major Marston was back at the MB, Quantico, where he attended and graduated from the MCS's Field Officers' course. One year later, on 8 June 1925, he was assigned to duty with the Office of the Chief Coordinator in Washington.

After four years he was on duty with the *Guardia Nacional* in Nicaragua, beginning on 1 May 1929. Major Marston was a colonel in the *Guardia* and was CO of the Eastern area from 7 May 1929 until 5 May 1931. He would be there while several mutinies among the *Guardia* occurred, greatly affecting the Marines on duty. He came back to the States in May and was back at MB, Quantico on 16 July 1931, as head of MCS, remaining there for several years. He was next at HQMC as Director of Personnel on 13 April 1934 and somehow forged ahead of a great number of his contemporaries, seeming to bypass his lieutenant colonelcy to colonel effective 30 June 1935.

Marston was back to foreign duty on 13 March 1937 when he arrived at Peiping to assume command of the MD at the American Legation and, technically, Commander of all U.S. Marine Forces in North China. While in that position he had an exchange of numerous letters with the MGC, Thomas Holcomb. Most were concerned with the reduction in personnel of his command and their increased responsibilities, all of which Holcomb was in agreement with, but could do little to correct. Marston had the interesting experience of having his son-in-law, Capt. John Letcher, as a subordinate. During his sojourn he was cited by a journalist as one who "acted ... coolly to protect American lives and help keep Peking on an even keel as the Japanese carried the war to [Peking's] very gates." He and his family returned to the States in July 1939 and his next assignment, to recruiting duty in Chicago, began in August 1939. This task was not to his liking. On 27 January 1940 Brigadier General Marston (1 October 1939) was at the Marine Corps Base, San Diego.

On 31 March 1940 he assumed the position of CoS of the Department of the Pacific. He would next command the developing infantry units of the newly formed 2dMarDiv for a period in 1941. In June 1941 his next move was to Iceland to command the 1st Provisional Brigade of Marines sent there to relieve the British forces. When the U.S. Army later sent troops and a senior general to the island, Marston briefly reported to him and soon after returned to the U.S.

Major General Marston (20 March 1942) became commanding general of the 2dMarDiv between 1 April 1942 and 1 April 1943. In order to maintain a relationship with the U.S. Army, he was not allowed to accompany his division to Guadalcanal in late 1942; although he was senior to the U.S. Army MG Alexander M. Patch, it was the latter who commanded all U.S. forces on the island (see de Carre above). Marston returned to the U.S. in April 1943 to command the Department of the Pacific until 1944. He then assumed command of Camp Lejeune from 1944 to mid-1946, when he retired from the Marine Corps in August 1946.

His awards appear to have been limited to various campaign and expeditionary medals, including those from the Mexican intervention of 1914, Nicaragua, China, and those various World War II medals from Iceland, then Pacific medals, with the World War II Victory Medal.

Major General John Marston III died on 25 November 1957.

MERRITT, Major General Lewie Griffith was born on 26 June 1897, in Ridge Spring, SC, and in 1917 earned a B.S. from the Citadel. Merritt accepted a commission as a second lieutenant of Marines on 10 August 1917 and promotion to first lieutenant on the following day. His first overseas assignment, beginning in June 1917, was with the Second Provisional Brigade in Santo Domingo. Capt. Merritt (1 July 1918) returned to the States in August 1918 and joined the AEF in France that November. His assignment is not known but he returned from Europe with the 4th Brigade in July-August 1919, so without a doubt he had been assigned as a replacement officer for occupation duty in Germany.

After a brief leave, on 3 November 1919 he was assigned duty at the MB, Boston Navy Yard. On 27 August 1920 he boarded the *New Mexico* to command the MD. On 4 June 1920 he, as with so many other captains, was confirmed in his rank. His next tour was with the Department of the Pacific in San Francisco, arriving there on 23 September 1922. On 29 June 1923 he reported for duty at the NAS, Pensacola, FL for training. He was designated a naval aviator in January 1924 and was assigned to the MB, Quantico, VA on 23 February 1924. On 19 May 1925 his next assignment was with the Office of Judge Advocate General in Washington D.C. While there, he was awarded an LL.B. from George Washington University in June 1928.

On the first of that month he was assigned duty with Marine air in Haiti, arriving on 25 July. That duty terminated in July 1930 when after his return on 14 August he became a student at the U.S. Army Air Corps Tactical School, Langley Field, VA. After graduation, his next assignment was at the C&GSS, Fort Leavenworth, KS, effective on 15 August 1931, remaining there until graduation in June 1933. He now had a well-rounded education: He was the holder of a graduate degree in law, a naval aviator, graduated from the Air Corps Tactical School, and a graduate of the Fort Leavenworth, C&GSS two-year course.

On 19 June 1933 Major Merritt (29 May 1934) was back at Quantico (the logjam for captains promoted in 1920 had finally been broken). On 13 July he reported for duty at San Diego, remaining there until transferred to the Bureau of Aeronautics on 24 May 1938. Merritt was again promoted, this time to lieutenant colonel, on 29 June 1938. He was back at San Diego on 28 June 1940. From 3 February until 18 November 1941, he was commanding officer of the airfield at Ewa. Then, like several other American flying officers, Col. Griffith (30 June 1942) had been to, and returned from Great Britain. He had spent time there (until March 1942) as an observer of the RAF in the Cairo area.

Upon his return, on 4 May 1942 he assumed command of Service Group, Pacific, from then until September 1942. In January 1943 Col. Merritt was given command of the combined El Toro, Santa Barbara, El Centro, and Mojave air bases, now the MarFairWest. Brigadier General Merritt (5 October 1942) became CG of the 4th Marine Base Defense Aircraft Wing in October 1943. This became, in the Task Organization, Central Force Pacific, Task Group 57.4, Ellice Defense and Utility Group. During his command, the 4th MBDAW moved forward, following the ground Marines; the first move was to Tarawa, then in March 1944 to Kwajalein in the Marshalls. Merritt was relieved as CG of the Wing on 16 May by BG Thomas J. Cushman. BG Merritt returned to the U.S. to become CG of the Fleet Marine Air, West Coast. From there he assumed command of the 1st MAW on 10 June 1945, remaining in charge until 10 August 1945.

He retired from the Marine Corps in June 1947 with the rank of major general, dated 5 October 1942.

His decorations included the Legion of Merit, dated September 1942 to August 1943, and the Bronze Star, Santo Domingo and Haitian expeditionary medals, plus the usual World War II campaign medals and Victory Medal.

Major General Lewie G. Merritt died on 24 March 1974.

MILLER, Major General Ivan "W.," was born on 16 July 1898, in Versailles, OH. He attended Ohio Wesleyan University, then was appointed to the Naval Academy and graduated in a three-year class in June 1920. He was one of six graduates selected to be Marine officers. He accepted a commission as a Marine second lieutenant on 5 June 1920 and as his first assignment he joined the 17th Company, 5th Marines at Quantico. In November of that year, Miller was assigned to the Pensacola NAS as a flying student. He and the other students, including Walter G. Farrell, qualified as naval aviators in 1921 and upon graduation his first assignment, reporting on 16 September 1921, was at Brown Field, Quantico. Then he briefly served in Santo Domingo with the First Air Squadron, mainly dropping supplies to the scattered garrisons and Marine patrols. Following which, on 6 June 1922, he went back to the Naval Academy at Annapolis to study aeronautical engineering. On 7 July 1923, Miller was assigned to a course at the Massachusetts Institute of Technology where he obtained an M.S. in 1924. On 27 September 1924 he assumed duties at the Bureau of Aeronautics, Navy Department. He was back with the First Aviation Group as assistant engineering officer with Service Squadron One at Quantico on 27 January 1925 and was promoted to first lieutenant on 3 June.

He arrived for service as the Engineering and Construction Officer with Observation Squadron 9M, First Marine Brigade at Port-au-Prince, Haiti, on 13 May 1926, remaining there until March 1928. His tasks were to keep the planes flying by supervising the enlisted mechanics in tearing down engines and other parts of their planes, then reassembling them. Upon return to the U.S., he was assigned duty at the NAS, North Island, San Diego, arriving on 5 May 1928. His next posting was back to Brown Field, Quantico, arriving on 11 August 1930 where he graduated from the Company Officers' course.

Next he was assigned to Nicaragua in June 1932, performing engineering duties with the air units of the Second Brigade. He remained there until December 1932 when he again returned to Brown Field. The following month, January 1933, he was assigned duty with the 1st Brigade of Marines, Haiti, arriving on 3 February 1933. Capt. Miller (29 May 1934) returned to Quantico on 13 August 1934; while there, he took and completed the Senior Officers' course at the MCS.

Capt. Miller arrived at the NAS, San Diego, on 30 June 1937 and the next year, on 29 June, he was promoted to major. On 23 May 1939 he was back at Brown Field, Quantico. During this period, as the war drew near, the Corps had many rapid promotions, and they were no longer based upon seniority. Lt.Col. Miller (1 January 1942) became the CO of the Marine Corps Air Station, Brown Field, Quantico. Then he was promoted to colonel as of 18 October 1942, and brigadier general on 21 January 1945.

He remained CO at the Air Station, Quantico, from 1941 until 1943. From assistant CoS to CoS of Four Section, Marine Aircraft, South Pacific from February 1943 until May 1944. This was followed by service with Aircraft, FMF, Pacific, from June 1944 to July 1945. Then on 24 July 1945 he was made CG, Marine Fleet Air, West Coast/Marine Air, West Coast, Air FMF Pac. BG William J. Wallace relieved him on 15 August and he next became CG of MASs at Miramar and El Toro, CA, until 1947. His next posting was as CG at the MAS, Cherry Point, NC, beginning in February 1947. Miller retired as major general in October 1951 and went to live at Pearl Harbor, HI.

His decorations included the Legion of Merit from 3 February 1944 to 13 July 1945 and of course the many expeditionary medals for service in Haiti and Santo Domingo and Nicaragua. He also earned the World War II Victory medal plus campaign medals. My research has not uncovered his date of death.

MILLER, Brigadier General Lyle Holcombe was born on 10 March 1889 in Athens, Michigan. He was awarded a B.A. from Albion College and then accepted a commission as a Marine second lieutenant on 1 July 1914. After a period of instruction at the MOS, MB, Norfolk, VA, on 31 August 1914, he was assigned duty, beginning 4 November 1915, at the MB, Port Royal,

SC, possibly as an instructor. First Lieutenant Miller (29 August 1916) was assigned to temporary recruiting duty in Illinois and while there became Capt. Miller on 26 March 1917.

Miller became the CO of Headquarters Company, in the 13th Marines, beginning a lengthy and positive relationship with Col. Smedley D. Butler. The 4th Marine Brigade was already in France and the 5th Brigade, composed of the 11th and 13th Marines, plus the 5th Machine Gun Battalion, sailed for France in September 1918. Upon arrival, General Pershing refused to accept another brigade of Marines for combat duty, and many of the officers and men were instead transferred into various kinds of non-combatant duties. Some were replacements for the numerous casualties of the 4th Brigade, and some for various U.S. formations in need of replacements. Miller remained in Europe, going to Germany on occupation duty, then returning to the U.S. with the Marines in July-August 1919.

After a leave he returned to the MB, Quantico on 1 October 1919 and while there his rank of captain was made permanent, effective on 26 March 1917. Beginning 16 September 1921, he would be one of the first Marine officers to attend the new U.S. Army Infantry School at Fort Benning, GA and then back at the MB, Quantico, on 29 May 1922 after graduating. Then he attended the MCS. After graduating from the Field Officers' course, on 28 June 1923 he boarded the *Arizona* to command the MD, remaining aboard until July 1925 when he went ashore for a brief leave. Then to recruiting duty in Seattle, WA, arriving there on 21 September 1925. The following year, 28 August 1926, he began studies at the C&GSS, Fort Leavenworth, KS. Beginning on 22 August 1927, he was once again at the MB, Quantico; he was now a graduate of three of the finest military school courses then available. While Major Miller (27 October 1928) was an instructor in the Field Officers' course, he was selected to work with Major Barrett (Major del Valle was later added to the group) and under the direction of Lt.Col. Price to develop a tentative text for a *Marine Corps Landing Operations Manual*.

In December 1931 he went back with the troops, arriving at the Marine Base at San Diego to be CO of the 2d Battalion, 4th Marines, then in residence there. At a special request from Col. Richard S. Hooker, then CO of the regiment in Shanghai, MGC Ben Fuller sent a battalion to the 4th Marines in Shanghai. This was the missing 2d Battalion and Miller was the battalion commander. His unit was composed of three infantry companies (9th, 10th, and 31st) and a machine gun company (32d). They arrived at Shanghai on 24 June 1932 and would remain there until October 1934. After arrival, Lt.Col. Miller's (29 May 1934) 2d Bn remained in Shanghai but the 3d Bn, plus (now alpha) Companies C and G were disbanded. Miller was relieved of command of the battalion and returned to Quantico on 12 November 1934, remaining there as an instructor, until assigned to duty at Parris Island, SC, arriving there on 8 April 1937.

He was promoted to colonel on 3 January 1939 while attending the NWC Senior Class, from which he graduated in May 1941. He was then assigned to the newly forming 2dMarDiv on 19 May 1941. When the war came, he was promoted to CoS of the Amphibious Force, Pacific Fleet, between March and April 1942; then to the Defense Force, Samoan Group, April 1942 until March 1944. In the meantime, Brigadier General Miller (26 August 1942) was taken ill and returned to the States, where he entered the hospital. This was followed by a lengthy stay prior to his retirement in June 1945.

Miller's decorations included the Legion of Merit from 28 April 1942 to 1 March 1944. Additionally, Miller was the recipient of a China expeditionary medal, a World War I Victory Medal, and numerous World War II campaign medals including a Victory Medal. My research has not uncovered his date of death.

MITCHELL, Lieutenant General Ralph Johnson was born on 25 September 1891, in New Britain, CT Upon graduation from the USNA, Annapolis, on 5 June 1915 he accepted a commission as a second lieutenant of Marines. His first assignment after attendance at the MOS, Norfolk, VA, was to the MB, Guam, arriving 1 May 1916. His promotions, like so many other Marine officers, were all temporary but in rapid succession: first lieutenant on 29 August 1916, captain on 26 March 1917, then to major on 1 July 1918. He had returned from Guam to the U.S. in November 1918 and the following 26 December was assigned duty with the 3d Provisional Brigade of Marines at Galveston, TX, watching Mexico. However, like so many other Marines, his rapid promotions during the war years evaporated back to captain and on 26 April 1919 he was assigned to the MB, Quantico.

On 29 November 1920 he was assigned to flight school at Pensacola, FL where he qualified as naval aviator in 1921. On 28 November he was reassigned to the MB, Guam. There, between 1921 and 1923, he helped to establish and build the NAS. He returned to the States in June 1923 and on 13 August reported for duty at HQMC.

On 18 September 1926 he arrived at the U.S. Air Corps Tactical School from which he graduated in 1927. On 20 August he was sent to attend the C&GSS, Fort Leavenworth, KS, from which he graduated in June 1928. Following this schooling and a leave, he was assigned to the NAS at North Island, San Diego, on 15 July. This was followed by promotion to major on 22 December 1928.

His next duty, beginning on 9 December 1929, was to command the Marine aircraft squadrons serving with the 2d Brigade of Marines in Nicaragua. Augusto Sandino had recently returned from his Mexican exile to create trouble for the Nicaraguan government and Marines. Marine troops and planes were again busy until the eventual withdrawal of Americans in 1934. Mitchell, however, was back at the MB, Quantico, effective 16 November 1931.

On 7 June 1932 he reported to the NWC, Newport, RI, and a year later (June 1933) graduated. His next posting was at HQMC, arriving on 30 June 1933. His education and experiences enabled him to be selected for and promoted to lieutenant colonel on 29 May 1934. On 21 November 1935 he was again assigned to duty at the NAS, San Diego, as commander of the 2d MAG and while there he was awarded the Distinguished Flying Cross. Col. Mitchell (1 February 1939) was on 1 March assigned as a senior Marine officer to the Bureau of Aeronautics, Navy Department.

On 1 March 1939 Mitchell was back with Marine aviation, as Director of Aviation at HQMC, which lasted through April 1942. In the meantime he was promoted to brigadier general on 30 March 1942, and major general on 28 September 1942. During this period he acted as assistant to the commandant of the Marine Corps for aviation from April 1942.

He went overseas and relieved MG Roy Geiger as CG of the 1st MAW, Solomon Islands, in April 1943. On 20 November 1943 MG Mitchell assumed command of Air Solomons (AirSols). This group consisted of four separate services, including the 1st & 2d MAWs, AAF's 13th AF, various USN units, and units of the Royal New Zealand AF. While in command, Mitchell brought about several different strategies that consisted of relentless bombing of Rabaul and fighter sweeps that decimated Japanese fighters in the vicinity. He was relieved on 15 March 1944 by MG Hubert R. Harmon, AAF, and then became ComAirSoPac; on 15 June his unit would come under the command of SoWesPac. Marine air was now subordinate to General Kenny's (USAF) command and pure and simple, Marine air would be shunted aside. Sent to assist the U.S. in the Philippines, Marine air was finally allowed to again participate in the active war. That was where Mitchell ended his overseas commitment and in June 1945 he returned to the U.S.

His next position was as CG of the Marine Corps Air Base at Cherry Point, then CG of the Second MAW from August 1945. He was promoted to lieutenant general upon retirement in May 1948.

Mitchell's decorations included two Distinguished Service Medals, two Legions of Merit, the Distinguished Flying Cross and two Air Medals, several Nicaraguan expeditionary medals plus the usual campaign medals from his World War II Pacific experiences.

Major General Ralph J. Mitchell died on 31 May 1970.

MOORE, Lieutenant General James Tillinghast was born on 5 September 1895, in Barnwell, SC. He earned a B.S. from the Citadel in 1916. Moore accepted a commission as a second lieutenant of Marines on 29 September 1916. His first assignment was with the Second Provisional Brigade in Santo Domingo, arriving on 10 December 1916 after a brief stint at the Marine Officers' School, MB, Norfolk, VA. While on the island, he was promoted to captain on 22 May 1917; it appears he entirely bypassed the rank of first lieutenant. During this sojourn he was "skipper" of the newly arrived 48th Company of the 4th Marines. The 48th Co. was based in Le Vega, at the end (beginning?) of the rail line in central Santo Domingo. With a total of 48 officers and men, his company and two others, the 33d Mounted and 25th, were in 3d Marine (Lt.Col. George Thorpe) territory and assigned to duty under Thorpe. They never made contact with rebel forces though they made several efforts to do so.

On 28 October 1918 his captaincy was confirmed as permanent. He returned to the U.S. in December 1919 and on the 22d of that month arrived at the MB, Navy Yard, Philadelphia. On 7 December 1920 he was assigned to duty at the Naval Ammunition Depot, Hingham, MA. Some time between this assignment and the following, Moore qualified as a naval aviator, in 1921. He was assigned duty at what was soon to be named Brown Field, Quantico, VA, on 26 January 1922, remaining there until 16 August when he reported for duty with the First Brigade of Marines, Haiti. Since the establishment and expansion of the *Gendarmerie d'Haiti*, the usually explosive situation in that country had cooled considerably. In September 1924 he returned to the States and was assigned duty at Brown Field, arriving on the 23nd of September. (Registers indicate that he was missing for one year, returning to Quantico on 24 September 1925—their mistake, I assume.)

On 3 May 1927 he was assigned duty with the 3d Brigade in China, as EO of the fighter and observation aircraft squadrons. This duty terminated in September 1928. Then briefly he was on duty at the Naval Station, Guam (September-November 1928). In December he was at the MB, Quantico, where he was CO of the Air Service, East Coast Expeditionary Force. In August 1929 he was at the Air Corps Tactical School from which he graduated in July 1930, returning to Quantico. During this period, Major Moore (20 May 1931) graduated from the MCS Field Officers' course.

On 14 May 1932 he again reported for duty with the First Brigade in Haiti. With the withdrawal from that nation of all U.S. personnel, Moore was back at Quantico on 14 August 1934. Lt.Col. Moore (30 June 1935) was the squadron commander on St. Thomas, Virgin Islands, on 9 August. He was back in the States in April 1937 and completed the course at the advanced flying school, then attended the NWC at Newport, RI, from 17 June 1937 and graduated the senior course in June 1938.

He was back at Quantico that month as EO of First MAG. The following year, in July, he was air officer with FMF at San Diego. From October 1940 until October 1942, Col. Moore (1 October 1940) was a member of the U.S. Aviation Mission to Peru, where he was named CG of the Peruvian Air Force. Brigadier General Moore (16 September 1942) became CG of the Fourth Marine Aircraft Base Defense Wing from October 1942 to May 1943. Chief of Staff, then deputy commander, and finally CG of the First MAW May 1943 to July 1944. Commanding general of Second MAW July 1944 to February 1945 then Aircraft, FMF, Pacific, February 1945 till August 1946. Moore was promoted to major general on 1 February 1944. He retired in November 1946 as a lieutenant general.

His decorations included a Distinguished Service Medal and a Legion of Merit while he was CG of the First MAW. Other decorations included various expeditionary medals from Santo Domingo, Haiti (2), China, plus a World War II Victory Medal and various campaign medals for the Asiatic-Pacific phase.

Lieutenant General James T. Moore died on 10 November 1953.

MOSES, Major General Emile Phillips was born on 27 May 1880, in Sumpter, SC. He attended the University of South Carolina from 1896 until 1899 and then the Georgia Institute of technology from 1901 to 1902. He accepted a commission as a second lieutenant of Marines on 2 April 1904 and the following month he attended the Marine Officers' School at Annapolis. On 18 February 1905 he arrived at the MB, New York, where he remained until the following December; on the 15th he arrived for duty at Camp Elliott, Panama Canal Zone. His CO was Major Charles G. Long, and the command consisted of eight officers and 200 enlisted Marines. Elections had been held and the "right people" elected, so there were no serious problems during this period.

On 30 December 1906 Moses arrived at the MB, Boston, becoming First Lieutenant Moses on 1 January 1908. In June 1908, more election disturbances in the Republic of Panama caused another intervention of a battalion of Marines to augment Lt.Col. John E. Mahoney's force. This latter group (totaling 19 officers and 706 enlisted Marines, and led by Lt.Col. Eli K. Cole) was withdrawn on 8 July. On 10 January 1909 Moses was at the MB, Honolulu, HI and the following November, after a brief return to the States, he boarded the *Washington* for service with the MD.

His seagoing duty ended in October 1911 and on the 5th of that month he arrived for duty at the newly moved (from New London, CT) Advanced Base School at the MB, Philadelphia. In late August 1912, Moses was one of the officers selected to accompany Col. Joseph Pendleton in our first major incursion into Nicaragua. There Moses was assigned as adjutant to the 1st Battalion, Major William McKelvey commanding, and with his battalion was involved on 4 October 1912 in the assaults upon both Barranca and Coyotepe Hills.

Returning to the U.S., Moses was assigned to the MB at Puget Sound, WA, arriving on 13 January 1913. Capt. Moses' (12 July 1914) next post was as "skipper" of the MD, aboard the *Galveston*, boarding on 27 November 1914 and remaining until June 1917. In the meantime he was promoted to major on 22 May 1917. From here on, his locations are not easily to determine. He arrived at his next post on 7 August 1917; then on 26 October 1918 he was at the MB, Quantico.

His next assignment was to the MB, Pearl Harbor, arriving on 16 May 1919 and remaining there until 17 October 1921 when he appeared at the MB, San Diego, to join the 5th Marine Brigade. On 11 November 1923 he was back at MB, Quantico, until 5 September 1925 when he arrived at the U.S. Army Field Artillery School, Fort Sill, OK, from which he graduated the following year. By 1 August 1926 he was at MB, Quantico, remaining there until he was assigned duty with the 3d Brigade destined for China, arriving there on 5 May 1927. Later that year, he was Lt.Col. Moses (7 September 1927) and detached from the Brigade on 26 September for duty with the Legation Guard Detachment, Peking, China.

He returned to the States in June 1929 and was therewith assigned 15 August 1929 to the AWC, from which he graduated in 1930, and then on 12 June attended the NWC from which he graduated the Junior course in 1931. On 8 August he arrived for duty at the MB, San Diego, followed by his reassignment to China, this time with the 4th Marines in Shanghai, arriving on 9 December 1932. He assumed command of the regiment on 24 December; briefly relinquished it to Col. Fred D. Kilgore on 13 March 1933, then assumed command once again on 7 May until 10 July 1933 when Col. John Beaumont arrived to assume command of the regiment. (I have assumed he then reverted to EO of the regiment.)

China was undergoing an invasion by the Imperial Japanese naval forces in and around Shanghai and the 4th Marines were kept very busy maintaining the independence of the International Settlement, doing their best with the limited numbers of Marines available. On the 2d of October, Col. Moses (20 March 1934) was in Washington D.C. Nearly a year later, on 1 September 1935, he arrived at San Diego where he assumed the post of CoS of the Fleet Marine Force (FMF).

In June 1938 he arrived at the NWC to attend the Senior course, which he successfully completed. Brigadier General Moses (1 February 1939) then returned to Quantico where on 23 May he was made president of the Marine Corps Equipment Board at which post he remained until August 1941. His next assignment was as CG of the MB at Parris Island beginning 19 September 1941. Major General Moses (28 September 1942) remained at that post until he retired in May 1944.

His decorations included expeditionary medals from the various interventions in Panama; Nicaragua; and China (several) plus World War II victory medal.

Major General Emile P. Moses died on 22 December 1965.

MULCAHY, Lieutenant General Francis Patrick was born on 9 March 1894, in Rochester, New York. He was awarded a Ph.B. from Notre Dame University in 1914. He accepted a commission as a second lieutenant of Marines on 15 August 1917 and was promoted to first lieutenant the following day. Mulcahy trained and became a naval aviator, Number 597 (USMC #695), at the NAS, Miami, FL on 17 April 1918. He served overseas with the Northern Bombing Group in Belgium in July 1918. Capt. Mulcahy (1 July 1918), while flying a DH-9 with the RAF on 29 September 1918, shot down a Fokker D-VII over Coremarche, Belgium, receiving credit for the first USMC victory in aerial combat. On 2 October 1918 Mulcahy flew one of three USMC planes that repeatedly dropped food and supplies from 100 feet to French forces under heavy enemy fire. For this he was awarded a Distinguished Service Medal, then ranked just below the Medal of Honor.

He and his unit returned to the U.S. in December 1918 and his first assignment, arriving on the 20th of that month, was with the 1st Aviation Force at the MB, Norfolk, VA. On 21 August 1920 Capt. Mulcahy (4 June 1920) arrived to serve with the First Provisional Brigade of Marines in Haiti. Back to the States on 21 May 1921 and duties assumed at Brown Field, Quantico, on that date. On 21 March 1922, he was assigned to duty with the Naval Bureau of Aeronautics in Washington D.C.

Then he was back with the 1st Brigade of Marines in Haiti on 26 November 1923; military activity in Haiti was slow at this period yet Mulcahy remained there until 27 November 1925 when he returned to the MB, Quantico. While in Haiti he had commanded the Observation Squadron. On 18 March 1926 he was reassigned to the Marine Corps Base, San Diego, and then arrived at the Army Tactical School, Langley Field, VA, on 2 September 1927 to attend that course, from which he graduated in 1928.

Next he arrived at the C&GSS, Fort Leavenworth, on 1 September 1928 and graduated in June 1929, followed by his next assignment beginning on 27 July at the MB, Quantico. Duty in Nicaragua followed and joining the 2d Brigade of Marines on 23 July 1931 again placed him in harm's way. He and his Marine comrades supported the *Guardia Nacional* patrols, usually led by Marines, and still after Sandino. In December 1932 he was headed back to Quantico, after which he was assigned to HQMC on 2 February 1933. Finally, the buildup of captains, post–World War I, was partially brought to a halt. Along with many other Marine captains, he was promoted to major on 29 May 1934.

His next assignment was to the NWC, Newport, RI, arriving on 25 June 1935. Mulcahy graduated from the NWC Senior course in June 1936. This was the dawn of selection for Marine officers and Lt.Col. Mulcahy (30 June 1936) was promoted, far ahead of many of his contemporaries. Then, on 25 May 1936, he was once again at Quantico.

On 21 June 1938 he arrived to serve in St. Thomas, Virgin Islands, returning to the States in July 1940. His next assignment was the course at the AWC beginning that same month. Upon graduation and now Col. Mulcahy, as of 1 July 1941, was sent as an observer with the British Western Desert Air Force in North Africa. Arriving on 31 August, he was in Libya and in Egypt sharing the fortunes and misfortunes of the British fighting against Rommel and the Africa Korps.

He returned to the U.S. on 18 February 1942 and assumed the role of CoS, then commanding officer, of the 2d MAW at Quantico. He took his unit overseas to Guadalcanal where he commanded all Allied air forces (Cactus Air Force) from December 1941 until February 1943. He then became CoS to the Commander, Air Forces, Solomon Islands, until April 1943. Brigadier General Mulcahy (20 September 1942) on 26 December 1942 assumed command of the 2d MAW and continued to command the wing until 16 March 1944 when he was returned to the States to become CG of MarFairWest, 14 May to 11 September 1944. Major General Mulcahy (5 February 1944) then went to AirFMFPac on 16 September 1944.

His next assignment, effective on 21 November 1944, was as CG of the Tactical Air Force, Tenth (U.S.) Army, and included numerous USMC and USAAF commands, too numerous to list. This was when Marine Air and Artillery supported MacArthur's Army in the retaking of the Philippines. But, because of serious illness, he was relieved of this command by MG Louis E. Woods on 11 June 1945.

General Mulcahy had a lengthy stay at the U.S. Naval Hospital in San Diego beginning in June 1945. He received a medical discharge and retirement on 1 April 1946 and was promoted to lieutenant general retroactive to 5 February 1944.

His decorations included the Distinguished Service Medal and a Legion of Merit for the period he was CG of 2d MAW. Expeditionary medals included Haiti (two) and Nicaragua. He was also the recipient of Victory Medals from both

World Wars, plus clasps for service in Belgium in 1918; then the European and Asiatic theaters campaign medals.

Lieutenant General Francis P. Mulcahy died on 11 December 1973.

NIMMER, Major General David Rowan was born on 14 October 1894 in St. Louis, Missouri. He was living in Los Angeles when he "ran away from home" and in November 1912 enlisted in the Marine Corps. He went to Mare Island for Boot Camp and after three months was shipped to the Philippines, stopping in between at Honolulu, Guam and Olongapo. He was back on Guam a few months later. Nimmer served enlisted until he accepted a commission as a second lieutenant on 17 July 1918 and the following day was promoted to first lieutenant. Assigned to duty with Headquarters Company in the newly created 5th Machine Gun Battalion, 5th Marine Brigade, Nimmer was shipped to France, arriving on 10 November 1918. The war was over the following day and he, like so many other Marines in the Brigade, was assigned various duties during the occupation of Germany. Following the Marines' return to the U.S. in August 1919, Nimmer resigned his captain's commission on 29 September 1919. He, however, returned to active duty in the Marine Corps as a captain in April 1921, with a date of commission, back to 4 June 1920.

His first assignment was in the Quartermaster Department and duty at the MB, Quantico on 8 June 1921. That service continued until, on 29 April 1925, he went aboard the *Mississippi* for duty as "skipper" of the MD, remaining aboard until May 1927 when he returned to Quantico. He was made an Instructor at Marine Corps Schools between 1927 and 1929. He went back aboard ship to command the MD on 4 September 1929; this time it was the cruiser *Pittsburgh*.

He served his next tour with the Fourth Marine Regiment in Shanghai from 1929 until 1930, then he, with special permission, went north to Harbin, in Manchuria, before the Japanese conquered it from China. In the period 1931–1932 he was assigned to the American Legation in Peking, China, where he learned the Russian language. He was the second Marine officer, after James Moriarity, to be a Russian language expert. His transfer back to the U.S. was to HQMC, and then to the Navy Department, assuming duty there on 12 December 1932. His next formal appointment was as Assistant Naval Attaché in Moscow from 1932 to 1935. (It wasn't until Roosevelt was president that the U.S. recognized the Soviet Union on 17 November 1933. The tale of his tenure in Russia is a whole fascinating story in itself.)

Major Nimmer (29 May 1934) was back in the U.S. and on 3 September 1935 was on duty at Quantico. During this period he graduated from both the Junior Officer and Senior Officer classes at the Quantico MCS. In June 1938 he was a student at the Senior course, NWC, Newport, RI. Lt.Col. Nimmer (29 June 1938) graduated the following year, 30 June 1939, and went back to Quantico where he had been assigned duty with the troops 29 May 1939. His posting was as operations officer with the 1st Marine Brigade (and later Division). This lasted until late December 1941-early January 1942 when there was a major shake-up of senior personnel in the division when MG Holland Smith reviewed its attainments, or, in his opinion, lack thereof. Major General Torrey was relieved as division CG and in his place, BG Alexander A. Vandegrift was appointed. At about this time, Nimmer's ulcers began acting up and his aide, Lt.Col. Gerald Thomas, succeeded him as D-3.

Upon partially regaining his health, on 14 April 1942 he was made CO of the Marine Corps Base, Guantánamo Bay, Cuba, serving until 1942, then as CO of the Ninth

Defense Battalion. Col. Nimmer's (1 January 1942) battalion was transferred to the Pacific in October 1942 and that November to Guadalcanal, remaining there until April 1943 when Nimmer's ulcers acted up once again and he was returned to the States for treatment. Nimmer's next duty was with the Pacific war section of the Joint War Plans Committee of the JCS, Commander in Chief, United States Fleet, from 1943 until October 1944.

Brigadier General Nimmer (in February 1944 but effective 4 April 1943) next commanded the IIIMAC Artillery from November 1944 and then, from April 1945 until that island was secured, the Marines' heavy artillery at Okinawa. During that prelanding period, his gunners needed extensive re-training and two of his batteries were sidetracked or arrived late. They in turn required extensive training, and that mainly on the job. His next promotion was to major general upon retirement in July 1947.

His decorations included the usual medals from service in World War I, the Victory medal with clasps, China expeditionary service, and the Legion of Merit for his services at Okinawa, plus the usual Pacific theater campaign medals and Victory Medal.

Major General David R. Nimmer died on 23 August 1975.

NOBLE, General Alfred Houston. was born on 26 October 1894 in Federalsburg, MD. He earned a B.A. degree from St. John's College, in Annapolis, MD and on 24 May 1917 accepted a commission as a reserve second lieutenant of Marines, which was then upgraded to a regular commission on 10 September 1917. At Quantico he was assigned as a platoon leader with the 83d Company, 3d Battalion, 6th Marines which in November that year arrived in France.

The 1st Battalion, 6th, had already arrived and was engaged in laboring work, as was the 5th Marines. Not until 2/6 landed in early February 1918 would the entire regiment be together, which with the 5th Marines and 6th Machine Gun Battalion, was the core of the 4th Marine Brigade. It, along with its comrades of the 3d Army Brigade, and ancillary units, composed the fire-eating 2d Division (Regulars).

After brief training, the 4th Brigade was entered into the lines in the Verdun Sector in mid–March and with activity but without major incident was relieved in mid–May with some experience in various trench-type combat situations. After a few weeks in western France, the 2d Division was directed to help the French 6th Army stop the advancing German Army, now east of Paris.

Arriving slightly to the west of Chateau Thierry, the 6th Marines took up positions off the north side of the Paris-Metz Road followed by the 5th Marines, who moved the line still further north. This was on 1 June 1918. The division stopped the enemy and on 6 June the 4th Brigade was ordered to recapture the Bois de Belleau (Belleau Wood). The 5th Marines launched attacks against the western face and the 6th attacked the southern face. The 82d Company began their advance and moved into the woods when they were stopped by the heavy machine gun fire. The 83d followed in support and fought its way to a clump of trees about 300 yards northwest of Bouresches. However, the losses suffered by 3/6 were heavy and the battalion was unable to do anything more than hold on for the next few days.

Noble showed his stuff when his CO was wounded; he became "skipper" of the 83d and earned a DSC, later supplemented by a Navy Cross, for actions between 6 and 8 June 1918. The award noted that he was "conspicuous for his judgment and personal courage in handling his company in attacks against superior numbers in fortified machine gun nests."

Noble fought the rest of the war as the

company "skipper" with courage, earning several more citations, later three Silver Stars, and a silver Croix de Guerre, at Blanc Mont and during the Meuse River campaign. He remained with the battalion through the occupation and returned home in August 1919. After the usual parades, the brigade was dissolved and officers and men desiring separation, were rapidly sent back to civilian life. Noble appeared to enjoy life as a Marine and remained with the Corps.

After a brief leave, in September 1919 he was assigned to duty at the MB, St. Thomas, the Virgin Islands, remaining there until June 1922. On 11 April 1921, he was promoted to permanent captain. After completing the Company Officers' course at MCS, Quantico, he remained there serving as an instructor, then adjutant and secretary and finally as CO of the school's MD. He left Quantico in July 1927 and the following month went aboard the *California* to command its MD. During this tour they landed in Nicaragua in support of the U.S. intervention, but made no significant impact and all returned shipboard soon after.

He returned to the MCS at Quantico, enrolling in the Field Officers' course, graduating and then serving as an instructor for several years. Major Noble (1 July 1932) next served as CoS of the 1st Marine Brigade in Haiti but his term expired in August 1934 as the Marines were withdrawn. Noble served at HQMC with the Adjutant and Inspectors Office until May 1937, then returned to Quantico where he was one of the four Marine members dedicated to revising the *Tentative Landing Operations Manual*. He continued with this duty through the several revisions to the final updated version.

Lt.Col. Noble's (1 August 1935) next role was as Assistant Commandant of Marine Corps Schools, remaining at that post from 1937 to 1939. Next he was made a battalion commander in the 5th Marines, and later the regimental CO from 27 May 1940 until 14 May 1941. This period was spent in

Alfred Houston Noble

the Caribbean, mainly based at Guantánamo Bay in Cuba, but in training and maneuvers at Culebra Island. Col. Noble (1 August 1940) was again ordered to HQMC on 19 May 1941.

There he was made Officer in Charge of the Material Section, Division of Plans and Policies, and later became Director of the latter organization. With the coming of the new war, there was promotion for everyone and Noble had an assignment as CoS for the newly minted 3d Division under the CG, MG Charles D. Barrett. While in New Zealand, when Barrett was transferred to command the IMAC, at Barrett's request Brigadier General Noble (16 September 1942) followed as his Deputy Corps Commander. For his services at Bougainville, Admiral William F. Halsey, USN, awarded Noble the Legion of Merit with a "Combat V."

After that campaign, Noble was back with the 3d Division as ADC under MG Allen Hal Turnage and for a period, beginning in February 1944, he was the CG of

Task Group A, IMAC. He then served again as ADC of the 3d Division through the Guam Campaign. When Turnage returned to the States in September 1944, Noble became the Acting CG of the Division from 15 September to 13 October 1944 when Graves Erskine assumed command. Noble had, however, received a promotion to major general, which was effective back to 18 September 1942.

For his planning and operations (because of Gen. Barrett's death, Noble was mainly responsible for the planning) as ADC of the 3d Division in the Guam Campaign, he earned another Legion of Merit also with a "Combat V." However, his time overseas was now up, and he returned to the U.S. in November 1944. Upon arrival, following a brief leave, he was made CG of Training Command at Camp Lejeune, which post he retained until the war terminated.

This was followed by his return to the Pacific where, from February through August 1946 he commanded the Marine Garrison Forces of the 14th Naval District at Pearl Harbor, HI. Sent to Tientsin next, he became ADC of the 1stMarDiv in North China. He hardly had time to unpack when he was sent back to Coronado, CA, where he assumed command of the Troop Training Command, Amphibious Forces, Pacific Fleet, remaining there until February 1948.

He continued moving about; next to Parris Island as CG of the Recruit Depot until August 1950 when he was back on the West Coast as CG of the MB at Camp Pendleton for a year. Next he was made CG of the Department of the Pacific at San Francisco for a year. Then to the Netherlands; they were fighting a losing war to regain their control over the Dutch East Indies (later Indonesia) where he was an advisor to their military command. In September 1954, he assumed the role of CG of Camp Lejeune for one more year. That was followed in September 1955 by elevation to lieutenant general and as CG of the FMF, Atlantic, based at Norfolk, VA. That November, he and several other notable Marines made the trek back to Belleau Wood where they witnessed the erection of a plaque dedicated to their 4th Brigade.

On 1 November 1956, at age 62, Noble was elevated to full general and retired with nearly 40 years' active service as a Marine.

His awards were primarily the eminent decorations earned during the first World War and the two Legions of Merit. Other awards included a Presidential Unit Citation with a bronze star; Victory Medals and clasps from both World Wars; World War II campaign medals; China Service Medal; several Haitian medals and the Order of the Orange Nassau with crossed swords from the Netherlands.

After a long life, General Alfred H. Noble died on 27 September 1983, a month before he would have had his 89th birthday.

OSTERMANN, Major General Edward Albert was born in Columbus, OH on 23 November 1882, a son of Mr. and Mrs. Seigmund Ostermann. He attended the public schools of Milo, Columbus, and Dayton, OH. After attending Ohio Northern University at Ada for two and a half years, he enlisted in the Army on 21 October 1899 to serve briefly during the Spanish-American War. Discharged a chief trumpeter at the expiration of a three-year enlistment, Ostermann remained a civilian for about one and a half years and then reenlisted in the Army on 28 April 1904. He was honorably discharged by purchase on 12 November 1905 as a chief trumpeter with the First Band, Artillery Corps.

Apparently military service continued to appeal to him and he accepted a second lieutenant's commission in the Marine Corps on 20 March 1907, though his date of entry in the records was listed as on 14 March. His first assignment was at MOS, Norfolk, VA, and then to the Norfolk MB on 14 December 1907. Ostermann's first overseas assignment was to the American Legation, MD at Peking, China, arriving on 15 November 1908. First Lieutenant Ostermann (23 April 1909) remained there until transferred to MB, Washington D.C. on 3 January 1910. On 10 December, he was transferred to the MB, Boston, MA.

On 26 May 1912, during the "troubles" in Nicaragua, he was assigned duty at Camp Elliott, the Panama Canal zone, then commanded by a man with whom he would serve several times in the near future, Major Smedley D. Butler. He was part of Butler's battalion command that landed in Nicaragua in August 1912 and was selected by Butler to travel forward to warn a so-called native "general" that the Marines were going through to Granada and he'd better not try to stop them. They didn't and Ostermann went on to serve there until the "troubles" were over. He was back in the States with the 1st Brigade, ABF, at the Philadelphia Navy Yard on 4 December 1914.

In 1915 the U.S. intervened in Haiti and the Brigade was the instrument of choice, landing began on 1 July. Ostermann was awarded the Medal of Honor in 1917 for his conspicuous gallantry in action incident to the capture of Fort Dipitie, Haiti, on 24 October 1915. The citation accompanying the Medal states that a Marine detachment was crossing a river in a deep ravine at night when it was suddenly fired upon from three sides by about 400 Cacos concealed in the bushes about 100 yards from the objective, Fort Dipitie. The Marines fought their way forward to a good position and maintained it throughout the night despite the continuous fire of the Cacos. At daybreak, the Marines, in three squads commanded by Lieutenant Ostermann, Capt. William P. Upshur and Gunnery Sergeant Daniel Daly, advanced in three different directions, surprising and scattering the Cacos. The squads of Ostermann and Upshur, with a total of 13 Marines, then went to the capture the fort. The fort was demolished and burned and the garrison was put to flight. "These men were in pitch darkness surrounded by ten times their number and fighting for their lives..." the citation relates. "Had one squad failed, not one man of the party would have lived to tell the story..." (The three award citations for Ostermann, Upshur, and Daly, were written for their leadership in driving off the surrounding Cacos, not, as is usually cited, for taking Fort Dipitie.)

Later in the Haitian campaign, on 11 November 1915, Ostermann was wounded in action and returned to the United States for hospitalization. Perhaps it was during this period that he met Katherine, who became Mrs. Ostermann. After some repairs, Ostermann was back in Haiti and by 29 April 1916 was assigned duty as an officer with the newly created *Gendamerie d'Haiti* where Capt. Ostermann (29 August 1916) served as a major. The U.S. was now at war

Edward Albert Ostermann

and Major Ostermann (22 May 1917) and those officers on active duty found themselves promoted more rapidly than usual.

On 1 August 1918 he was at the MB, Quantico and on 30 July 1919 he was back in Haiti with the 1st Provisional Brigade, returning to the States again in August 1921, his majority having been confirmed on 4 June 1920. On 14 August 1921 Ostermann was on duty with the Adjutant and Inspectors Office based at the MB, Parris Island, SC and on 18 April 1923 he was at HQMC, followed in December 1925 by transfer to the MB, San Diego, CA. On the following 5 May he became the FMO of the Scouting Fleet, while serving aboard the *Wyoming*. In July 1927 he went ashore, took annual leave and on 30 August 1927 assumed a role at the MB, Quantico, VA. On 25 June 1928 he was back at HQMC, where he would remain for a number of years.

By November 1933 he had arrived for duty at Guantánamo Bay, Cuba, and a month later, on 24 December, he was promoted to lieutenant colonel. Col. Ostermann (30 June 1935) was, as of 20 June, attending classes at the NWC in Newport, RI from which he graduated on 26 May the following year, after which he was back at Quantico.

Ordered to HQMC in 1938 to become the Assistant Adjutant and Inspector of the Marine Corps, on 1 February 1939 Ostermann was advanced to the post of Adjutant and Inspector with the rank of brigadier general, for a period of four years. With the coming of World War II, General Ostermann requested combat duty as either a brigadier general or as a colonel. In refusing the request as "impracticable at this time," the Major General Commandant expressed his full appreciation of the offer to the Adjutant and Inspector.

On 1 January 1943 BG Ostermann was retired due to physical disability. Because of having been "specially commended for his performance of duty in actual combat" by virtue of the award of the Medal of Honor, Ostermann was promoted to the rank of major general on the retired list. He and Katherine retired to a farm called Wakefield Manor at Huntly, VA, and lived happily and comfortably for a number of years.

During the course of his long service, he earned the following medals and decorations: Medal of Honor, Purple Heart, Cuban Pacification Medal, Marine Corps Expeditionary Medal with two stars, Mexican Service Medal, Nicaraguan Campaign Medal, Haitian Campaign Medal, Victory Medal (World War I) with West Indies clasp, American Defense Service Medal, American Area Campaign Medal, World War II Victory Medal, and the Republic of Haiti's Distinguished Service Medal in the grade of Officer.

Major General Edward A. Ostermann died at age 87 at a nursing home in Fairfax, VA, on 18 May 1969 and was buried with honors at Arlington National Cemetery.

PECK, Major General DeWitt was born on 29 May 1894 in Bakersfield, CA. Awarded an appointment at the Naval Academy, he graduated in June 1915 and was commissioned a second lieutenant of Marines. He trained briefly at Gettysburg, PA and at the MOS at Portsmouth, VA and his first assignment was to the 1st Marine Brigade in Haiti, serving there from 4 January 1916 until 23 March 1917. First Lieutenant Peck (29 August 1916), along with a large segment of the Marines in Haiti and in Santo Domingo, was withdrawn and returned to the U.S. and incorporated into the 5th Marine Regiment. When Congress declared War on 6 April 1917, now Capt. Peck (26 March 1917) was assigned to the 5th Marines but didn't arrive in France until 8 June 1918. His first assignment within the regiment is not apparent, but possibly he was sent to one of the newly created AEF officers' schools. He doesn't appear as a member of the 55th Company until late

September 1918 when he became "skipper," leading them at the Battle for Blanc Mont in October. He was wounded in action on 4 October and was out of commission for the balance of the war but he went with the division into Germany and served in the occupation until returning home in June 1919. Effective on 1 July 1918, Peck had been promoted to major but his rank was reduced to captain in 1920.

As of 26 March 1920 he was stationed at the MB, Quantico. His next overseas assignment was at Guantánamo Bay, Cuba, arriving on 24 July 1922 and remaining there until his transfer to the 1st Brigade of Marines in Haiti on 17 November 1923. In June 1924 he was back in the U.S., had taken a leave and was at the MB, Quantico, in August. He graduated from the Field Officers' class and then served as an instructor at MCS in 1925. Peck then went to school at Fort Leavenworth in 1927, graduating from the C&GSS in 1928 and returning to MB, Quantico, on 17 July. For the following year he taught at the MCS. Next, on 17 May 1929, Major Peck (2 January 1929) came sea duty aboard the *Galveston* as SMO in the special service squadron. While attached, he was assigned ashore to the Nicaraguan Electoral Mission in 1929 as an intelligence officer aiding the U.S. Electoral officers in their mission to insure an "honest election."

He was back in the States in June 1931 and at the MB, Quantico, as of 3 August 1931. There he was once again instructor at MCS until 1933 where by this date he was listed as an interpreter in both French and Spanish. Lt.Col. Peck (29 May 1934) on 22 June 1935 attended the NWC, graduating in 1936, but they retained him in Newport as an instructor until 1937. On 17 June 1938 he was back with the troops at San Diego, where he was assigned to duty with the FMF. Now Col. Peck (1 February 1939) was assigned as the CO of the 4th Marines stationed in Shanghai, China, on 16 December 1939. His term as CO would last from 3 January 1940 until 13 May 1941 when, lucky for him, he would be replaced by unlucky Col. Samuel L. Howard.

Peck's experiences in China would include some close encounters with the invading Japanese military and naval forces then engaged in an undeclared war with China. The Japanese were anxious for all foreigners to leave China to their tender mercies; most of the other occupiers would depart or had already removed themselves. France already had, and hard-pressed Britain, still in residence, would eventually go. Meanwhile, after Italy joined the Germans and declared war on Britain in June 1940, those two nations had adjacent territory in the International Settlement and their differences became positively volatile for a time.

Peck, fearing trouble between the two, called on each commander and both quickly agreed to be discreet in their handling of the opposite's troops on liberty in their sector. The Japanese, however, were not so considerate. They tried numerous attempts at intrusion in the American zone, each of which was put down by the 4th Marines under Peck's direction. One situation became serious. Twenty-five armed Japanese soldiers entered the American zone and the CO of 1/4, Lt.Col. Eugene F. Collier, immediately went out and picked up 16 armed Japanese soldiers. Some refused to surrender their arms, a few became rambunctious, others resisted arrest and had to be picked up bodily and thrown into the trucks. Finally MG Saburo Miura, IJA, came to see Col. Peck to apologize for the "unpleasantness" caused by his men. Peck thereupon released the Japanese soldiers to the general, and after a few outbursts by the Japanese about how cruelly their troops had been treated, once again, quiet reigned in the American settlement.

The end of Peck's tenure arrived and he went back to the U.S. in June 1941. But on the first of the following month, he was assigned to Headquarters, Commander in Chief, United States Fleet. Brigadier General Peck's (March 1942) role was as Assistant CoS for War Plans to the Commander South Pacific Area and South Pacific Force, May 1942 through July 1943. This was followed by assignment as Director of the Marine Corps Division of Plans and Policies, 1943–1944. Major General Peck (1 January 1944) was Assistant Commandant of the Marine Corps between 1944 and 1945.

He managed to get back with the troops when he was assigned duty as CG of the 1stMarDiv in August 1945, retaining that post in China until late 1946. He retired from the Marine Corps in November 1946 after 30 years of service. Peck returned to active duty briefly in 1953 and served as deputy director of manpower utilization in the Department of Defense.

General Peck's decorations included two Legions of Merit, the first for his planning services with the Navy and the second for command of the 1stMarDiv and its entry into China. He was awarded the Purple Heart, for his wounds received at Blanc Mont in October 1918, and Victory Medals from both World Wars, plus the World War II campaign medals.

Major General DeWitt Peck died on 13 January 1973.

PEPPER, Lieutenant General Robert Houston was born on 22 April 1895 in Georgetown, DE. He earned a B.A. from the University of Delaware in 1917 and soon after accepted a commission as a second lieutenant of Marines on 15 August 1917. The following day, like so many others, he was promoted to first lieutenant. After a few weeks training at the MOS he was shipped to the Caribbean.

Pepper served with the 1st Provisional Brigade in Haiti from 15 December 1917 and, now captain (1 July 1918), remained there until December 1919. Following a brief leave he was at the MB, Quantico, on 3 January 1920 but, like so many others, now reduced to first lieutenant. Pepper was selected to journey to France in May 1920 to help in preparing maps of the battlefields there, returning that December. For the next two years he was at the MB, Quantico.

He was back in Haiti on 18 May 1922 as an aide to the American Commissioner to Haiti, BG John H. Russell, USMC; he would remain until August 1924. On 24 August, Capt. Pepper (20 August 1924) arrived back at the MB in Quantico where he was next a student at the USA Transport School, Fort Holabird, MD, graduating in June 1925. On the 17th of the following month, he arrived at Marine Base, San Diego, where he became part of MG Smedley Butler's 3d Brigade. With that brigade, he arrived in China on 24 February 1927. Two years later, the Brigade returned to the States and Pepper arrived at the MB, Quantico, on 30 August 1929.

He was next an instructor in the Correspondence School, Quantico, from 30 August 1929 through the summer of August 1931. This was followed by two years of sea duty, beginning on 21 August 1931, as skipper of the MD aboard the *Oklahoma*. Back ashore he assumed responsibilities at San Diego on 15 August 1933 then attended the Army Coastal Artillery School at Fort Monroe, VA, from July 1934 to June 1935.

Major Pepper's (1 May 1935) next assignment, on 28 July, was at HQMC, as Artillery Assistant in the War Plans Section of the Division of Plans and Policy where he, and a group led by Col. Charles D. Barrett, played key roles in fully developing the concept of Marine defense battalions; primarily artillery units. The then "latest" concept was toward developing Marine units (Defense Battalions) to defend national territory (islands in the Pacific), and with a few larger units (think brigades or even divisions) for the taking of enemy Pacific holdings. The thinking being that the navy of the obvious potential enemy, Japan, would be defeated by the U.S. Navy. Of course, as we know, the enemy gave no time for our fleet to do anything but die at Pearl Harbor and in a few battles soon after.

Major Pepper became battalion commander with 15th Marines from June to September 1939. On 1 October, the 90mm antiaircraft was removed to form the 3d Defense Battalion, FMF, formed on that date at Parris Island, SC, Lt.Col. Pepper (1 October 1939) becoming CO of that organization. He and his unit left P.I. bound for Hawaii in April 1940. For a time, a third of his unit was sent to Midway Island in September 1940 and early the following year the balance of the battalion was sent to Midway. They returned to Pearl, however, in October 1941 and Pepper was in command of this unit during the defense of Pearl Harbor on 7 December 1941. Following that defense, Col. Pepper (20 May 1942) led his command throughout the early months of the Guadalcanal Campaign in the Solomon Islands in 1942, receiving the Legion of Merit with Combat "V" for his outstanding performance.

Pepper became EO of the 11th Marines from August 1940 until March 1943, serving at Cape Gloucester. Then when Pedro del Valle was promoted to command the division, Col. Pepper assumed command of the Regiment in March 1943, participating with it during much of the Cape Gloucester (New Britain) operation, kicked off in late December of that year.

In February 1944, Pepper returned to the U.S. to become CoS at Camp Lejeune, NC, leaving this post in June 1945 to command the VAC Artillery (with headquarters at Guam) until the war ended. Late in 1945 he served Deputy CoS of the FMF, Pacific, until returning stateside in May 1946. In the meantime, effective 7 December 1943, he was now Brigadier General Pepper.

From 1946 to 1949, he was, initially, Assistant Director, and then Director of Marine Corps Personnel. On 13 April 1949, the Commandant, General A.A. Vandegrift, appointed Pepper CG of Test & Training unit, Amphibious Training Command, Norfolk, VA. From August 1950 to February 1952 (with the Korean War in progress), he commanded the Marine Corps Recruit Depot at Parris Island; retroactive back to 7 December 1943, he was a major general. He then became CG of the 3dMarDiv at Camp Pendleton, CA, sailing with it to Japan in August 1953. From May to July 1954, he commanded the 1stMarDiv in Korea before moving to Pearl Harbor to lead the FMF, Pacific, a position he held until September 1955 and as a temporary lieutenant general on 2 August 1954. (According to the following year's register, he was back to major general.) At the end of that month, he undertook his final assignment as CG, Department of the Pacific at San Francisco, serving in this capacity until his retirement at the rank of LG on 1 May 1957, after almost 40 years of continuous active service. He was recalled to active duty on several occasions in later years to serve as a member of various Defense Department or Marine Corps study groups, and in 1964 was back to lead the Pepper Board, a special study group focusing on the role of Women Marines in peacetime.

His decorations included the Legion of Merit and two Commendation Ribbons. Additionally, he was awarded numerous expeditionary medals from Haiti, China, and the World War II various campaign medals.

Lieutenant General Robert H. Pepper died of cancer at the U.S. Naval Hospital, Bethesda, MD, on 2 June 1968, at age 73.

PFEIFFER, Major General Omar Titus was born on 24 November 1895, in Toledo, OH. He earned a B.A. from the University of Minnesota in 1917 and was one of the numerous students from that university to volunteer to become a Marine officer, accepting a commission as a second lieutenant of

Marines on 10 August 1917. The following day he, like so many others, was promoted to first lieutenant. On 30 October 1917 he went aboard ship and served with the Atlantic Fleet in World War I. Another promotion, this time to captain, became effective on 1 July 1918.

When the war terminated he was at the MB, Navy Yard, Norfolk, VA, effective on 13 December 1918. He decided he liked being a Marine and managed to obtain a permanent position as a Marine officer. This was followed by assignment to the 2d Provisional Brigade in Santo Domingo on 1 September 1919. Pfeiffer remained there until September 1921, after which he was assigned to duty at the MB, NAS, San Diego on 7 November 1921. In the meantime, like so many other junior officers postwar, his lineal grade was greatly reduced though he remained a captain as of 4 June 1920. This caused a great turmoil which was aided by two separate boards of inquiry, Russell's and Neville's. (His sojourn at San Diego was apparently interrupted, with no available information as to when and where he went. However, he is later listed as returning to the same post at the NAS in San Diego, on 16 July 1924. Another, though questionable record, places him at the MB, Guam, between March and December 1925.)

On 22 December 1925 he was shipped to the MB, Naval Station, Cavite, Philippine Islands, as a company commander, returning to the MB, Quantico on 16 December 1927. (During the latter period he may also have been sidetracked to the American Settlement in Shanghai, according to a sometimes questionable source.) He then attended the MCS and graduated from the Company Officers' course.

Pfeiffer was then assigned to the MB, Navy Yard, Pearl Harbor until July 1931, followed on 13 August 1930 to the Fourteenth Naval District (Hawaii). He remained there until his return to the U.S. and assignment at the Norfolk Navy Yard on 28 March 1933. On 13 January 1934 he was assigned to duty at HQMC and promoted to major on 29 May that year. In June 1936 he attended the NWC, graduating in May 1937. This was followed by lengthy duty in the War Plans section at the MB, Quantico, from 17 May 1937. Lt.Col. Pfeiffer (29 June 1938) next became Assistant War Plans officer with the Commander in Chief, Pacific Fleet, on 16 April 1941. His role was as the Commandant's representative in Admiral Kimmel's office. Holcomb preferred that Kimmel realize that the Marine Corps was a separate entity, not belonging to the Navy; therefore he wanted to keep an eye on what the admiral was doing and thinking. In later years Pfeiffer related how he was, more or less, a go-between for Vandegrift and Rear Admiral R.K. Turner at Guadalcanal and later between Turner and LGC Holcomb. Pfeiffer would remain in this sensitive post until June 1943. Col. Pfeiffer (29 April 1942) was promoted to brigadier general on 5 October 1942.

Pfeiffer remained as staff Marine officer at Commander in Chief United States Fleet (now Admiral Ernest King) between June 1943 and November 1945. While in this post, he was awarded a Legion of Merit. This was followed by duty in the office of the Chief of Naval Operations until February 1946. Next he was FMO with the Commander of the Seventh Fleet between February 1946 and May 1947.

Back to the troops when on 1 May 1946 he became CG of the FMF, Western Pacific, until October 1947. This organization had a T/O & E of a Headquarters & Service Bn, two infantry bns, the 12th Service Bn, and AirFMFWesPac. Its job was to provide security for various naval installations plus protection of American citizens in North China. In October, after establishing a flourishing command, Pfeiffer was then replaced by his old comrade "Jerry" Thomas.

Between October 1947 and July 1948 Pfeiffer becoming CoS of the Marine Barracks and Marine Training and Replacement Command, at Camp Pendleton. He was promoted to major general upon retirement in May 1950.

Decorations included the Legion of Merit and Bronze Star and various expeditionary medals for Santo Domingo, China(?), and the various World War II campaign medals plus Victory Medals for both world wars.

Major General Omar T. Pfeiffer died on 1 March 1979.

PICKETT, Major General Harry Kleinbeck was born on 9 January 1888, in Ridgeway, SC. Awarded a B.S. from the Citadel in 1913, Pickett accepted a commission as a second lieutenant of Marines on 6 February 1913. His original assignment, on 25 March, was to the MOS at MB, Norfolk, VA. After graduation came duty at the Navy Yard, Mare Island, CA beginning on 8 June 1914. His first overseas assignment was at the MB, Guam Naval Station, from 28 April 1915 until August 1917, and during this sojourn he was promoted to captain effective on 23 September 1916. (I have no record of his being a first lieutenant but it was probably on 29 August 1916 when so many junior officers became 1stLts.)

Major Pickett (1 July 1918) became CO of 1/11 on that date, and with the infantry regiment as part of the 5th Marine Brigade, went over to France, arriving on 13 October 1918. They were too late to participate in the war but did remain for occupation duty in Germany, returning home in July-August 1919 with the rest of the Marines.

Upon his return, he, like many other war-time promoted Marines, was reduced to his previous rank of captain. After a short leave he was assigned duty with the MB, Navy Yard, Charleston, SC, arriving on 5 September 1919. A year later, 20 September 1920, he was on recruiting duty at Memphis, TN. In another year, on 31 October 1921, Pickett was with the 2d Brigade in Santo Domingo. This was at a time when the anti-bandit activity took on a new impetus and Pickett was right at the heart of the action. Patrols were now utilizing air support and messages directing them toward observed enemy location and potential ambuscades.

He returned to the States in June and, after leave, on 5 July reported for duty at the MB, Quantico. While there he graduated from the MCS Field Officers' course and the next year, on 1 August 1924, he was posted to HQMC. Major Pickett (28 July 1925) was on 25 August 1925 assigned to duty with the Quartermaster Department at the MB, Norfolk Navy Yard, arriving on 4 September and remaining there until he was sent to join the 1st Brigade in Haiti on 13 June 1928, still assigned duty with QM.

He was back at HQMC on 31 January 1930 and was selected for promotion to lieutenant colonel effective 29 May 1934. On 1 July 1935 he was at Quantico, remaining there until 14 October 1936 when he transferred to the Naval Base at San Diego. Col. Pickett (29 June 1938) was on duty in New York and during this period he completed a course at the USA Coast Artillery School. This was in preparation for his duties in developing the Defense Battalion concept, which concept was popular in the Corps at that time.

Following graduation he was once again back at San Diego on 19 December 1938 and remained there until transferred as the Marine Officer to the 14th Naval District, and also CO of the MB, Honolulu, the Hawaiian Islands. He helped establish the 1st Defense Battalion, elements of which later made a splendid defense of Wake Island in December 1941. His unit also had detachments at Pearl Harbor, Johnston Island and Palmyra Island, as well as at Wake, a total of 50 officers and 953 men. He temporarily replaced Col. Pepper as CO of the 3d DB on 23 August 1940. Pepper was lauded for his drive and energy plus obtaining necessary equipment for his respective commands on the various atolls.

When Pearl Harbor was attacked by the air and naval forces of Imperial Japan on 7 December 1941, Col. Pickett and his local units went into action immediately. On 13 December, all Marine ground forces in the Islands were placed in his capable hands. His first move afterward was to send strengthening units from the 1st, 3d and 4th DBs to various outlying islands like Palmyra, Midway, Wake, and Johnston. As we know, the reinforcements for Wake were returned to Pearl Harbor by Adm. Fletcher, who made the decision not to close with any Japanese naval forces.

Brigadier General Pickett (1 January 1942) assumed duties as the CG of Marine Garrison Forces in the 14th Naval District and soon after, he was major general on 28 September 1942. Then Pickett became CG of the Troop Training Unit, Training Command, Amphibious Forces, Pacific Fleet May 1943 until July 1946. MG Pickett was retired on 1 November 1946 after 33 years' service.

His decorations included two Legions of Merit, one for the period from 28 August 1940 until 19 May 1943, and the second for the period from August 1943 until January 1945. Other decorations included campaign and Victory medals for World War I, World War II, and expeditionary medals in Santo Domingo.

Major General Harry K. Pickett died on 19 March 1965.

PRICE, Lieutenant General Charles Frederick Berthold was born on 18 September 1881 in Hamburg, Germany, the son of American parents temporarily residing there. It appears that all his schooling was in the U.S. and he graduated from the Pennsylvania Military College in 1902 with a degree in Civil Engineering. His first employment was with the Pennsylvania Railroad and while there he served as a member of the Pennsylvania National Guard, in the 2d Troop, Philadelphia City Cavalry. Deciding upon a military career, Price accepted a commission as a second lieutenant of Marines on 30 December 1905. His active duty beginning at the School of Application, Annapolis MB, on 8 February 1906, he remained there for about six months. On 8 October 1906 he and numerous other Marines were called upon to serve on expeditionary duty with the 1st Provisional Brigade of Marines in Cuba. First Lieutenant Price's (14 May 1908) sojourn lasted until 31 December 1908, when he was en route back to the States.

On 11 December 1909, Price was assigned to Major Smedley D. Butler's command at Camp Elliott, the Canal Zone. This location was established mainly to keep an eye on what was going on in Nicaragua. When Butler and his battalion went into Nicaragua in early 1910, Price was with him. He was back in the U.S. on 6 May 1910 at the Rifle Range in Winthrop, MD; several months after arrival, he assumed command of the post.

During the next three years he was at the rifle range then, on 11 November 1913, he was assigned to duty at the MB, Norfolk, VA. After service with the Marine landing force at Vera Cruz in April 1914, Price's next duty was once more as the CO of the Winthrop Rifle Range effective 20 July 1915. Many superb Marine riflemen would have been trained at this range during his tenure and the German army would certainly learn to respect the "graduates."

Capt. Price's (29 August 1916) next posting was as skipper of the MD, *Arkansas,* arriving on 4 December 1916; on 22 May 1917 he became Major Price. That rank would become permanent on 4 June 1920.

In October of 1918 he sailed with the 11th Marines, 5th Marine Brigade, for France arriving too late for combat service but remaining for the occupation of Germany. He was selected to head up the 15th Separate Battalion, 18 officers and 737 enlisted men designated to oversee the forthcoming Schleswig-Holstein vote which would decide if the citizens should remain within Germany or join Denmark. The battalion came home later, nearly forgotten by everyone but their families.

Upon returning to the U.S., Price was to have gone to the MB, Philadelphia Navy Yard, but it appears those orders were changed and he remained at the MB, Quantico, from 30 December 1919. During this period he graduated from the Field Officers' course in June 1922. On 1 September 1922 he entered the next C&GSS class at Fort Leavenworth, graduating in June 1923. His first assignment after graduation was as an instructor in tactics at MCS, Quantico, reporting on 28 July 1923.

When the Asiatic Fleet began maneuvers in the Hawaiian Island waters, he was temporarily detached to participate. Overseas duty with the American Legation in Peking came next, Price reporting on 12 October 1925. His post was as Intelligence Officer and Officer in charge of Operations and Training. He remained at Peking until September 1927, when he returned to the States, took leave and then in November 1927 returned to the MB, Quantico.

His next overseas assignment was with the American Electoral Mission in Nicaragua, arriving there in July 1928 and remaining until November. In December he returned to MB, Quantico. This would not be the last time he would serve with the Electoral Mission in Nicaragua. He was back in 1930, 1931, and 1932 and received praise for his services from President Calvin Coolidge, his Secretary of State, and the Nicaraguan President. Lt.Col. Price's (29 October 1931) base remained at Quantico during the entire period. He is credited with being the Director of the Field Officers' course and, with Charles Barrett and Lyle H. Miller, for preparing the text for the vaunted *Marine Corps Landing Operations* manual.

In April 1936, Col. Price (1 February 1935) was shipped out to Shanghai, China, to assume command of the 4th Marines, relieving Col. John C. Beaumont on 7 May. Upon arrival he had 58 officers and warrants, plus 978 enlisted men, barely a battalion, with which to attempt to dissuade the Japanese from infringement on the International Settlement. Those numbers increased in September 1937 to 70 officers and 1279 enlisted but were still nowhere near sufficient for the job at hand. During this period, Price proved to be a superb soldier, negotiator, politician, and trainer of his command. It was when the Japanese were doing their utmost to upset the various foreign elements in the International Settlement, and the Marines were constantly in their way. His lone two battalions were supplemented by the arrival on 19 September 1937 of the 6th Marines, Col. Thomas S. Clarke commanding. The 6th would

Charles Frederick Berthold Price

remain only a few months in China, and when they left, the situation was just as it had been before.

Certainly this period was a highlight of Price's Marine career. He was awarded the Distinguished Service Medal for his "excellent tact, judgment, initiative, and administrative ability of a high order." Returning to the U.S. on 23 October 1938, Price had a brief leave and was then assigned duty as a member of the Examining Board (for promotions) at HQMC. Brigadier General Price (1 August 1940) remained at that post until 15 February 1941 when he assumed command of the Department of the Pacific, San Francisco, CA, remaining there until 31 October.

While still in command at the DoP, Price joined the newly forming 2dMarDiv, assuming command on 9 December 1941. When the Headquarters, Samoan Area Defense Force was created, Major General Price (1 February 1942) was its first CG. He and his staff arrived at Pago Pago on 28 April 1942 and, though his force was never called upon to conduct a defense of the island chain, they were ready. His term at Samoa was up in May 1944 and Price returned to San Diego, assuming command of the Training and Replacement Command. He was ordered home to await retirement on 1 October 1945, and was advanced on the retired list to lieutenant general on 25 October 1948. He served just a bit less than 40 years as a Marine.

His decorations included the Distinguished Service Medal and Legion of Merit for his services in command in Samoa. Other awards included various World War II Pacific area medals, China Service Medal, Second Nicaraguan Campaign Medal, World War I Expeditionary and Victory Medals, Mexican Campaign Medal, Cuban Pacification Medal and the Nicaraguan Presidential Medal of Merit.

Lieutenant General Charles F.B. Price died at age 72 in the Naval Hospital at San Diego in January 1954.

PURYEAR, Major General Bennet Jr. was born on 9 January 1884, in Richmond, VA. He attended local schools until his family moved to a farm in Madison County, VA, in 1895. Afterwards his schooling was intermittent; mainly instruction from his father, who was a Latin scholar and later Chairman of the Faculty and Professor of Science at Richmond College. Bennet's older brother was a mathematics professor, which helped. Bennet later attended Texas A&M between 1903 to 1905.

He was appointed to the Marine Corps from Texas and accepted a commission as a second lieutenant on 12 September 1905. His first assignment was at the School of Application, Annapolis MD, and while in training he, with so many other young lieutenants, was assigned to the First Provisional Regiment of Marines on duty in the Isle of Pines, Cuba, from 8 October 1906. First Lieutenant Puryear (13 May 1908) was promoted while still in Cuba but in January 1909 he returned to the U.S. and on 11 February 1909 was at the MOS then at Port Royal (now Parris Island) SC, where he served as an instructor in the School of Application. As instructor he taught nearly everything, including gunnery, but no drill. Some of his students included Vandegrift, Roy Geiger and Julian C. Smith. In addition to his other duties, he became captain and Assistant Quartermaster on 1 April 1911. He joined the Quartermaster's Department and was sent to Philadelphia. On 5 December 1911, as QM, he joined the 1st Brigade at Cavite in the Philippine Islands, remaining there until 1914.

Puryear returned to the States and after a leave reported to the MB, Mare Island, CA, on 18 June 1914, as Post QM. With the declaration of war in 1917 came a great increase in personnel and subsequent rank, and Major Puryear was promoted effective on 22 May 1917. He was selected to ship out with the 5th Marines when they sailed to join the AEF in France in June

1917. According to the records he was listed as a "Staff Administrator" with the Second Division, but actually was in charge of the Division QM operations. In that role he served commendably. Puryear later claimed that the "service chain worked very well." Some of the enlisted men and a few officers might have found fault with that comment.

Commenting later about the clothing and shoes issued to the Marines, just before Blanc Mont, he stated "they got English shoes, and they had a hell of a time with them. The British shoes didn't fit." (But they were probably cheaper than American-made shoes.)

Puryear was awarded a Navy Cross for service ranging from Toulon to the Meuse Argonne; the citation was lengthy but essentially ended by stating that his services "were conspicuous, highly meritorious, and in duty of great responsibility." He was also awarded a Silver Star citation, later the medal, and the French awarded him a Croix de Guerre, Gilt. According to some records he was also awarded a Purple Heart. He was surprised that any staff member received any medals and someone put him in for an Army DSM, which was refused because he was just a major.

Puryear returned from Europe in May 1919 and after a leave on 2 June took up duties with HQMC where he, unlike so many others, retained his rank of major, confirmed on 4 June 1920. Puryear also remained in Washington for many years, not leaving until he arrived as QM at the Marine Constabulary Detachment at the headquarters of the *Gendarmerie d'Haiti* on 6 July 1925. During this period he received a "promotion to colonel" in the *Gendarmerie* which increased his salary by $200 a month, a fantastic sum in 1928. He remained at that post until July 1928 and after a month's leave he was back at the QM, at HQMC on 24 August 1928.

The following year, on 12 August 1929, he was at the Depot of Supplies in Philadelphia. PA. The following year, 6 October 1930, Puryear was back at QM, HQMC, soon after Lieutenant Col. (1 December 1930). Col. Puryear (1 October 1934) was shipped out to San Diego, arriving in July 1936, but by 8 June 1937 he was back at Quantico. So far his only schooling had been to graduate earlier from the MCS, Field Officers' course.

On 5 February 1942 he left Quantico for HQMC, still a QM officer, and remained there until 1944. During the period he traveled to the Pacific with LGC Thomas Holcomb on a fact-finding tour to determine what Marines needed (everything) at war. Meanwhile, Puryear had complained about seeing his friends being promoted but he remained a colonel. He was promoted to brigadier general on 28 March 1942 and major general upon retirement in May 1944, retroactive to 28 March 1942.

His decorations included the Navy Cross, Silver Star, Legion of Merit, for his services while at HQMC, and a Purple Heart, plus a World War I Victory Medal. Because he traveled to the South Pacific, he was also entitled to the usual campaign medals of World War II plus that World War II Victory Medal.

Major General Bennet Puryear Jr. died on 11 February 1982 at the advanced age of 98.

PUTNAM, Brigadier General Russell Benjamin was born on 7 January 1878, in Abbeville, Louisiana. He earned a B.S. from Centenary College in 1894 and an M.E. from Cornell University in 1901. Appointed from New York, he accepted a commission as a second lieutenant of Marines on 16 January 1904. After a sojourn at the School of Application, on 28 December 1904 Putnam boarded the *Kearsarge* to serve with the MD. On 31 March 1905 he transferred to the newly constructed *Maine*, then went ashore on 18 May 1906 and served as an aide to the MGC George F. Elliott. On 1 July he was promoted to first lieutenant, remaining in that post for several years.

Capt. Putnam (31 January 1909) switched from line duty to the Paymaster's Department effective 18 May 1909. On expeditionary duty with the First Brigade Marines in the Philippine Islands from 1909 until March 1912 he, upon return to the U.S., assumed a role at the Paymaster's Department, HQMC on 19 April that year. He was, however, detached for duty as paymaster with the Marines intervening in Nicaragua until April 1914 when he was part of the force sent in to take the city of Vera Cruz, Mexico. He remained with the rest of the Marines, as paymaster, until he moved to the 1st Brigade of Marines, ABF (then stationed at the Philadelphia Navy Yard), on 5 January 1915.

On 19 June 1916 he moved once again, to Santo Domingo, to serve as Regimental Paymaster with the 4th Marines. At a meeting of officers, Col. "Uncle Joe" Pendleton complained that Adm William Caperton, in overall command of the intervention, had only given him $15,000 to run the entire operation. Putnam spoke up and said, "I've got $150,000 and will make it available if required." Although Pendleton was dubious of Putnam's authority to spend payroll money, Putnam assured him that Pendleton needn't worry, because Putnam would take care of the matter (this from a taped interview with Putnam). Major Putnam (26 March 1917) returned to the States the following May and on 1 September 1918 he had returned to HQMC. Apparently he was right about the 150K; Pendleton spent it without rancor, as far as I can tell.

Putnam was destined to go back to the tropics and on 9 April 1919 he was transferred to the 1st Provisional Brigade of Marines in Haiti, followed by a return to HQMC on 18 August 1921. Two years later, on 2 October 1923, he was at Quantico and had graduated from the MCS Field Officers' course. On 22 July 1924 he was assigned to the Department of the Pacific in San Francisco and while there, on 3 June 1926, he was promoted to lieutenant colonel. A year later, on 23 September, he was back at Quantico where he remained until shipped to the Marine Corps Base at San Diego effective on 3 July 1930.

He became Col. Putnam (1 January 1934) while still at San Diego, then returned to the DoP in San Francisco on 31 July 1934. This lasted a relatively short period; on 2 October 1935, he was back serving in the office of the Paymaster General, HQMC, until 1938. That year he was promoted to brigadier general on 1 May as Paymaster of the Marine Corps 1938, serving in that post until retirement in February 1942.

He held the customary campaign and expeditionary medals for service in the Philippines, Nicaragua, Mexico, Haiti and Santo Domingo.

Brigadier General Russell B. Putnam died on 29 May 1959.

REA, Major General Leonard Earl was born on 14 March 1897 in Auburn, New York. At age 20 in April 1917 he enlisted in the Marines, and served as a corporal in the 17th Company, 1st Battalion, 5th Marines at Toulon, Belleau Wood, and at Soissons. He accepted a commission as a second lieutenant on 15 August 1918 and assumed command of a platoon in the 66th Company, 1/5. He then served at Marbache, followed by St. Mihiel. Rea was wounded in action during the bloody 4th of October at Blanc Mont when his battalion was nearly decimated (130 officers and men out of the 1,300 that began the day). Though wounded, he refused to leave his men until his skipper finally ordered him off the field. His reluctance to desert his men on a troubled field was noted and he was awarded a Distinguished Service Cross, plus later a Navy Cross and a Silver Star along with a much later issued Purple Heart. After hospitalization, Rea served during the Meuse River campaign and then went into Germany and served with the 4th Brigade on occupation duty until returning to the U.S. in August 1919.

Like so many other temporary appointments, 1stLt Leonard E. Rea decided to accept a discharge from the Corps rather than a reduction to enlisted rank. He was honorably discharged on 16 July 1919. This, however, was not his complete termination of service with the USMC. As with so many others, he returned to active duty at the MB, Quantico as a Marine captain effective on 1 July 1921, serving with the 6th Marines. He joined the Quartermaster's Department and was posted to the 2d Brigade, Santo Domingo, on 23 July 1923 but on 9 August that year he was at the MB, Parris Island, SC serving as Purchasing, Finance, and Clothing Officer.

He spent several years at PI with the QM department. Then on 9 August 1927, he went back with the troops, aboard the *New Mexico*, as skipper of the MD, remaining until June 1929. On 6 July 1928 he was ashore and serving with the 2d Brigade in Nicaragua. There he, a major in the *Guardia*, was CO of the Marine detachment at Chinandega. During that period, the war really began to heat up. Many Marine patrols were attacked by the so-called rebels.

Returning to the States in June 1929, his next assignment effective 29 August was at the MB, Quantico, where he attended the MCS and graduated from the Company Officers' course. His next posting was as EO and Post QM at the MB, Charleston, SC Navy Yard beginning on 25 July 1930.

It wasn't long before he was back in Nicaragua, now as QM with the *Guardia d'Nacional*, beginning on 14 May 1931; his service continued, according to the records of the *Guardia d'Nacional*, between 10 April 1932 and 1 January 1933, as a member of G-4 (QM) in Nicaragua. In January 1933 that situation ended and he was transferred to the MB, Boston Navy Yard as EO, arriving on 21 February 1933. While at Boston he was a recipient of a newly reinstated Purple Heart and two Silver Star medals, all for his services in France. On 29 May 1934 he was jumped over numerous other more senior officers, to the rank of major. (This was when "selection" took over from "seniority.") On 15 October that year he returned to MB, Quantico as Assistant Post QM.

His next assignment, a most desirable one for any Marine, was as Post QM to the American Legation Guard at Peiping, China, arriving on 18 December 1936. His detachment commander at that time was Col. Alexander A. Vandegrift. It was a time of great trouble in China. Not long after Rea's arrival, the Japanese started a full-blown war with the Chinese government and soon assumed complete control over the city and its surrounding environs, making life difficult for the foreigners as well as the native population. In the meantime, Lt.Col. Rea (29 June 1938) was, like all Marines in Peking and Shanghai, kept very busy.

His next assignment was back at the MB, Quantico, arriving on 30 September 1939 to duty as Brigade QM to the 1st Marine Brigade. When the brigade was expanded to become the 1stMarDiv, he moved up to become Division QM from May 1941 until 1943, then Assistant to the Officer in Charge, then Officer in Charge, of the Supply Division of the QM Department at HQMC. Following this, he became EO of the QM Department at HQMC, from 1943 until August 1946. Brigadier General Rea (May 1944) served in the Pacific with MG Barrett as Assistant, for Supply Services, 1st Amphibious Corps (IMAC). He was in fact one of the last two officers to speak with MG Charles Barrett just minutes before he died. Their conversation had to do with providing supplies for the forthcoming Bougainville operation.

Following the war, he became Depot QM at the Depot of Supplies in August

1946. This lasted until October 1950 when he became Chief of the Supply branch at HQMC. He remained at that post until retirement as a major general in November 1953.

His decorations included the Navy Cross, Distinguished Service Cross, a Silver Star, plus an Oak Leaf Cluster for a second; the Legion of Merit, for services between December 1941 and September 1945 at Headquarters, and a Purple Heart. Additionally, he was awarded campaign medals for Nicaragua, China Service, Nicaraguan Medal of Merit, and a Netherlands Order of Commander of the Orange Nassau with Swords; plus two Victory medals, and campaign medals for his service in the Pacific.

Major General Leonard Earl Rea died in Syracuse, NY on 12 May 1972.

RILEY, Lieutenant General William Edward was born on 2 February 1897 in Minneapolis, MN. After attending local schools he earned a B.A. from the College of St. Thomas. He enlisted as a Marine private in April 1917, and in June reported for active service to the Marine Corps Rifle Range at Winthrop MD as a second lieutenant in the Marine Corps. According to the registers, his acceptance of his commission as a second lieutenant of Marines is dated on 27 August 1917. He was soon assigned as a platoon leader in the 74th Company, 1st Battalion, 6th Marines, which would be the first battalion of the regiment shipped to France, arriving in October 1917.

His service included the trenches in the Toulon Sector, where most of the company, including Riley, were gassed. One of the few not in serious condition, he was able to return and remained with the 74th for a few months. Later, because his skipper was wounded, Riley took his place at Belleau Wood in June 1918. He was promoted to first lieutenant effective 1 July 1918. On 19 July at Soissons, he was wounded seriously enough to be evacuated to the United States in December 1918. His World War I decorations include the Silver Star, an Oak Leaf Cluster in lieu of a Second Silver Star, and the Croix de Guerre with Gold Star.

Soon after arrival in the States and a brief leave, he elected to remain a Marine and was shipped off to Haiti for service with the 1st Provisional Brigade of Marines. That term lasted but a relatively short period, and he was back in the U.S. at the MB, Charleston Navy Yard, SC, on 14 November 1919. On 12 January 1920 he went to the MB, Brooklyn Navy Yard. Capt. Riley's (4 June 1920) next assignment was recruiting duty at the Des Moines IA office, beginning 21 October 1921.

He went back on active field service: to Santo Domingo, with the 2d Provisional Brigade arriving on 23 October 1923. In December 1924 he returned to the U.S. and duty at the MB, Quantico. On 31 July 1925 Riley was stationed at the MB, Parris Island, SC and one year later, on 21 July 1926, he was back at the MB, Quantico, having graduated from the U.S. Army Infantry

William Edward Riley

School, Fort Benning, GA, Company Officers' course. (During the foregoing period, some records indicate that he served in Cuba and in Puerto Rico; however this does not show up in his official records.) He was now an instructor at MCS and would remain there until 6 April 1927 when he arrived at his next duty station at MB, Philadelphia Navy Yard.

On 25 July of the following year, he was in Haiti serving with the *Garde d'Haiti*. This appointment ended in June 1931 when he returned to the States. After a brief leave he arrived on 25 August at Fort Leavenworth to attend classes at the C&GSS, graduating in April 1933. His next duty station, effective on 24 May 1933, was at Evanston IL where he became an instructor at the Northwestern University Naval ROTC classes, which posting lasted two years. Major Riley's (29 May 1934) commitment as instructor terminated in May 1935, and he was back at Quantico on 3 June.

On 11 June 1937 he arrived at the NWC in Newport RI. Lieutenant Col. (29 June 1938) graduated from the NWC in May 1940 and became SMO then FMO with the Atlantic Squadron in May 1940. This appointment concluded 22 April 1942 and he was reassigned for duty with the War Plans Division at Headquarters, Commander in Chief, United States Fleet. He served in that capacity until 1943. His first award in World War II was the Commendation Ribbon, received for outstanding service after the outbreak of war, on the staff of Admiral King.

Col. Riley (1 January 1942), then Brigadier General Riley on 1 April 1943 was now Assistant War Plans officer on the staff of Admiral Halsey, Commander, South Pacific Area and South Pacific Force Commander. While in these positions he was awarded three medals for outstanding services. His first award, the Distinguished Service Medal, while in the latter position; then as Assistant CoS, War Plans, he was awarded the Legion of Merit, and then a second LoM for service in a similar assignment when Admiral Halsey commanded the Third Fleet.

His wartime achievements are illustrated by the following excerpt from a citation: "...General Riley prepared concepts for the occupation of Palau and coordinated the plans the Expeditionary Force Commander with the broader operational plans of the Task Fleet Commander. Because of his grasp of the general situation, he was able to render valuable service to Admiral Halsey as liaison officer to the Commander in Chief, Southwest Pacific Area."

A year later, he entered a series of important assignments in the Pacific: as ADC from 12 May 1945 until 20 October and the next day as CG of the Third Marine Division. Unfortunately, his role was limited to being the last CG of the division and he "closed the books" on the 3dMarDiv on 28 December 1945.

After he returned from the Pacific he served as Director, Division of Public information and Division of Recruiting at HQMC, from June 1946 until 31 May 1948, at which time he was detached to the Second Marine Division, Camp Lejeune, NC. In the summer of 1948 he was temporarily attached to the United Nations Mediation Commission in Palestine, and on 1 August 1949, he was detached to HQMC for administrative purposes, although still on duty in the Mediterranean with the State Department.

Later in his career, he was Major General Riley (effective back to 3 April 1943) and served from August 1949 until June 1953 as CoS of the United Nations Truce Supervision Organization for Palestine. Riley had retired from active duty as a lieutenant general (effective back to 3 April 1943) on 31 May 1951.

Then he served as Deputy Director for Management for the Foreign Operations Administration from September 1953 until

May 1955. He next served with that administration as Director of the United States Operations Mission in Turkey.

In addition to the Distinguished Service Medal, Letter of Commendation with Ribbon, Silver Star Medal and Oak Leaf Cluster in lieu of a Second Silver Star, and the Croix de Guerre with Gold Star, his decorations and medals include several foreign awards including the Purple Heart with Oak Leaf Cluster, Victory Medal, Asiatic-Pacific Campaign Medal, American Campaign Medal, World War II Victory Medal, American Defense Service Medal, and the Philippine Liberation Ribbon.

Lieutenant General William E. Riley died at the U.S. Naval hospital at Annapolis, MD, on 28 April 1970 at age 73 and was buried at Arlington National Cemetery, to later be joined by his wife, Katherine Donahue Riley.

ROBINSON, General Ray Albert was born on 1 July 1896 in Los Angeles, CA, where he attended the University of Southern California before enlisting in the Marine Corps on 21 May 1917. After completing his recruit training he accepted a commission as a second lieutenant of Marines on 15 September 1917, and during the next year, he completed the course at the Officers' Training School, Quantico, VA, and joined the newly activated 13th Marine Regiment. He embarked with that regiment for France in September 1918. Overseas, "Torchy" Robinson saw service as Aide-de-Camp to BG Smedley D. Butler, with whom he would serve with once again in China.

The 5th Marine Brigade arrived too late to see combat in France but served with the remnants of the 4th Brigade on occupation duty in Germany. Robinson, however remained with Butler in his assignment at the Camp Pontanezan receiving-dispersing station near Brest.

Robinson returned from France with the rest of the Marines in July 1919 having made the decision to remain a Marine. After a short leave he was stationed at Quantico until September 1921. He was promoted to captain, effective 4 June 1920.

He arrived on 21 November 1921 to begin a two-year tour of duty at the MB, Pearl Harbor, HI. Capt. Robinson returned to the mainland and on 14 December 1923 served briefly at the Department of the Pacific, San Francisco, CA, before he was ordered in February 1924 to San Diego CA. There he served in a number of capacities including, on 11 April, duty aboard the receiving ship at the destroyer base. On 18 April 1926 he was transferred to the MB on the base and served with the staff of the CG, BG Smedley D. Butler of the Western Mail Guard, during a wave of railway mail robberies. Butler, in a letter to his mother, stated "hard-pushed mail guards and sent all my favorite 'sons'—Vandegrift, Torchy, Hunt etc. so am now alone..."

On completing that assignment, he joined the 4th Marine Regiment, which was based there, on 24 February 1927, sailing with that unit for China the following month. Upon arrival in China he was once again serving on the staff of BG Smedley D. Butler, CG, 3d Marine Brigade, at Shanghai and at Tientsin. Butler once remarked at how much he liked "Torchy" Robinson and his work and how close they were.

The brigade remained in China for nearly two years and, when called home, left the 4th Marines behind in Shanghai. Capt. Robinson returned from China in March 1929. On 29 April 1929, he reported to Quantico where he was attached while serving that summer as Officer in Charge of the MD at President Herbert Hoover's summer camp. He was Officer in Charge of the MD which built Hoover's initial summer camp on the Rapidan River near Criglersville, VA.

In September 1929 he entered the Company Officers' course in the MCS at

Quantico, which he completed in June 1930. He then served briefly at San Diego before going to sea on 18 October 1930 as skipper of the MD aboard the *Colorado*. Completing that tour of duty on 26 September 1932, he was ordered to the MB at the Puget Sound Navy Yard, Bremerton, WA, where he served in various capacities for almost three years. On 29 May 1934 he was promoted to major. On 1 August 1935 Major Robinson (29 May 1934) was again ordered to Quantico, where he served as Post Maintenance Officer and Safety Engineer before entering the Senior course, MCS, in August 1938.

Lt.Col. Robinson (29 June 1938) graduated in May 1939 and was ordered once more to China. Upon arrival 10 July 1939, he served successively as Executive and Operations Officer of the MD at the American Embassy, Peiping; then as commander of the MD at Tientsin, and later as commander of Marine Forces, North China, including the embassy detachment at Peiping.

He returned to the United States in June 1941, and the following month, on 22 July, he reported to HQMC to become Assistant Officer in Charge of the Personnel Section, Division of Plans and Policies. Col. Robinson (1 January 1942) took charge of that section in April 1942 and served in that capacity until October 1943, when as Brigadier General Robinson (2 April 1943) was named Officer in Charge of the Operations and Training Section.

Leaving Washington in January 1944, the general embarked for the Pacific theater, becoming CoS of the 3dMarDiv the following month. He was subsequently named CoS of the 5th Division in October, serving in that capacity during the invasion and battle for Iwo Jima, and until June 1945 when he was named ADC of the 5th Division. Robinson was given command of the Fukuoka Occupation force which proceeded to organize the occupation of that part of northwestern Kyushu. He returned with the division from Japan in December 1945, and after the division was disbanded, he went back overseas in March 1946, as FMO on the Staff of the Commander in Chief, Pacific Ocean Area. He held that position until September 1946, when he became CoS, FMF.

In August 1947, BG Robinson reported again to HQMC in Washington, where he served as Director of the Division of Plans and Policies for almost two years. Major General Robinson (1 February 1948) was Inspector General of the Marine Corps from July 1949 until June 1950, when he assumed command of the 2dMarDiv at Camp Lejeune, NC. He served in that capacity until December 1951, and subsequently, as CG of Camp Lejeune until August 1952, when he was appointed CG of the Department of the Pacific at San Francisco, CA. He left San Francisco in June 1954, and two months later was ordered to The Hague as Chief of the Military Assistance Advisory Group to the Netherlands.

Transferred to Norfolk in October

Ray Albert Robinson

1956, the general served there as CG of the FMF, Atlantic, from 1 November 1956 until his retirement from the Marine Corps on 1 November 1957. He was advanced to four-star rank on retirement by reason of having been specially commended for heroism in combat. He was awarded two Legion of Merit medals. The first was for outstanding service in July and August 1944, as CoS of the 3dMarDiv during the planning and execution of the recapture of Guam. The second was for outstanding service from October 1944 to March 1945, as CoS of the 5thMarDiv during the preparation and combat phases of the Iwo Jima campaign.

In addition to the Legion of Merits, Robinson was awarded the Bronze Star Medal, Presidential Unit Citation Ribbon with one bronze star; the Navy Unit Commendation Ribbon with one bronze star; the World War I Victory Medal with one bronze star; the Marine Corps Expeditionary Medal; the Yangtze Service Medal; the China Service Medal; the American Defense Service Medal with Base clasp; the American Area Campaign Medal, the Asiatic-Pacific Area Campaign Medal with two bronze stars; the World War II Victory Medal; the Navy Occupation Service Medal; and the National Defense Service Medal.

General Ray A. Robinson, a veteran of more than 40 years in the Marine Corps, died in Seattle, Washington, on 26 March 1976.

ROCKEY, Lieutenant General Keller Emrick was born on 27 September 1888 in Columbia City IN. He earned a B.S. from Gettysburg College in 1909 and attended Yale University Forestry School in 1910–1911. He accepted a commission as a second lieutenant of Marines on 20 August 1913 and his first assignment was to attend the MOS at the MB, Norfolk Navy Yard, arriving on 29 November. Of the 21 second lieutenants attending that class, all same date of commission, eight would become general officers during World War II. After graduation on 10 June 1915 he went aboard the *Nebraska* to serve with the MD. That duty terminated on 16 October 1916 and First Lieutenant Rockey (29 August 1916) boarded on 3 January 1917 the *Nevada*.

Capt. Rockey (26 March 1917) had been assigned to duty with the first Marine regiment going to France. He was briefly skipper of the 67th Co, 1st Battalion, 5th Marines, following which he served as the Adjutant of the 1st Battalion. On 6 June 1918 he was cited for his distinguished service in bringing up support and placing them in the front lines at great personal exposure, showing exceptional ability and extraordinary heroism. For this he was awarded a DSC, later a Navy Cross and Silver Star. Major Rockey (26 March 1917) continued to serve with the Brigade in Germany until after the war, returning home (February 1919) to a brief leave.

Like most everyone else, Rockey was reduced to the next rank down, in this case captain. He was assigned duty in Haiti with the First Provisional Brigade, arriving there 23 April 1919, and subsequently serving as a major in the *Gendarmerie d'Haiti*. This was a time when the *Cacos* were being led by an overly efficient Charlemagne Peralte who would cause many serious problems for Marines and the members of the *Gendarmerie*. The latter was, however, fool enough to get in the way of Sgt. Herman H. Hanneken and Cpl. William R. Button, officers in the *Gendarmerie*. They delivered Peralte's body to the local authorities on 1 November 1919.

Rockey remained in Haiti with the *Gendarmerie* until returning to the States in August 1922, then was assigned to the MB, Washington Navy Yard, on 28 August. On 9 August 1923 he was reassigned to duty at HQMC. On 29 September 1924, Rockey was a student at the MCS, Quantico, graduating from the Field Officers' course the following spring. His next appointment was at Fort Leavenworth and the C&GSS, arriving on 28 August 1925. He graduated from there the following June, and on the 29th he was back at Quantico as an instructor at MCS. On the following 3d of January he was promoted to major. He served as an instructor at the schools until 19 January 1928 when he was sent to join the Marines of the 2d Brigade, already in Nicaragua.

Most Marines in that country were engaged in trying to track down Augusto Sandino, a remarkable leader of guerrillas, and Rockey was no different. His assignment was as CO of the 1st Bn, 11th Marines. (The regiment was then infantry, not artillery.) His first role was to organize a unit of men mounted on native horses. He would be a fine battalion commander and patrol leader during the entire period and earn a second Navy Cross, or rather a Gold Star, for services from January to November 1928.

He returned to the States in July 1929 and on the 13th he was assigned duty as a recruiting officer in Baltimore, MD and on 10 May 1930 he was at the MB, San Diego, as the Base Intelligence, Operations, and Training Officer. He was later appointed CoS of that base. He remained at San Diego until his arrival at HQMC on 10 June 1934.

Meanwhile, Lt.Col. Rockey (29 May 1934) was at his new post as Chief of the War Plans Division and became part of the board of officers reviewing the *Tentative Landing Operations Manual* and later heading a new board to make revisions. His next assignment was as FMO, Battle Force, beginning on 17 January 1937 and lasting until June 1939. Col. Rockey (29 June 1938) assumed duties in the Office of the Chief of Naval Operations between 31 July 1939 and 14 August 1941.

His next assignment, effective 14 August 1941, was as CoS of the newly formed 2dMarDiv, which position he held when the U.S. declared war upon Japan. Brigadier General Rockey (28 March 1942) was made Director of the Plans and Policy Division at HQMC, and in August 1943 was made Assistant to the Commandant. That same month he was been promoted to major general.

Rockey was given an opportunity to be back with the troops when on 4 February 1944 he replaced BG Thomas Bourke as CG of the newly formed 5thMarDiv. With several other veterans of the 4th Brigade plus numerous Marine veterans of the Pacific war, they rapidly put together a quality unit fit to help take Iwo Jima. For his services as CG he was awarded a Distinguished Service Medal.

After that bloody battle on 30 June 1945 Rockey was made CG of the IIIMAC for the balance of the war. He and the three divisions of the Corps were back at Guam to prepare for the anticipated invasion of Japan, earning a second DSM for his role as CG of IIIMAC. However, the war was now over and two of his divisions went to

Keller Emrick Rockey

China where he became CG, Marine Forces, China.

Assignments after the war included CG of the FMF, Atlantic, in August 1947, remaining in command until 1949, and then CG of the Department of the Pacific between 1949 and 1950. Rockey retired as a lieutenant general on 1 September 1950.

Decorations included a Navy Cross and Gold Star, an Army DSC, two Distinguished Service Medals, Navy and Army, Presidential Unit Citation, Iwo Jima, Mexican Service Medal, 1916, Victory Medal, World War I, Haitian Campaign Medal and Haitian Expeditionary Medal, Second Nicaraguan Campaign Medal, World War II Campaign Medals and several foreign medals from Haiti, Nicaragua, and France.

Lieutenant General Keller E. Rockey died on 6 June 1970 at Harwichport, MA, at age 81 and on 11 June 1970 was buried with full honors at Arlington National Cemetery.

ROGERS, Major General Ford Ovid was born on 23 March 1894 in Waco, TX. He attended Annapolis for three years (1913–1917), then enlisted as a private in the Marine Corps at Baltimore, MD on 14 July 1917. Rogers was appointed as a second lieutenant of Marines on 15 September 1917. He had earlier decided upon a career in flying and after commissioning was sent for pilot training at the NAS and Marine Flying Field, Miami, FL. After training on 14 April 1918 he was designated naval aviator #560. Rogers went overseas in July 1918 with the First Aviation Force as part of the Day Wing of the U.S. Navy's Northern Bombing Group, led by Major Alfred A. Cunningham. He was assigned a member of USMC Squadron 8, which was based at Field D, Oye, France. First Lieutenant Rogers (1 July 1918) and his fellows aviators had to wait for airplanes with which to enter combat with the enemy German planes bombing French, British, and Belgian trenches in Flanders.

Between 18 and 25 September he and several other Marine pilots were assigned to duty with the British Pilots Pool at Audembert, France, and then between 8 and 22 October with the RAF Squadron No. 218. He flew DeHaviland 4 bombers with Sgt. Ross W. Winkler as his observer-gunner and during this brief period he flew numerous bombing missions against German bases in Belgium, earning a Navy Cross for "distinguished and heroic service during September, October and November 1918, bombing enemy bases, ammunition dumps, railroad junctions, etc."

He returned to the U.S. in December 1918, and after a brief leave was assigned on 20 December to the 1st Marine Aviation Force, MB, Norfolk Navy Yard, followed on 19 June to the MB at Parris Island, SC, for ground duty. He was transferred on 2 May 1921 to the MB, Quantico, and the following year, on 3 April 1922, he was in Santo Domingo as a member of the 1st Air Squadron, serving with the 2d Marine Brigade. Their job was to bomb and strafe the rebel forces opposed to the Marines. When peace had been restored, the squadron was withdrawn with the balance of the Marines on 24 July 1924. Rogers, however, had left in April 1923 at his request so he could participate in the Pulitzer Air Races at St. Louis, MO. He held the record for flying the longest distance by any American flyer up until that time. During the following period Rogers won fame as a test pilot and he took part in stunt flying for five years.

By 14 May he was on duty at the NAS in Anacostia, Washington D.C. and on 28 September 1925 he attended the U.S. Army Tactical School at Langley Field, VA, graduating the following June. He was then at HQMC on 27 September 1926. This was during his period removed from air service, which was intermittently required of most flying Marines; Capt. Rogers (9 April 1927) was no exception.

In 1929 he took part in the National

air races at Cleveland, OH, as a stunt flyer. On 30 October 1929 he was transferred to Haiti, joining VO-9M, and remaining there providing aerial support for the 1st Brigade until withdrawn on 12 August 1931. Beginning on 24 June 1932 Rogers was to ferry planes to Marines in Nicaragua from the Aircraft Factory, Philadelphia Navy Yard. By 2 June 1934 he had returned to the MB, Quantico, and promotion to major on 1 September 1935.

On 5 July 1938 he was assigned duty at the NAS, San Diego, CA and became Lt.Col. Rogers on 14 August 1939. In June 1940 he was assigned to the U.S. Marine Air Station, St. Thomas, the Virgin Islands, where in 1941 he became the CO. His next assignment was as Chief of the U.S. Naval Aviation Mission to Peru between 1942 and 1944. On 20 May 1942 he was promoted to colonel, and much later to brigadier general, retroactive to November 1943.

His next post was as the CG of the Third Marine Aircraft Wing, 1 to 7 January 1945; then duty with the Air Defense Command on Okinawa 1945 and 1946. He was island commander of Peleliu on 7 August 1945. When he learned of the atomic bombs dropped on Japan, Rogers, on his own, prepared a surrender document and had it approved by Adm Murray, ComMarianas. The document was subsequently used in all surrenders in Murray's control areas.

Major General Rogers was promoted upon retirement on 1 November 1946 but effective back to 25 November 1943.

General Rogers, known as the "Flying Texan," received such decorations as the Navy Cross in World War I, plus a Victory Medal with several clasps, and a Distinguished Flying Cross for services in World War II. A Letter of Commendation for the period, 1941–1942, Virgin Islands; Santo Domingo Expeditionary Medal; various World War II campaign medals; the Peruvian Order of the Sol, Commander's rank; and Peru's Aviation Cross 1st Class.

Rogers later wrote that he, like many of his peers for various reasons, hated duty aboard the new Marine escort carriers. (See introduction for more details.)

Major General Ford O. Rogers died at the U.S. Naval hospital, Bethesda, MD, age 78, on 12 September 1972 and was buried with full military honors in Arlington National Cemetery on the 15th. Rogers had a son, Robert H. Rogers, who served in the war in the Pacific as an enlisted Marine.

ROGERS, Major General William Walter was born on 25 December 1893 in Thorntown, IN. He was educated in local schools, then was awarded a B.S. from Miami University of Ohio in 1914. Rogers enlisted in the Marine Corps on 30 June 1917 and became a corporal in Hdqs Co, 6th Marines. He served in that capacity at Toulon, Belleau Wood and Soissons. Enrolled as a second lieutenant from the field on 15 August 1918, he served as a platoon leader in the 82d Company, 3d Battalion, 6th Marines. He fought the platoon at St. Mihiel in September and at Blanc Mont in October; he was seriously wounded on 6 October (some records say the 7th). During this period he was awarded three Silver Star citations and a Croix de Guerre, Gilt. He recovered and served on occupation duty, returning with the Marines in early August 1919. A few days later (15 August), along with many other wartime appointments, Rogers resigned his commission as a first lieutenant.

He returned to the Corps as of 4 June 1920 and became Capt. Rogers effective 1 July 1921. His first duty was with the recruiting office in Pittsburgh, PA beginning on 21 December that year. Upon his return he was assigned to the Quartermaster Department on 20 March 1924 and two months later in that position, as QM to the MD, American Legation Guard, Managua, Nicaragua. In August 1925 he returned to the U.S. and on the 18th was QM in the MB, Quantico. A few other 4th Brigade combat veterans were added to that department and in December 1927 he went to serve with the *Gardia Nacional* in Nicaragua, with an effective date of 27 January 1928. On 6 August 1929, he was with the 2d Brigade of Marines. This was at a time when the Marines and *Gardia* were very busy chasing Sandino and his rebel army with modest success.

By 17 November 1930 he had returned to the States to the MB, Quantico. On 15 December 1931, he was at the MB, Washington Navy Yard. During this period he attended and graduated from the U.S. Army Industrial College. On 11 November 1932, he was at Quantico and on duty with the Seventh Marines. During this period the Silver Star medal had been created and he now had two of them plus a Purple Heart. The registers listed him as an interpreter proficient in spoken French and Spanish.

Major Rogers (29 May 1934) was transferred on 15 August 1934 to HQMC, returning to Quantico in June 1936. One year later he was at Newport, RI, where he completed the NWC's Senior course and was made DMO, Battle Force, Division Two, effective on 18 June 1938. Lt.Col. Rogers (29 June 1938) was back at HQMC in July 1940.

Rogers was assigned to the Plans and Policies Division at HQMC in July 1941 and would remain there until 1943. Col. Rogers (20 May 1942) went back to the troops when he was appointed CoS of the Fourth Marine Division on 16 August 1943. He remained in that position all through the Marshall Island campaigns and the ensuing landings and conquest of Saipan and Tinian. He is credited with the concept of seizing off-shore islands on which to land the division artillery to support the nearby troop landings. He was also noted as proclaiming that the lack of the DUKWs (which the Army had) was serious for Marine landings and should be rectified, and it eventually was.

Still CoS of the 4th Division at Saipan and later Tinian, Rogers was also credited for the planning for the satisfactory divisional operation on Iwo Jima. Brigadier General (January 1945) and moved up 1 March 1945 to CoS under the CG, MG Harry Schmidt, for V Amphibious Corps. Through his efforts, on D-Day there were more Marines ashore than Japanese. Since Schmidt was the CG ashore, Rogers' position was very important and noted as important to the successful conclusion of that campaign. Rogers was the recipient of three Legion of Merit awards: one for the Marshall Campaign, one each for Saipan and Tinian, and a Distinguished Service Medal for Iwo Jima.

He was promoted to major general upon retirement in December 1946, effective on 4 April 1943. His decorations included the DSM, three LoM, two Silver Stars and the Purple Heart. Additionally he was the recipient of a World War I Victory Medal, several clasps, another Victory Medal for World War II, the campaign medals for the various World War II battles plus expeditionary medals for his service in Nicaragua.

Major General William W. Rogers died at age 82 on 15 October 1976.

ROWELL, Lieutenant General Ross Erastus was born on 24 September 1884 at Ruthven, IA, attending grade and high schools there. He was graduated from Iowa State College and then studied electrical engineering for two years at the University of Idaho. Before his appointment from Idaho as a second lieutenant in the Marine Corps on 3 August 1906, he worked for two years as topographer and draftsman for the U.S. Geological Survey at Sanke River Valley, ID.

His first Marine assignment was at the MOS, Annapolis, MD on 7 September 1906. Following his initial Marine Corps schooling, which he would not complete,

Rowell was sent on 8 October to the First Provisional Brigade stationed in Cuba. First Lieutenant Rowell (17 June 1906) commanded the post at Palmira, Santa Clara Province, ending in December 1908 and on the 31st of that month he was en route back to the States.

He next went to the MB, Portsmouth, NH, then aboard the *Prairie* followed by the *Buffalo* for a trip to the Philippines. Upon arrival there he joined the 1st Brigade of Marines at Cavite, remaining for six months. His next duty, on 11 November 1909, was aboard the *California* to command the MD. He remained aboard until reporting for duty at the recruiting office in San Francisco, CA on 6 June 1912 and he was also later on recruiting duty in Los Angeles and at Denver CO.

His next assignment, effective 13 April 1914, was to the American Embassy Legation Guard, Managua, Nicaragua. Returning in April 1916, he was assigned duty as Officer in Charge with the Marine Corps Publicity Bureau in New York City on 27 April and promoted to captain on 29 August 1916, then to major on 22 May 1917.

During this period he put the Marine Corps forward in the best possible light, including personally posing for the famous James Montgomery Flag poster depicting a Marine officer in campaign hat, drawing a pistol with the U.S. flag draped behind him stating "First in the Fight, Always Faithful, etc." He was also involved in assisting the professional making of the recruiting films *The Peacemakers* and *U.S. Marines Under Fire in Haiti*. When in June 1917 the Fifth Marines sailed from Philadelphia for New York and then France, he was on hand with Marine photographers to record the event.

In August 1917 he was back at Quantico as battery commander of the Mobile Artillery Force, sailing to Guantánamo Bay on 20 December 1917 to command the 3d Battalion, 3d Provisional Brigade, and early in 1918 to Haiti as adjutant with the 1st Provisional Brigade. Six months later he returned to the States and sailed for France in command of the 12th Replacement Battalion. He arrived too late for combat but was assigned duty with the 15th Separate Battalion, the Schleswig-Holstein Bn, and remained in Europe until returning to the U.S. with that unit in December 1919.

He was selected as a battalion CO of the 10th Artillery, based at Quantico. Then like many others, he was selected to train at the Quartermaster Department, arriving on 18 November 1920. On 28 December he was transferred as Brigade QM, 1st Provisional Brigade, Haiti. While there he learned to fly with the 4th Air Squadron. The brigade CO, Col. John H. Russell, recommended that Rowell be designated a Student Naval Aviator. The QM, BG McCawley, raised hell, stating in writing that "Rowell should have his time fully occupied in the legitimate duties of his office, etc."

Rowell petitioned MGC Lejeune in February 1922 requesting his detail to Marine aviation, and not just as a student.

Ross Erastus Rowell

Although McCawley objected, the request was approved. After 17 years' service, the 39-year-old Major Rowell was designated a Naval Aviator. He then took a course at the USA Air Corps, Kelly Field, where he qualified as a pursuit (fighter) pilot. In July 1924 he assumed command of the Observation Squadron 1 (VO-1M) at San Diego. He was commended in writing by the Secretary of the Navy for attaining the highest bombing score in aviation for the years 1924–1925. Over the following years he was cited more than a dozen times for his and his unit's efficiency.

His command, VO-1M, sailed to Nicaragua in early 1927 to join the 2d Marine Brigade. Soon after, VO-4M also arrived, and Rowell was designated CO of both units. During his stay in that country, many aerial innovations were developed by Rowell and his men. Two of his flyers, 1stLt Hayne (Cuckoo) Boyden and GySgt Michael (Polish Warhorse) Wodarczyk, were instrumental in softening up the Sandinistas' attack upon Octal, making the defense of that town somewhat easier for Capt. Gilbert D. Hatfield and his Marines. Rowell came in later with the balance of his command and dropped bombs and fired their Lewis guns, tearing up the Nicaraguan formations and causing numerous losses to Sandino. Rowell earned a Distinguished Flying Cross for invoking the first dive bombing (really glide bombing) against an armed enemy. His fliers were genuine pioneers in close ground support, developing concepts used extensively in a later major war. Rowell would remain committed to close ground support and, some might say, paid for it (see Information section for more details).

It wasn't long before the DeHavilands were replaced by more modern Corsairs and Falcons, making flying somewhat safer. However, his so-called "terrorism" in bombing people on the ground was frequently castigated by the news media (ain't it always the truth?) and consequently Sandinistas would hide in towns and villages because it was "off limits" for the planes to attack.

Regardless of the media, Ross Rowell continued to innovate and lead in this new concept of warfare. Leaving Nicaragua on 4 August 1928, he reported to the Air Corps Tactical School, Langley, VA, graduating with high honors the following June 1929. In the meantime he had been awarded a Distinguished Service Medal for his turn in Nicaragua. His next half dozen years saw him as CO of various formations, specifically Aircraft One and Aircraft Two, East and West Coasts. He was promoted to lieutenant colonel in August 1932. In May 1935 he arrived at HQMC as Director of Marine Aviation, assuming the rank of colonel in June.

In March 1939 Rowell was relieved as Director of Aviation and designated Naval Attaché and for air at the American embassy in Havana, Cuba. Brigadier General Rowell (October 1939) was the first Marine aviator to attain the rank of general. In April 1940 General Rowell reported to San Diego where he served a year as Force Air Officer on the staff of the CG of the FMF, BG William P. Upshur.

His next few assignments placed him in the ONI and then took him to London, England, in the office of the Naval Attaché. While there, he, like several other Marine airmen, served with the RAF as an observer in their North African campaign. Returning to the U.S. in August 1941 he assumed command of the 2d MAW and a year later, after war with Japan was declared, Major General Rowell (January 1942) commanded the newly created MAWPac, with Geiger's subordinate "Cactus Air Force" going to Guadalcanal.

His command eventually increased to four Marine aircraft wings and support units. In September 1944 he was relieved by MG Francis P. Mulcahy and was directed to command a new air mission to Peru. He had argued for less (or none) carrier flying Marines, to instead have more Marine aviators and planes flying direct infantry support. He was considered, by his seniors, wrong. General Rowell retired as a lieutenant general almost as soon as the war ended, after having served as a Marine since 1906—40 years of dedication and loyalty.

Among other decorations and medals, he earned the Distinguished Flying Cross and the Distinguished Service Medal for services in Nicaragua and in September 1944, he was awarded the Legion of Merit for outstanding service as Commanding General, Marine Aircraft Wings Pacific, during the period from August 1942 to September 1944. His other decorations include the Cuban Pacification Medal, Expeditionary Medal with two bronze stars (Panama, 1909, Nicaragua, 1914, and Haiti, 1921), the Victory Medal with West Indies clasp, the Second Nicaragua Campaign Medal, several Nicaraguan medals, and several American World War II medals.

Lieutenant General Ross E. Rowell died on 6 September 1947 in the U.S. Naval Hospital in San Diego.

RUPERTUS, Major General William Henry was born in Washington D.C., on 14 November 1889. His schooling was local. Between 1907 and 1910, he had some enlisted service in the District of Columbia National Guard. He was appointed to and graduated on 20 August 1913 from the United States Revenue Cutter Service School, later the Coast Guard Academy, at New London, CT, and accepted a commission as a second lieutenant in the Marine Corps. His first assignment, on 29 November 1913, was as a student at the MOS, then located at the MB, Norfolk, Navy Yard. I believe he served briefly at Vera Cruz, Mexico, in April 1914, then went back to school.

Rupertus went aboard the *Florida* to join the MD on 20 December 1915. While still aboard, First Lieutenant Rupertus (29 August 1916) became "skipper" of the detachment, then captain on 26 March 1917, at which time his ship was attached to the British Grand Fleet. Major Rupertus' (1 July 1918) sea duty terminated when he left the ship in October 1918. After a month's leave, he went to the MB at Quantico on 11 November 1918, Armistice Day.

Rupertus was soon reduced to captain and in a year, beginning 10 September 1919, was serving with the 1st Provisional Brigade of Marines in Haiti. He arrived there just in time for the New Year's Day (1920) offensive in an all-out campaign to permanently crush the rebels (Cacos). Capt. Rupertus was a company commander in the 8th Marines and his term in Haiti would be lengthy: He remained there until April 1923.

Back in the States his first assignment after leave was at HQMC on 20 June 1923, which was followed by reassignment to the MB, Quantico, on 29 September 1924. On 1 September 1925 he was studying at Fort Leavenworth at the C&GSS and in June 1926 he graduated with distinction. He was promoted to major on 3 June 1926. He was back at MB, Quantico, attending the MCS and in June 1927 graduated from the Field Officers' course. On the 18th of that month he reappeared at HQMC, remaining there for two years.

He went to China on 27 June 1929 for duty with the MD, American Embassy Legation in Peking. While there, Rupertus was the victim of a very severe and perhaps career-affecting tragedy. His wife and two of his children were victims of the Scarlet Fever plague then afflicting China's inhabitants and he was allowed to bring them back for interment in the U.S. in the spring of 1931. His next assignment, as of 30 July 1931, was once again at the War Plans Section, HQMC, where he would remain until 3 April 1933 when he arrived at the MB, Sunnyvale, CA, as the CO of that Marine Aviation air station. Rupertus was a

Distinguished Marksman and had been a member of the 1915 Marine Team. Consequently he put much effort behind his unit's rifle team. Of the six Sunnyvale Marines who went to the NRA Regionals, four later became Distinguished Marksmen and a fifth won two medals toward the treasured Gold Badge. Rupertus was perhaps best known as the creator of the "Marine's Creed" ("This is my rifle...").

On 26 November 1934 Lt.Col. Rupertus (29 May 1934) was back at the MB, Quantico. In June 1936 he headed to San Diego where he served until, on 23 March 1937, he transferred to Shanghai, China, and service with the 4th Marines as EO, and also CO of the 1st Battalion. He had arrived just in time for the second "incident," as the Japanese called the invasion of China. The trouble in Shanghai was expected to overflow into the International Settlement, and Col. Charles Price was proactive in calling out his Marines to stem any incursion, no matter which combatant tried to enter, defending Chinese or aggressor Japanese. 1/4 was ordered to protect the left or north flank and Lt.Col. Roswell Winans with 2/4 the right or south of the American Zone. This line ran along the famous Soochow Creek near where the main rail lines ran on the north side of the river. The Japanese certainly made an effort to broach the American zone, but were "eased out" by careful, diplomatic efforts on the part of Price and his officers. Consequently, very little antagonism resulted and no shooting. While still in Shanghai, Rupertus was promoted to colonel on 29 June 1938.

On 3 October he was back in the U.S., now commanding the MB in Washington D.C. On 17 September 1940, he was CO of the MB, Guantánamo, Cuba. At that time, it was believed that the Germans might try to take control of the French possessions in the Caribbean, especially the French fleet based at Martinique. The Roosevelt administration had decided that the USMC would be responsible for any required overt actions to preclude any shift in the status quo.

It didn't happen but Rupertus was where the action might be if it had. He was also a part of the emerging 1stMarDiv. Soon after his appointment as CG, MG Vandegrift selected Rupertus to be his ADC of the Division. During the Guadalcanal invasion, Brigadier General Rupertus (January 1942) led the Marines ashore at Tulagi, Gavutu, and Tanambogo Islands while Vandegrift's force landed on the main island. Both landings were successful, but immediately Rupertus' force ran into a stiff fight right from the beaches. Rupertus was awarded a Navy Cross for his skill, personal courage, and leadership in those landings.

In July 1943 Major General Rupertus (July 1943) replaced Vandegrift in command of the Division and had the less than pleasant state of affairs that occurred on a supposed rest resort on Pavavu Island. It was not a good place for any unit, let alone one which had gone through the hell of Guadalcanal. Conditions were worse than primi-

William Henry Rupertus

tive and disease was widespread. Though he was essentially blameless for the selection of that island, he was held responsible by many critics.

Next came the Division's various amphibious landings between 28 December 1943 and April 1944 in clearing the Western part of New Britain and driving the enemy to the Rabaul area. Cape Gloucester was one of his greater successes and Douglas MacArthur personally congratulated him. Rupertus added an Army DSM to his collection of awards.

Next came the disaster at the taking of Peleliu beginning on 15 September 1944. The problems were many; he was very ill and should have requested relief, but his pride refused that alternative and, although the ultimate taking of the islands was successful, his reputation suffered through overall mismanagement, by himself and several senior subordinates.

General Rupertus was a personal friend of MGC Vandegrift, and was recalled to the U.S. where in November 1944 he became Commandant of MCS at Quantico. While serving in that role, and while on an excursion to Washington D.C., he suffered a heart attack and died on 25 March 1945. He was buried with full honors at the Arlington National Cemetery.

His awards were a Navy Cross, a U.S. Army Distinguished Service Medal and numerous campaign medals including those for Haiti; and China, several; plus the usual World War I Victory Medal with appropriate clasps.

SANDERSON, Brigadier General Charles Roosa was born on 25 June 1889 in Washington D.C. and after attending local schools he matriculated at George Washington University in Washington. On 3 February 1904 he accepted a commission as a second lieutenant in the Marine Corps and like most new officers, he was first stationed at the MB, Annapolis, MD, where he attended the Marine Corps School of Application. Upon graduation in December 1904, he was ordered to foreign shore duty, reporting on 1 January 1905 at San Juan, Puerto Rico, where he served as Post Quartermaster and Aide to the Governor of Puerto Rico. First Lieutenant Sanderson (16 June 1906) assumed duties at the MB, Washington D.C., on 18 October 1907, then in June 1908 went on temporary duty for a short period of two months with an expeditionary force to the Isthmus of Panama, returning to the States in August of that year.

Capt. Sanderson (14 May 1908) in the Quartermaster's Department and on 30 October that year was stationed at Cavite in the Philippine Islands as Officer in Charge of the Marine Corps Depot of Supplies. From January 1909, he had additional duties as QM of the First Marine Brigade. Still remaining in the Philippines, he was transferred to Olongapo in June 1909, where he became Post Quartermaster and Commissary of Subsistence.

He returned to the States in October 1910, and on 26 November was attached to the MB Norfolk, in the same capacity as in the Islands. The MB, Philadelphia, PA, on 6 July 1911, was his next stop, and for a lengthy period. He went on temporary foreign shore duty in Nicaragua in August 1912, in the intervention led by Smedley Butler, and then in November into the Canal Zone which lasted until February 1913. That is, until he was detached on 6 July 1915 for duty at HQMC.

Sanderson was next assigned duties as QM of the First Advanced Base Regiment. He participated with the Regiment in maneuvers in the Caribbean Area at Culebra, Puerto Rico, and in April 1914 took part in the occupation of Vera Cruz, Mexico, following which he returned to this country to become Post QM at the MB, Philadelphia. On 6 July 1915 Sanderson joined the QM Department, HQMC, where he remained for the next three years.

The war in France called for a second brigade of Marines and Major Sanderson, effective 26 March 1917, was detached for duty with the Thirteenth Regiment at Quantico in July 1918. As CO of the Supply Company, they sailed for France in September 1918, and he remained overseas until November. After the Armistice he was detached to the U.S. and rejoined the QM Department at HQMC on 26 December 1918. He received a special Letter of Commendation for his services with the 5th Brigade.

In April 1920 Major Sanderson again went to the Caribbean Area, where he joined the Second Provisional Brigade Marines in Santo Domingo, remaining there for two years. On 15 April 1922 he returned to duty at HQMC, where he was stationed until 25 September 1925, when he was ordered to the MB at Quantico. Here he was assigned as a student at the Field Officers' course, MCS, and upon graduation in May 1926, Lt.Col. Sanderson (19 January 1926) remained at Quantico as Post QM.

Ordered to Nicaragua in January 1928 where he assumed duties as Brigade QM of the Second Brigade of Marines on the 16th of that month. For his outstanding services in the above capacity he was awarded the Distinguished Service Medal.

He was back in April 1929 and from 7 May 1929 to 8 July 1934 he was on duty in the Quartermaster Department, HQMC. Col. Sanderson (1 September 1933) was ordered to the Depot of Supplies in Philadelphia where he was EO of the Depot until July 1936, when he was named Depot QM. On 1 June 1939, Col. Sanderson was transferred to the retired list at his own request.

Like numerous other retirees, he returned to active duty in June 1940, and was assigned to the QM Department, HQMC. In October of that year he was named Officer in Charge of the Purchase Division of the QM Department, in which position he remained for the duration of the war. For his outstanding services he was awarded the Legion of Merit between 1 October 1941 and 30 July 1945. He was promoted to brigadier general on the retired list effective on 23 December 1944, but he continued at HQMC until 16 December 1945 when the general was transferred for the second time to the retired list at his own request. On 6 February 1947, he was again recalled to active duty, on this occasion as a member of the Advisory Council of the War Assets Administration, Washington D.C.

In addition to the Distinguished Service Medal and the Legion of Merit, his decorations and medals include the Marine Corps Expeditionary Medal with two Bronze Stars, Panama 1908, Nicaragua 1912–13, Dominican Republic 1920–22; Nicaraguan Campaign Medal, Nicaragua 1912; Mexican Service Medal, Vera Cruz 1914; Victory Medal with Maltese Cross and Silver Star; Second Nicaraguan Campaign Medal, 1927–29; American Defense Service Medal; American Campaign Medal; World War II Victory Medal; and the Nicaraguan Medal of Merit. He has also been awarded two Letters of Commendation by the Navy Board of Awards.

Brigadier General Charles R. Sanderson died on 22 December 1961 at age 79 in Washington D.C.

SANDERSON, **Major General Lawson Harry McPherson** was born on 22 July 1895 in Shelton, WA, where he attended local schools then the University of Washington and earned a B.A. from the University of Montana in Missoula in 1917. He enlisted in the Marine Corps on 19 September 1917, serving a year and eight months in that role (exactly where and how he served is not evident from the available records). He requested and was approved for Marine Air training and upon winning his wings became a Naval Aviator. Sanderson was commissioned a second lieutenant in the Marine Corps on 20 January 1919 (register makes it on 1 June 1919 but USMC records the date shown). On 29 March 1919 Sanderson went to Haiti and joined Squadron E, then attached to the First Provisional Brigade Marines at Port-au-Prince. Capt. Harvey Mims was the CO and the command consisted of seven HS-2 seaplanes and six Jenny land planes. The Marines were after Charlemagne Peralte and the air service was beginning to provide close air support in the form of reconnaissance observation. Sanderson, however, began experimenting with what later became known as glide bombing. He had a makeshift rack made up and when he spotted groups of Cacos, he went down to about 250 feet and released the bomb in the same pattern as the plane was flying. The technique was readily adapted and soon every pilot was using it.

He returned to this country on 27 February 1920 for duty and instruction at the Officers Training School, at the MB, Quantico. He again went overseas on 22 April, 1922, rejoining the First Brigade Marines in Haiti where he flew one of two planes, the other by Lt. Basil G. Bradley, which flew from Quantico to Santo Domingo, till then the longest flight over water. Each of the four participants (including the observers) were awarded a Distinguished Flying Cross.

After completing a one-year tour of duty with the Brigade, in April 1923 he was ordered to the Navy Department in Washington for duty with the Bureau of Aeronautics. In October of the same year he was assigned as a student in the Company Officers' course, MCS, Quantico. First Lieutenant Sanderson (31 October 1923) remained there as an instructor until 29 December 1928 when he went to foreign shore duty with the Second Brigade of Marines in Nicaragua as Squadron Commander of Observation Squadron 7-M. That lasted until 27 May 1930 when he returned to Quantico. At Quantico he was attached to Aircraft Squadron, East Coast Expeditionary Force, and attended the Company Officer course at the MCS. He stayed at Quantico for some years and during that period, on 29 May 1934, he was promoted to captain.

Next he was assigned as a student at the Air Corps Tactical School, Maxwell Field, Montgomery, AL, in August 1934, and upon graduation in June of the following year returned to Quantico for duty at Brown Field. While there he attended the Senior course, MCS, and upon completion of his studies went to the West Coast in July 1936 for aviation duty at the Marine Corps Base, San Diego. In January 1937, he was named Squadron Commander of Fighter Squadron Four-M.

Major Sanderson (29 June 1938) returned to the East Coast on 12 July and was again stationed at Brown Field, Quantico as Squadron Commander, Aircraft One, of the First Marine Brigade. In June 1939, he was named Operations Officer of the First MAG and in July, 1941, became Wing Operations Officer of the First MAW.

Following this country's entry into World War II, Lt.Col. Sanderson (1 January 1942) departed with the Aircraft Wing for the West Coast and, in September 1942, sailed for Guadalcanal. As Operations Officer of the First MAW, the so-called "Cactus Air Force," on Guadalcanal from October through December 1942, Col. Sanderson (15 October 1942) was awarded the Legion of Merit for his outstanding services.

Col. Sanderson was appointed CO of MAG Two, based on New Hebrides, in January 1943, remaining until March when he returned to the U.S. to become Group Commander of Marine Base Defense Aircraft Group Forty-Two at the Marine Corps Air Station, Santa Barbara, CA. Brigadier General Sanderson (5 June 1944) was appointed CO of MarFairWest in September 1944. In January 1945 he became CG of the

Fourth MAW in the Marshalls-Gilbert Area from May 1945 to March 1946. In this capacity, he accepted the surrender of the Japanese on Wake Island in September 1945. Japanese Admiral Sakaibara, CO of the island, refused at first to believe that Japan had surrendered and it was touch and go for a short period. Finally he was notified of the facts and then turned the island over to Gen. Sanderson. Would the Fourth MAW have enjoyed attacking and thereby forcing Wake Island's surrender? Possibly, but who can say at several decades' distance?

In March 1946 he was attached to Aircraft, FMF, at Guam, and three months later joined the First MAW at Tientsin, China, as CG and then became Deputy Commander of the same wing in October 1947, when that unit's headquarters returned to the United States.

Brigadier General Lawson H.M. Sanderson served as Deputy Commander, Aircraft Fleet Marine Force, Atlantic, and Second MAW at the Marine Corps Air Station, Cherry Point, NC. However, upon the arrival of MG Louis E. Woods on 27 August 1949, Sanderson became Deputy Commander. He remained in that role until retiring as a major general in December 1951.

During his earlier flying service, Sanderson was, like so many other aviators of the period, especially interested in air races. Participating in several races in Europe, he had an occasion in Germany to meet Ernst Udet, the noted ace of the German Air Force in World War I. Later, Udet was responsible for the creation of the dive-bombing program in the Nazi era. He obviously spent enough time with Sanderson to learn some details of the skill the latter had developed. He was also a victim of running poor luck, having several instances of crashes but without major injury at any time.

In addition to the Legion of Merit, Sanderson's decorations and medals include the Distinguished Flying Cross, Dominican Republic 1921; Presidential Unit Citation, Solomon Islands 1942; Victory Medal, World War I; Haitian Campaign Medal, 1919–20; Expeditionary Medal, Haiti 1922–23; Second Nicaraguan Campaign Medal, 1928–30; American Defense Service Medal; American Campaign Medal; Asiatic-Pacific Campaign Medal with three Bronze Stars; World War II Victory Medal; and the Nicaraguan Medal of Merit with Silver Star, 1928–30.

Major General Sanderson died on 11 June 1979.

SCHILT, General Christian Frank was born 19 March 1895, in Richland County, Illinois, and after local schools attended Rose Polytechnic Institute at Terre Haute, IN. He enlisted in the Marine Corps 23 June 1917 and served at Ponta Delgada, in the Azores, with the 1st Marine Aeronautical Company, a seaplane squadron assigned to anti-submarine patrol. This was the first organized American air unit of any service to go overseas during World War I. The unit was commanded by Major Francis T. "Cocky" Evans and included 12 officers and 133 enlisted men. An aerial gunner, Schilt, in a later oral history interview, summed up the overall experience of the force. "We saw a few [German submarines] out there; in fact we dropped a few bombs, but as far as we know we didn't damage anything ...But we kept them submerged, I think."

Returning to the United States as a corporal, he entered flight training at the Marine Flying Field, Miami, FL. He graduated and was designated a Naval Aviator on 5 June 1919, and commissioned a second lieutenant five days later but effective 1 June 1919. On 9 October, he began his first tour of expeditionary duty as a member of Squadron "D," (later OS-7M) Marine Air Forces, 2d Provisional Brigade, in Santo Domingo. He returned to the United States in February 1920, to enter the Marine Officers' Training School, Quantico.

Completing the course in August, he went overseas again the following month, joining Squadron "E" of Marine Aviation Forces, 1st Provisional Brigade, at Port-au-Prince, Haiti, on 22 September 1920. He was transferred to the 2d Brigade the following March to make an aerial survey and mosaic map of the coastline of Santo Domingo and, after completing that assignment, returned to Quantico on 2 October 1922.

Schilt remained at Brown Field, Quantico, for the next five years. However, he served temporarily at the NAS, Pensacola, FL, from January to July 1923, and First Lieutenant Schilt (29 May 1924) completed a three-month photographic course at the Air Service Technical School, Chanute Field, IL, in 1925. While attached to Quantico, he won second place in the Schneider International Seaplane Race at Norfolk in November 1926.

In November 1927, Schilt was ordered to Managua, Nicaragua, where he joined Observation Squadron 7-M on the 27th. It was during this tour of duty that he earned the Medal of Honor when he flew an O2U Corsair (which had no brakes) into besieged Ocotal, landing on cleared and flattened ground. His plane was stopped by Marines on the ground catching his wings and holding on. He would then take off with wounded Marines in need of medical treatment, making numerous trips and carrying out 18 Marines in all.

He returned to the U.S. in August 1929, and on the 14th became CO of Fighter Squadron 5-N at Quantico. Schilt was named Chief Test Pilot and Flight and Aerological Officer at the Naval Aircraft Factory, Philadelphia, on 18 June 1930. He served in that capacity for two years before returning to Quantico on 10 June 1932, to enter the Company Officers' course at the MCS. He completed that course in July 1933, and on 26 August 1933 entered the Air Corps Tactical School at Montgomery, AL.

Capt. Schilt (29 May 1934) graduated from the tactical school in June 1934 and began another four years at Quantico, where he was Air Officer on the Staff of the CG, FMF, and later a squadron commander with Aircraft One, FMF. He then served from 26 May 1938 as EO of the Marine Corps Air Station at St. Thomas, Virgin Islands, where he had been promoted to major on 29 June 1938. After St. Thomas he returned to Quantico in June 1940 to complete the Senior course in the MCS and to serve with Base Air Detachment 1, FMF.

Major Schilt left Quantico on 19 May 1941 when assigned to the American Embassy in London as an Assistant Naval Attaché for Air. In that capacity he traveled through England and Scotland and served as a naval observer in North Africa and the Middle East. He returned to the States on 25 August 1941 and was assigned to Quantico as Engineer and Supply Officer of the 1st MAW. Lt.Col. Schilt (1 January 1942) was promoted to colonel on 18 October, after he had arrived at Guadalcanal in September 1942, as Assistant CoS, 1st MAW. After that he was commander of MAG 11, then CoS of the 1st Wing and CO of the Strike and Search Patrol Commands, Solomon

Christian Frank Schilt

Islands. He returned to the U.S. in September 1943, and commanded the Marine Corps Air Station at Cherry Point, NC, until March of the following year.

From April to June 1944, Schilt headed the 9th MAW during the organization of that unit. He then served for six months as CoS of the wing and for another month as its commander before returning to the Pacific theater in February 1945. This time Brigadier General Schilt (7 June 1944) was Island Commander, Peleliu, from March to August 1945, and CG, Air Defense Command, 2d MAW, on Okinawa until October 1945, when he assumed command of the 2d Wing.

Returning from Okinawa in March 1946, the general reported to the NAS at Glenview, IL, the following month. There he headed the Marine Air Reserve Training Command until July 1949, when he was ordered to Norfolk as CoS, FMF, Atlantic. He served in that capacity until he assumed command of the 1st MAW in Korea in July 1951. In 1952 he was promoted to major general, effective back to 7 June 1944.

In April 1952, Major General Schilt returned from Korea to serve in Hawaii as Deputy Commander, FMF, Pacific, until February 1953 when he became CG, Aircraft, FMF, Pacific, at the Marine Corps Air Station, El Toro, CA. He left El Toro in July 1955, and Lieutenant General Schilt (1 August 1955) assumed his duties at HQMC as Director of Aviation on 1 August 1955. He served in this capacity until retirement from the Marine Corps on 1 April 1957, when he was promoted to his present rank of general.

His medals and decorations, in addition to the Medal of Honor, Distinguished Service Medal, Legion of Merit, Distinguished Flying Cross, Bronze Star Medal and Air Medal with Gold Stars in lieu of four additional awards, include the Presidential Unit Citation Ribbon with one bronze star; the Marine Corps Good Conduct Medal; the World War I Victory Medal with Overseas clasp; the Marine Corps Expeditionary Medal with one bronze star; the Second Nicaraguan Campaign Medal; the American Defense Service Medal with Base clasp; the Asiatic-Pacific Area Campaign Medal with two bronze stars; the American Area Campaign Medal; the World War II Victory Medal; the Navy Occupation Service Medal with Asia clasp; the National Defense Service Medal; the Korean Service Medal with one silver star; the United Nations Service Medal; the Nicaraguan Medal of Merit with silver star; the Nicaraguan Cross of Valor; the Korean Order of Military Merit TAIGUK; and the Korean Presidential Unit Citation.

General Schilt died 8 January 1987, and was buried with full military honors in Arlington National Cemetery.

SCHMIDT, General Harry was born in Holdrege, NE, on 25 September 1886. He attended Nebraska State Normal College before entering the Marine Corps as a second lieutenant on 17 August 1909. Following instruction at the MOS at Port Royal, SC, which began on 15 September, he reported at the MB, Guam, in the Marianas Islands on 25 January 1911. While attached to this station he accompanied an expeditionary force to Chefoo, China. There had been a series of attacks upon American personnel and interests and from mid–October 1911 till mid–March 1912, Marines were being landed at various points and eventually were relieved. In October 1912, Schmidt was ordered to duty in the Philippines where he remained until detached to the United States in April 1913.

His first assignment after his return was with the Recruiting Service in St. Paul, MN, arriving on 1 July 1913. This was followed by a tour of duty at the MB, New

Orleans, LA, then Vera Cruz, Mexico, in April, followed by joining the 1st Marine Brigade at the Philadelphia Navy Yard on 7 December 1914. After his return he was soon aboard the *Kearsage* for temporary duty on 11 January 1915. He next posting, according to the official handout, was sea duty aboard the *Oklahoma* but instead he went aboard the *Montana* on 2 May 1916 and soon after, on 29 August, became a captain. (We have no date when he was promoted to first lieutenant.)

He served as CO of the MD, *Montana*, and led that ship's landing force ashore in Cuba from 25 February to 22 March 1917. Once ashore the MD joined with Marines at the MB, Guantánamo, and then moved into the city of that name, to prevent destruction of American property. This was the so-called "Sugar Intervention" created by the desperate need of that product; the revolutionaries taking the terrorism tack to force an American intervention in accordance with the Platt Amendment.

Leaving the *Montana*, on 23 September 1918, Major Schmidt (1 July 1918) spent most of the next two years at the MB, Navy Yard, Norfolk. Caught up in the postwar rank reductions, he was reduced to captain. Schmidt was again at sea, as of 3 June 1920, when he went aboard the *Tennessee* to command the MD, leaving them in July 1922 and the following month arriving at the MB, Quantico. There he attended the MCS from August 1922 until graduating the Field Officers' course in June 1923. In the meantime he had been again promoted to major, effective 2 January 1923, and began serving as an instructor at MCS for several years.

Then followed a year in recruiting at St. Paul, MN and a six-month tour of foreign service with the Sixth Regiment in China. The regiment was part of the 3d Brigade which arrived in China in December 1927 and remained there until 1929. Schmidt's length of service there was much less, however, when he returned to the States and then was shipped off to assist the Marines of the 2d Brigade in Nicaragua, arriving there 5 February 1928.

At this time, the rebels in Nicaragua, under the leadership of "General" Augusto Sandino, were raising hell and every Marine ashore was involved in the efforts to squash them. From February 1928 to June 1929, Major Schmidt was Brigade Intelligence and Operations Officer and was awarded a Navy Cross for the period he was there. He returned to the U.S., had a brief leave, and then attended the U.S. Army C&GSS, Fort Leavenworth, KS, on 19 August 1929, graduating the two-year course on 18 June 1932.

On 29 June 1932 he was assigned to duty with the Paymaster Department, serving variously at HQMC and with the Department of the Pacific, San Francisco. Lt.Col. Schmidt (29 May 1934) reported for duty with the 4th Marines in Shanghai, China, as paymaster on 10 August that year. He remained in Shanghai until May 1936, then returned to the U.S. to assume a post

Harry Schmidt

at San Francisco that month and on 18 June 1937 he arrived for duty at the MB, San Diego.

In June 1937, Col. Schmidt was assigned to the Second Marine Brigade, sailing with that unit for Shanghai, China, in August where he served as CoS until detached to the United States in April 1938.

Col. Schmidt (1 December 1937) was assigned to HQMC, on 13 July 1938, as Executive and Personnel Officer of the Paymaster Department in July 1938, in which capacity he was in upon the U.S. entry into World War II. Brigadier General Schmidt (21 December 1941) was still in line to be Paymaster General. Nonetheless, Major General Schmidt (28 September 1942) had been made Assistant to the Commandant in January 1942, retaining that post until August 1943. He must have requested reassignment with the troops because he was next ordered to the 4thMarDiv as CG, which command he assumed on 18 August 1943.

He commanded the Division in the seizure of Roi and Namur of the Marshall Islands Group and in the battle for Saipan. On 12 July 1944, he assumed command of the Fifth Amphibious Corps and led that command in the assault and capture of Tinian Island. For exceptional meritorious service in the seizure and occupation of the Marshall Islands and in the assault and capture of Saipan and Tinian, the general was awarded a Distinguished Service Medal and a Gold Star in lieu of a second Distinguished Service Medal.

Continuing in command of VAC, he led it through the successful Iwo Jima Operation, earning another Gold Star in lieu of a third DSM. Following the conclusion of hostilities, he led the Corps in the occupation of the Japanese homeland. During this period, while in the war zone, MG Schmidt earned a Legion of Merit from 2 June to 31 December 1945. On 15 February 1946, Lieutenant General Schmidt (1 March 1946) was ordered back to the United States to assume command of the Marine Training and Replacement Command, San Diego Area. Upon return, he was promoted to full general on 1 March 1946, serving in that capacity when he concluded his brilliant 39-year career as a Marine on 1 July 1948 and retired at the age of 61.

In addition to the Distinguished Service Medal with two Gold Stars, his decorations and medals include the Navy Cross, Nicaragua 1918; Legion of Merit (Army), Japan 1945; Bronze Star Medal, 1945; Presidential Unit Citation with One Bronze Star, Saipan and Tinian 1944; Navy Unit Commendation, Iwo Jima 1945; Expeditionary Medal with Two Bronze Stars, China 1911, Cuba 1917, China 1927–28; Mexican Service Medal, 1914; Victory Medal with Convoy and Escort Clasp, 1918; Yangtze Service Medal, China 1927; Second Nicaraguan Campaign Medal, 1928–30; China Service Medal, 1937–38; American Defense Service Medal; American Campaign Medal; Asiatic-Pacific Campaign Medal; World War II Victory Medal; Nicaraguan Medal of Distinction (with Diploma); and the Nicaraguan Medal of Merit with Silver Star.

General Harry Schmidt died on 10 February 1968.

SHEPHERD, General and 20th Commandant Lemuel Cornick, Jr. was born on 10 February 1896 in Norfolk, VA. After attending local schools he graduated from the Virginia Military Institute and was commissioned a second lieutenant in the Marine Corps on 11 April 1917, reporting to the School of Application at the MB, Port Royal, SC, on 19 May. Less than a month later, 2dLt Shepherd sailed for France with 5th Marines as part of the first elements of the American Expeditionary Forces (AEF).

On 10 August, First Lieutenant Shepherd served as a platoon leader, 4th Platoon, in the 55th Company, 2/5, in the vicinity of

Verdun (Toulon Sector) and participated in the Belleau Wood campaign where he was twice wounded in action during the June 1918 fighting. The first was in the neck on 3 June at the defense of Les Mares Farm. The second was on 7 June when he, acting "skipper" of the 55th, was hit in the leg.

Upon returning to the front in August, Capt. Shepherd (1 July 1918) rejoined the 55th Company and saw action at St. Mihiel and Blanc Mont where he received his third injury (the other leg). He was now out of this war but for his gallantry in action at Belleau Wood, Captain Shepherd was awarded the Distinguished Service Cross, the Navy Cross, the French Croix de Guerre, Gilt, and was cited in the general orders of the 2d Infantry Division, AEF.

After duty with the Army of Occupation in Germany, Capt. Shepherd sailed for home in July 1919. In September, he returned to France for duty in connection with the preparation of relief maps of the battlefields on which the 4th Brigade of Marines had fought. Upon his return to the U.S. in December 1920, on the 20th he was assigned as White House aide and Aide-de-Camp to MGC John Lejeune. In July 1922, he was assigned duty in command of a select company of Marines at the Brazilian Exposition at Rio de Janeiro. On 11 June 1923, Capt. Shepherd was ordered to sea duty as CO of the MD, *Idaho*. This tour was followed by duty at the MB, Norfolk Navy Yard, on 15 June 1925, where he commanded the Sea School. In April 1927, he sailed for expeditionary duty in China, where on 5 May he served briefly in the 15th Marines, a regiment in the 3d Marine Brigade in Tientsin and Shanghai. Shepherd was then reassigned to the 4th Marines (then in residence in Shanghai), in which he served as adjutant until his tenure in China ended in January 1929 and he returned to the U.S. on 1 March 1929. He attended and graduated from the Field Officers' course at MCS, Quantico. This was followed on 2 July 1930 by a transfer to the *Garde d'Haiti* serving as the CO of *Caserne Dartiguenave* until May 1932, then Major Shepherd (1 April 1932) became Chief of Police and Commander of the Port-au-Prince Department until June 1933. On 4 September 1934 he was back commanding the MD at the MB, Washington D.C.

Promoted to lieutenant colonel on 27 July 1935, he received several newly created medals: three Purple Hearts and two Silver Stars to wear with his NC and DSC. On 4 June 1936, he began classes at the NWC, Newport, RI, graduating in May 1937. Then back with the troops on the 17th, to Quantico as CO of 2/5, part of the newly formed FMF, Atlantic, which was being extensively employed in the development of amphibious tactics and techniques.

In June 1939, he was ordered to the Staff of MCS, Quantico, where he served during the next three years as Director, Correspondence School; Chief of the Tactical

Lemuel Cornick Shepherd, Jr.

Section; Officer in Charge of the Candidates Class; and Assistant Commandant of the schools. When war came, Col. Shepherd (8 July 1940) bombarded the MGC for permission to return to the troops but was told to train the new officers coming along. In March 1942 his persistence (which angered some senior officers) paid dividends. Col. Shepherd was assigned as CO of the newly formed 9th Marines at Camp Elliott on 16 March 1942 and in September his now highly trained regiment was assigned as part of the 3dMarDiv and sent to New Zealand in February 1943 and to Guadalcanal in August of that year.

Brigadier General Shepherd (16 September 1942) became the ADC of the 1stMarDiv and with them served at the hard-fought Cape Gloucester, New Britain campaign, from December 1943 through March 1944; he was awarded a Legion of Merit for distinguished service in command of operations in the Borgan Bay area. On Easter morning of 1944 he received orders to report to Pearl Harbor where he became CG of the newly formed 1st Provisional Marine Brigade, composed of the newly reconstituted 4th Marines, and the 22d Marines. His brigade was assigned to the Guam invasion with the 3dMarDiv. Shepherd led this organization in the invasion and subsequent recapture of Guam during July and August of 1944 and for distinguished leadership in this operation, BG Shepherd received his first Distinguished Service Medal and was promoted to major general, effective 16 September 1942.

His next project was to successfully create the 6thMarDiv from components in his brigade. M.G. Shepherd commanded the Division throughout the Okinawa Operation and for exceptionally meritorious service as CG from 1 April to 21 June 1945 he was awarded a Gold Star in lieu of a second DSM. General Shepherd subsequently took the Division to Tsingtao, China where, on 25 October 1945, he received the surrender of the Japanese forces in that area.

Several months later, MG Shepherd returned to the United States and, in March 1946, organized the Troop Training Command, Amphibious Forces, Atlantic Fleet, at Little Creek, VA. On 1 November of the same year, he was ordered to duty as Assistant to the Commandant and CoS of HQMC. He remained at this post until April 1948, when he was assigned to Quantico, where he served as Commandant of the MCS until June 1950.

When the Korean War erupted, Shepherd was in command of the FMF, Pacific, with Headquarters at Pearl Harbor. In this capacity, he participated in the landing of the 1st MarDiv at Inchon and the evacuation of U.S. forces from Hungnam following their December 1950 withdrawal from the Chosin Reservoir in North Korea. On 1 January 1952 President Harry S Truman appointed him the twentieth Commandant of the Marine Corps and he held that post as a general until 31 December 1955.

During Gen. Shepherd's four years as commandant, he initiated a number of important policies that resulted in increased military proficiency for the Corps. He was the first commandant to become a Joint Chiefs of Staff member and, upon his retirement on 1 January 1956, he was awarded a third DSM.

Two months after his retirement, Gen. Shepherd was recalled to active duty and appointed Chairman of the Inter-American Defense Board. During his three and a half years of service with this international organization, Gen. Shepherd, through his leadership and diplomacy, made substantial contributions towards plans for the defense of the continent. He also promoted military solidarity among the military forces of the republics of the Western Hemisphere. He relinquished his duties with the Inter-American Defense Board on 15 September 1959.

In addition to the aforementioned World War I and World War II decorations, he was awarded an Oak Leaf Cluster in lieu of a second Legion of Merit, China 1945; Bronze Star, China 1945; Purple Heart with two Oak Leaf Clusters, France 1918, and one Gold Star, Okinawa; Presidential Unit Citation with three Bronze Stars, Okinawa and Korea; Navy Unit Commendation with one Bronze Star, Guam and Cape Gloucester; Victory Medal World War I with four Bronze Stars plus numerous Expeditionary Medals; China 1927–28, Haiti 1930; Yangtze Service Medal, Shanghai, China, 1927; World War II Campaign Medals with four bronze stars; World War I decorations from France and Montenegro; and many from Caribbean and South American republics.

94-year-old General Shepherd died on 6 August 1990 at his La Jolla, CA home from bone cancer. He was buried with full military honors at Arlington National Cemetery.

SILVERTHORN, Lieutenant General Merwin Hancock was born in Minneapolis, MN on 22 September 1896. After local schools he attended the University of Minnesota. Then he enlisted in the Marine Corps as a private on 27 April 1917. In August of that year, he sailed for France with the 16th Company, 3d Battalion, Fifth Marine Regiment. He was now a sergeant and would also serve with the 45th Co. of the same battalion. He was commissioned a second lieutenant on 9 June 1918 and assigned to the 20th Co., 3d Bn and promoted to first lieutenant on the 16th of August. While in France, Silverthorn fought at Belleau Wood, Soissons and in the Marbache Sector, and in the Blanc Mont assault. He had been selected to attend an Army school and had missed most of the St. Mihiel campaign. His decorations for gallantry in action during the war include the Navy Cross, Distinguished Service Cross, Silver Star Oak Leaf Cluster, Purple Heart and the French Croix de Guerre with Silver Star. He was also entitled, like the other members of the 4th Brigade, to wear the French Fourragere, and was thrice cited in general orders of the 2d Division, AEF.

After World War I he remained in Europe with the Army occupation of Germany until ordered to the United States in September 1919. After leave he reported to the MB, Mare Island, Navy Yard, CA on 20 November 1919. Capt. Silverthorn (1 July 1921) had returned on the 30th of April to the MB, Quantico. Silverthorn later related his experiences and especially working on the famous (or infamous, depending upon one's perspective) stadium built with donated materials and Marine labor.

On 8 May 1923, he reported for duty in Haiti with the First Brigade of Marines and in March 1924 he was transferred to the *Gendarmerie d'Haiti*, serving with that organization as District Commander, Aux Cayes, and Chief of Police at Port-au-Prince. He remained there for three years,

Merwin Hancock Silverthorn

returning to the States in May 1926 and reporting to the MB, Quantico, on 3 June. He would remain there for nearly four years and on 31 December 1927 served as an assistant quartermaster and was assigned to the MB on Guam on 22 April 1930, in the same QM role. He was detached to the U.S. in January 1932 and on 22 August of that year attended the U.S. Army QM Subsistence School in Chicago. Upon graduation, on 17 May 1933 he was assigned duty as Inspector-Instructor with the 24th Regiment of Marine Reserves based in Chicago, the first regular Marine officer to be so empowered. On 29 May 1934, still I&I in Chicago, he was promoted to major.

On 14 September 1935 he returned to the MB, Quantico to attend the MCS, Senior course. After graduation he served as instructor at the school and after two years Lt.Col. Silverthorn (29 June 1938) entered the NWC at Newport, RI, in July 1938. Completing the course in May 1939, Silverthorn began a tour of sea duty on 26 June which included service as SMO in the Navy's Scouting Force aboard (consecutively) the cruisers *Indianapolis*, *Enterprise*, *Houston* and the *Chester*.

He left shipboard in July 1941 returning to Washington in August, and was attached to the War Plans Section of the Operations Division, Navy Department, when the U.S. entered World War II in December 1941. Col. Silverthorn (1 January 1942) was then assigned to Headquarters, Commander-in-Chief, U.S. Fleet, where he served as a naval member of the Joint U.S. Strategic Committee, Joint Chiefs of Staff, from January 1942 until June 1943. He remained in Washington for the next six months as Chief of the Amphibious Warfare Section at the Army-Navy Staff College, winning the Letter of Commendation Ribbon from the Army for his service in that capacity.

In January 1944, Col. Silverthorn joined the IMAC in the Pacific theater, serving as CoS of that unit until it was redesignated the IIIMAC. He then served in the same capacity with the IIIMAC until June 1945. The following month he became CoS, FMF Pacific. Brigadier General Silverthorn (1 April 1943) remained with FMF Pac until September 1946 and the following month assumed command of the Troop Training Unit, Training Command, Amphibious Forces, Atlantic Fleet, at Little Creek, VA.

Silverthorn returned once more to Washington in September 1947, serving as the Marine Corps Liaison Officer with the Office of the Chief of Naval Operations until 3 May 1949, then as Director of the Marine Corps Reserve at HQMC. He was promoted to major general effective back to 1 April 1943. In his new role, Silverthorn realized the reserve would continue to play a huge role in the future Marine Corps, and so stated. Under his predecessor the reserve maintained a population of 38,403, but under Silverthorn that number grew to 123,000. He was, however, vocal in his annoyance when only 70 percent of those officers attended Summer camp. His activity on behalf of the reserves was a moving factor in the Corps' ability to field a division in June 1950.

He was named Assistant Commandant of the Marine Corps in July 1950, and was temporarily promoted to the rank of lieutenant general the following 22 February 1951, when the office of Assistant Commandant was elevated to that rank. He assumed command of the Marine Corps Recruit Depot at Parris Island in February 1952, reverting to the rank of major general for that assignment, and was again promoted to lieutenant general upon retirement in July 1954, retroactive to 22 February 1951.

On 31 July 1956, General Silverthorn reentered government service in a civilian capacity as an Assistant Director of the Office of Defense Mobilization, Executive

Office of the President, Washington D.C., resigning that role in September 1957.

In addition to the Navy Cross, Distinguished Service Cross, Distinguished Service Medal, Silver Star with Oak Leaf Cluster, Legion of Merit, Letter of Commendation Ribbon (Army), Purple Heart, and Croix de Guerre with Silver Star. General Silverthorne's decorations and medals include the Presidential Unit Citation Ribbon with one star, Okinawa 1945; Victory Medal with Aisne, Aisne-Marne, Meuse Argonne and Defensive Sector Clasps, 1918; Army Occupation of Germany Medal; Expeditionary Medal, Haiti 1923–24; American Defense Service Medal with Fleet Clasp, Indianapolis, 1939–41; American Campaign Medal; Asiatic-Pacific Campaign Medal with three Bronze Stars; World War II Victory Medal; and the National Defense Service Medal. In 1956 the University of Minnesota awarded him the gold medal of its Outstanding Achievement Award in recognition of his achievement in the field of military affairs.

Lieutenant General Merwin H. Silverthorn died on 14 August 1985 and was buried with full military honors in Arlington National Cemetery that month.

SMITH, General Holland McTyeire was born on 20 April 1882 in Seale, AL. He received a B.S. degree from Alabama Polytechnic Institute in 1901, then obtained his Bachelor of Laws degree from the University of Alabama in 1903. (Later he was awarded an honorary Doctor of Laws degree by Alabama Polytechnic Institute.) He practiced law in Montgomery, AL, for a year. He had no interest in law and wanted to join the Army. No Army appointments were available, and it was suggested that he apply to the U.S. Marines. "What is the Marines?" he asked. Smith applied and he was appointed a Marine second lieutenant on 10 March 1905.

In April 1906, after completing the School of Application at Annapolis, "Howlin Mad" Smith sailed for the Philippines (arriving on 11 May), where he served on expeditionary duty with the 1st Marine Brigade until September 1908. During that period, on 13 May 1908, he was promoted to first lieutenant. He returned to the U.S. in October and was stationed at the MB, Annapolis, from 21 December until one year later when he embarked for expeditionary duty in Panama. Returning from there in April 1910, he again served at Annapolis; then Puget Sound, WA, on 8 November 1910. Col. Charles A. Doyen, CO of the Puget Sound MB, was ordered to San Diego, there to form a regiment to be known as the 4th Provisional Regiment of Marines. Smith was one of the junior officers who went along. While there at North Island, Smith had a rifle range constructed and instituted rifle training. At the end of May the regiment was disbanded and the Puget Sound Marines were back in Washington state. On 3 July 1911 Smith was

Holland McTyeire Smith

at the Recruiting Station in Seattle, WA, before sailing in September 1912 to rejoin the 1st Marine Brigade in the Philippines, arriving on 2 October.

Smith remained with the 1st Brigade until April 1914, when he assumed command of the MD aboard the *Galveston*. He served in Asiatic waters until July 1915 and returned to the U.S. the following month. After leave, on 7 September he arrived for duty at the Navy Yard at New Orleans. Capt. Smith (June 1916) was ordered to the Dominican Republic as a member of the 4th Marine Regiment, 2d Provisional Brigade. During that unit's operations against rebel bandits, he saw action in the march to Santiago and engagements at La Pena and Kilometer 29. Smith returned to the U.S. on 30 May 1917, and then Major Smith (22 May 1917), now CO of the 8th MG Company, sailed for France just two weeks later.

In France, Major Holland Smith was sent to the Army General Staff College at Langres, from which he was graduated in February 1918. He was then named Adjutant of the 4th Marine Brigade, in which capacity he served in the Verdun Sector and at the epic Battle of Belleau Wood. Transferred to the 1st Corps, 1st Army, in July 1918, he served as assistant operations officer in charge of liaison during the Soissons, Marbache, St. Mihiel, and Meuse-Argonne offensives. After the Armistice, he participated with the Third Army and served with the General Staff, U.S. Army, during the occupation of Germany. For his service at Belleau Wood the general was awarded the Croix de Guerre with Palm by the French government. He also received a Meritorious Service Citation from the Commander in Chief, AEF, for which he was later awarded the Purple Heart Medal.

Smith returned to the U.S. in April 1919 and on 7 June his first assignment was at the MB, Norfolk Navy Yard. On 1 December 1920 he attended classes at the NWC, Newport, RI, graduating and on 28 November 1921 was assigned duty at Headquarters, Office of Naval Operations, with the War Plans Section, the first Marine officer to serve on the Joint Army-Navy Planning Committee. Leaving Washington in May 1923, he served aboard the battleships *Wyoming* and *Arkansas* as FMO, U.S. Scouting Fleet, until 7 September of that year, when he returned to HQMC.

In 1924, after serving at HQMC and in the West Indies in connection with joint Army-Navy maneuvers, Smith joined the First Marine Brigade on expeditionary duty in Haiti, serving as that unit's CoS and Officer in Charge of Operations and Training. He returned in August 1925 to serve as CoS of the 1st Marine Brigade at Quantico, from 9 September until September 1926.

He attended and taught at the MCS, Quantico, from then until 28 June 1927, at which time he graduated from the Field Officers' course. He followed this with an unwanted career change as Post QM of the MB, Philadelphia Navy Yard, until March 1931. While on duty with the QM he was promoted to lieutenant colonel on 9 July 1930.

He managed, however, to change the direction of his career when, on 22 April 1931, he began another tour of sea duty, this time aboard the *California* as Aide to the Commander and as FMO of the Battle Force, U.S. Fleet. He served in those capacities until June 1933, when he went ashore and on the 27th became CO of the MB at the Washington Navy Yard. Col. Smith (29 May 1934) on 1 March 1935 assumed duties as CoS, Department of the Pacific in San Francisco. On 31 March 1937, he was back at HQMC as Director of the Division of Operations and Training. This put him in a position to become Assistant Commandant of the Marine Corps under Major General Commandant Thomas Holcomb from April till 28 September 1939.

On 29 September, Brigadier General

Smith (14 August 1939) was back at Quantico and assigned to command the 1st Marine Brigade. With his command he went to Guantánamo Bay in October 1940 for extended amphibious training and in February 1941, when the brigade was re-designated the 1stMarDiv, he became that organization's first CG. He returned with the division to Quantico in April 1941, and in June of that year he was detached from it to take command of the organization which became the Amphibious Force, Atlantic Fleet. Major General Smith (1 October 1941) had under his command the 1stMarDiv and the 1st and 9th Army Divisions, which received their initial training in amphibious warfare under his direction.

Moving to San Diego in August 1942, the general assumed command of the Amphibious Corps, Pacific Fleet, under which he completed the amphibious indoctrination of the 2d and 3d Marine Divisions before they went overseas and then the 7th Army Division and other units later involved in the Aleutians operation. Smith directed extensive Army, Navy, and Marine amphibious training programs which was a major factor in the many successful U.S. landings in both the Atlantic and Pacific. Later he helped prepare U.S. Army and Canadian troops for the Kiska and Attu landings, then led the V Amphibious Corps (VAC) in the assaults on the Gilberts, the Marshalls, and Saipan and Tinian in the Marianas.

In the latter operation, besides the VAC, Lieutenant General Smith (28 February 1944) commanded all Expeditionary Troops in the Marianas, including those which recaptured Guam. In August 1944 he served as the first CG of FMF, Pacific, based at Pearl Harbor, and headed Task Force 56 (Expeditionary Troops) at Iwo Jima, which included all the assault troops in that battle.

General Smith returned to the U.S. in July 1945 to head the Marine Training and Replacement Command at Camp Pendleton, CA. A lieutenant general when he retired on 15 May 1946 after a 41 year career, the 64-year-old Smith was promoted to general, effective 28 February 1944, on the retired list for having been especially commended in combat.

General Smith resided in LaJolla, CA, where he was active after his retirement in youth activities and pursued his hobby of gardening. He was also the main author of his military biography *Coral and Brass* which provided some interesting exchanges between the USN and USMC until, because of the controversy, the latter effectively disowned it.

He was awarded the Distinguished Service Medal for his part in training America's amphibious forces on both coasts; a Gold Star in lieu of a second for his planning and execution of the Gilbert and Marshall Islands operations; a Gold Star in lieu of a third for similar service in the Marianas; and a Gold Star in lieu of a fourth for his part in the invasion and capture of Iwo Jima. Plus the Croix de Guerre with palm and the Purple Heart Medal. His other medals and decorations include the Marine Corps Expeditionary Medal with three bronze stars; the Mexican Service Medal; the Dominican Campaign Medal; the World War I Victory Medal with five sector clasps; the Army of Occupation of Germany Medal; the American Defense Service Medal with Base clasp; the American Area Campaign Medal; the Asiatic-Pacific Area Campaign Medal with one silver star in lieu of five bronze stars; the World War II Victory Medal; the Dominican Order of the First Merit; and the British Order of Commander of the Bath.

General Holland McTyeire Smith died at age 84 after a long illness on 12 January 1967 at the U.S. Naval Hospital, San Diego, CA. Funeral services were held on 14 January at the Marine Corps Recruit Depot Chapel. He was interred with full military honors in Fort Rosecrans National Cemetery overlooking San Diego harbor and North Island.

SMITH, Major General Joseph Thomas was born on 11 August 1895 in Livermore, CA and after attending local schools he earned a B.A. from the University of California in 1917. Smith accepted a commission as a second lieutenant of Marines on 10 August 1917 and the following day was promoted to first lieutenant. While on duty on Guam, Capt. Smith (1 July 1918) was promoted and remained there until February 1920. His next posting was to the MB, Philadelphia Navy Yard, arriving on 17 May 1920. On 8 August 1922 he was stationed at the MB, Quantico. There had been a huge reshuffling of officer ranking positions and he was moved far behind most of the officers who had fought in France (see references to the Russell/Neville boards). During this period he did, however, graduate from the Company Officers' course at MCS and remained a captain.

On 25 June 1923 he took up a post at the MB, Naval Station, in the Virgin Islands, remaining there two years, until June 1925. He returned to the States and on 14 August reported for duty at the MB, San Diego. The following 17 April 1926 he was aboard the Receiving Ship at San Diego.

On 16 January 1928 he joined the 2d Brigade in Nicaragua, which posting terminated in August 1929. Returning to the U.S., after a brief leave he was assigned to the MB, Boston Navy Yard, on 7 September. On 18 August 1930, he was at the MB, Philadelphia Navy Yard, and the following December he was at the Department of the Pacific in San Francisco. On 19 September 1932 he was to have boarded the *Wyoming* to command the MD but instead boarded the *West Virginia* for the same duty, remaining until March 1934.

Smith then reported to the MB, Quantico, for his next assignment, beginning in April 1934 and lasting until July 1935. Major Smith (29 May 1934) attended and graduated from the MCS Senior course, and on 18 June 1936 was on duty at the MB, San Diego. He was back at Quantico on 27 June 1938 and two days later promoted to lieutenant colonel. While at Quantico, he served as an instructor at the MCS.

On 8 April 1942, Col. Smith (1 January 1942) was assigned as CoS to the 3d Marine Brigade, FMF. They were shipped to Western Samoa to protect that American possession and Wallis Island, a French possession, from an anticipated Japanese assault. Smith was located there from March 1942 until May 1943. Marine brigades were then a combined arms formation with one infantry regiment (7th Marines, later the 22d Marines), an aircraft group and assorted support units. This 3d Brigade remained on the island until disbanded on 8 November 1943. Brigadier General Smith, retroactive to 3 April 1943, became CG of the South Pacific Echelon and deputy CoS of FMF, Pacific, until October 1944, then served as G-5 (Government) for Holland Smith's VAC command at Kwajalein during January and February 1943, and also after the retaking of Guam in July and August 1944. He was made a major general upon retirement in November 1946, retroactive to 3 April 1943.

His decorations during World War II included the Legion of Merit and Bronze Star, campaign and Victory medals, as well as various Nicaragua expeditionary medals.

Major General Joseph T. Smith died on 27 May 1965.

SMITH, Lieutenant General Julian Constable was born on 11 September 1885 in Elkton, MD, where he attended local schools and was a 1907 graduate of the University of Delaware. He accepted an appointment as a second lieutenant of Marines on 6 January 1909 and underwent his basic training as a Marine officer at the MOS, Port Royal, SC.

On 27 December 1909 he went aboard the *Rhode Island* to serve with the MD, with that tour ending in July 1911. On the 15th, he went to serve at the MB, Philadelphia. First Lieutenant Smith (22 August 1912) on 23 December joined the MD at Camp Elliott in the Canal Zone, remaining there until January 1914 as part of the two battalions commanded by Major Smedley D. Butler. Smith then went to Philadelphia and joined what then constituted the ABF, later identified as the 1st Brigade of Marines. As a member of that expeditionary force, he departed from Philadelphia to take part in the occupation of Vera Cruz, Mexico, from April to December 1914, and returned to the ABF, Philadelphia, on 5 December.

In August 1915, he began a tour of expeditionary duty in Haiti, and in April 1916, was transferred to Santo Domingo with the 2d Battalion, 1st Regiment, 1st Brigade of Marines. In December of the same year, he was ordered back to the ABF at the Philadelphia Navy Yard. Following his promotion to captain in March 1917, retroactive to 29 August 1916, he was ordered to a course of instruction at the NWC in Newport, RI. On 20 August 1918 Major Smith (1 July 1918) was assigned to Quantico, as an instructor in the Marine Officers' Training Camps.

On 26 January 1919, he sailed for Cuba in command of the Second Machine Gun Battalion; there they joined the Sixth Marine Brigade. After his brief service there, he and his battalion returned to the Navy Yard at Philadelphia on June 1919, and on 6 August he transferred to HQMC. On 1 October 1920, Smith again assumed duties at Quantico, and on 5 July of the following year, he was ordered to sea duty as FMO, Battleship Force, *Wyoming*, on the staff of the Commander, Scouting Fleet. Two years later, on 4 June 1923, he again returned to Washington, this time to serve in the office of the Chief Coordinator, Bureau of the Budget.

He left Washington to enter the Army C&GSS, Fort Leavenworth, on 30 August 1927 and, after graduation in 1928, was again ordered to HQMC. He captained the Marine Corps Rifle and Pistol Team Squad for the year of 1928, while detached to temporary duty at Quantico, on 8 October 1928, and also headed the 1930 shooting squad.

Major Smith's next assignment was with the Marines at Corinto, Nicaragua, where he began a tour of expeditionary duty on 31 August 1930. His first assignment was area commander, Central Area, from 28 October 1930 to 5 April 1932. This was interrupted when he served as colonel and acting *Jefe* (Director) with the *Guardia Nacional* between 16 August and 5 October 1931.

On 2 January 1933 he returned to Quantico, where he had been assigned the duty of heading up a group preparing a detailed examination of the experiences of the *Gardia* operations and organization (it was

Julian Constable Smith

published in 1933). In the meantime, he was awarded a Navy Cross for services rendered during the period from October 1930 to 2 January 1933. Remaining at Quantico, he was assigned duty with the 7th Marines, then in residence at that post. Lt.Col. Smith (29 May 1934) was at HQMC on 15 May 1935.

Following another short tour of duty in Philadelphia, he returned to HQMC for duty with the Division of Operations and Training. Col. Smith (27 July 1935) was named Director of Personnel. Meanwhile he completed a mail order course on strategy and tactics with the NWC. On 1 July 1938 he was back at Quantico and in command of the 5th Marines, 1st Marine Brigade. Brigadier General Smith (1 March 1941) was then ordered to London, England, where he served as a Observer with the Naval Attaché, American Embassy. He returned to the U.S. in August 1941, and reported to Quantico on the 15th.

Upon appointment to major general on 26 October 1942, he assumed command of the FMF Training Schools at New River, NC. Followed by being appointed CG of the 2dMarDiv in May 1943 as it was reorganizing in New Zealand. He would be CG at Tarawa, and, upon learning from a New Zealander who had spent considerable time in the Gilberts that the tides were notorious for their unreliability, became greatly concerned for the welfare of his men. He made sure that his troops were made aware that their LCVPs might not clear the reefs. Smith was also limited to two (rather than three) regiments, with no idea of when the third would be released to him. Not liking the plan, Julian insisted that Gen. H.M. Smith give him his orders in writing so he would be covered in the event the landing was unsuccessful. The landing was eventually successful, though very costly. As an example, his 2d Amphib Tractor Bn lost 323 officers and men out of 500, including the battalion CO, Major Henry C. Drewes.

MG Julian Smith continued as CG of the division until April 1944.

At that time he was appointed CG of Expeditionary Troops, Third Fleet, followed by his appointment as Deputy Commander, VAC, stationed at Pearl Harbor. He was also placed in command of the planning group for the taking of the Palaus island group, known as X-Ray Provisional Amphibious Corps (re-designated IIIMAC). He was the man selected to command Operation STALEMATE II, the taking of the Palaus; he was made CG of Expeditionary Troops, while his subordinate, MG Roy Geiger, CG, IIIMAC, was ground commander. It was another very costly assault, but with help from the USA, eventually successful.

In December 1944, General Smith assumed command of the Department of the Pacific, with headquarters in San Francisco. From there, he was ordered to Parris Island, SC, where he commanded the Marine Corps Recruit Depot from February 1946 until his retirement on 1 December that year, after 38 years' service. Upon retirement he was promoted to lieutenant general retroactive to 26 August 1942.

In addition to the Distinguished Service Medal with Gold Star in lieu of a second and the Navy Cross, the general's decorations and medals include the Presidential Unit Citation Ribbon; the Expeditionary Medal with two bronze stars (Cuba, 1912, Haiti, 1916, and Santo Domingo, 1916); the Mexican Service Medal (1914); the Haitian Campaign Medal (1915); the Dominican Campaign Medal (Santo Domingo, 1916); the Victory Medal (1917–18); the Second Nicaraguan Campaign Medal (1930–33); the American Defense Service Medal with one bronze star; the Asiatic-Pacific Campaign Medal with two bronze stars; the American Campaign Medal; the World War II Victory Medal; the Nicaraguan Medal of Distinction with Diploma (Nicaragua, 1930–33); the Dominican

Order of Military Merit, First Class with White Insignia (Santo Domingo, 1916); and the British Distinguished Service Order.

After his November 1975 death, Lt.Gen. Julian C. Smith was buried with full honors in Arlington National Cemetery.

SMITH, General Oliver Prince was born 26 October 1893 in Menard, TX. He attended local schools, then the University of California, Berkeley, from which he graduated in 1916. He reported for active duty as a Marine Corps second lieutenant on 14 May 1917 but officially on 10 August 1917 and was promoted to first lieutenant the next day. On 13 September 1917, he was assigned his first overseas tour at Guam, the Marianas Islands, where he served with the MB, Naval Station, and was promoted to captain effective on 1 July 1918. In March 1919, he returned to the United States for duty with the Marine Barracks at Mare Island, CA, arriving there on 6 May and remaining two years plus.

Ordered to sea duty on 12 October 1921, Capt. Smith served as CO of the MD aboard the *Texas* until May 1924, when he was ordered to HQMC for duty with the personnel section, arriving there on the 17th of that month. On 13 June 1928 he joined the *Garde d'Haiti* at Port-au-Prince, as Assistant CoS. During this period, the functions of the *Garde* were greatly increased and many more Haitians were hired on but not with a consequent decrease of U.S. Marines. Strong efforts were being made to educate the enlisted Haitians to fill roles normally held by enlisted Marines and the primary function of the *Garde* was, as always, mainly as a rural police force.

Following his June 1931 return to the States, he became a student at the Field Officers' course, Army Infantry School, Fort Benning, GA, on 17 September. On 30 June 1932 he was back at Quantico, where he was ordered to duty at the MCS as an instructor in the Company Officers' course. In September 1933, he was named Assistant Operations Officer of the 7th Marine Regiment at Quantico.

The next jump was a serious career move. He was appointed to duty with the Office of the Naval Attaché at the American Embassy in Paris on 17 January 1934, and promoted to major on 29 May 1934; this was informally an opening for him to attend the famed French *Ecole Supérieure de Guerre*. He attended classes there from November 1934 until graduating in July 1936.

Major Smith returned to the U.S. in July 1936 and joined the staff of the MCS at Quantico on 24 August, as an instructor in the Three Section (Operations and Training). He was now credited with being both a translator and interpreter of the French language. On 9 July 1939 Lt.Col. Smith (1 May 1938) was transferred to California, where he joined the FMF as Operations Officer at the Marine Corps Base, San Diego.

On 31 May 1941 he became CO of the

Oliver Prince Smith

1st Battalion, 6th Marines, and on that date the Regiment sailed for Iceland where Col. Smith (1 January 1942) remained until March 1942. In May of 1942 Col. Smith was ordered to HQMC where he became EO of the Division of Plans and Policies. He remained in this capacity until January 1944, when he joined the 1stMarDiv on New Britain, briefly as CoS. Next he exchanged places with Col. John T. Selden and assumed command of the 5th Marines, subsequently leading the regiment in the Talasea phase of the Cape Gloucester operation.

In April 1944, he was named ADC of the 1stMarDiv and participated in the initial planning of operations against the Japanese in the Peleliu operation, while MG Rupertus was in Washington arranging for replacements. The campaign took place during September and October 1944. On D-Day, Smith and a skeleton staff went ashore. The 7th Marines were badly shot up and Rupertus committed the Recon Co. to the 7th as replacements. Smith was not in agreement with that use for the company but was overruled. He was the recipient of a Legion of Merit award for his role during that campaign and had been retroactively promoted to brigadier general, effective on 1 October 1942.

B.G. Smith's next performance was at Okinawa during Operation ICEBERG in April 1945. In November 1944 he had been selected to join U.S. Army Gen. Simon Buckner's staff at Tenth Army, as his Marine Deputy CoS. Smith managed to become involved in much of the Tenth Army planning and decision-making. He was particularly concerned that much of Buckner's XXIV Corps would be composed of exhausted Army units still fighting on Leyte. They were, however, what the Army had "available" and what they would go with. He was awarded a second Legion of Merit, from the U.S. Army, during this exhausting campaign.

In July 1945, General Smith returned to the United States and became Commandant of the MCS, Quantico. While there, on 4 February 1946 he was assigned command of the 1st Special Marine Brigade, formed at Quantico, at the direction of LGC Vandegrift. Sometime during this period he was retroactively promoted to major general dated 1 October 1942. Under his command, the 1st Brigade only participated in one training exercise, that in the Caribbean area in May 1946. In January 1948 he was named CG, MB, Quantico, in addition to his duties at the school. Three months later he became Assistant Commandant of the Marine Corps and CoS at HQMC.

General Smith was named CG of the 1stMarDiv in June 1950. He was given command of a badly under-populated, under-staffed division, with less than half the required infantry, and even less support forces. (The Secretary of Defense, Louis Johnson, at the urging of President Truman, had cut the Marine Corps below its Congressionally designated manpower limits.) In a very few weeks, the Marine Corps managed, by calling up Marine Reserves, to collect two regiments of infantry plus some support forces. One regiment, the 5th Marines reinforced, was already on the scene and doing wondrous things at the Pusan Perimeter.

The division was scheduled by the Chiefs of Staff in Washington, to proceed to the west coast of Korea to effect an amphibious landing. This was something the Army members had pooh-poohed as not being necessary ever again (see CoS Omar Bradley's remarks). General Smith led his division through the bitter campaigns of the Korean conflict, from the late summer amphibious assault at Inchon and the taking of the capital at Seoul until the incursion of the Chinese in the latter part of 1950.

In November 1950, the 1stMarDiv was surrounded and vastly outnumbered at the Chosin Reservoir, but fought its way out of the trap. In the face of sub-zero temperatures and the onslaught of eight Chinese Communist divisions, his division broke the enemy stranglehold and completed a fighting 70-mile march to the seaport of Hungnam in 13 days. It was the only success the U.S. military forces had during that period. Smith continued to lead the 1stMarDiv, at the first UN Counter-Offensive and the fight against the Communist China Spring Offensive of 1951.

General Smith returned to the States in May 1951 and was assigned duties as CG of the Marine Corps Base, Camp Pendleton, CA. In July 1953, he assumed his final duties as CG FMF, Atlantic, and served in this capacity until his retirement on 1 September 1955. He had been advanced to four-star rank on retirement (1 September 1955) by reason of having been specially commended for heroism in combat.

His medals and decorations include: the USA Distinguished Service Cross; the Distinguished Service Medal (Navy); the Distinguished Service Medal (Army); the Silver Star Medal; Legion of Merit with Combat "V" and Oak Leaf Cluster; Bronze Star Medal with Combat "V," the Air Medal, the Presidential Unit Citation with three stars; the Navy Unit Commendation; World War I Victory Medal; the Marine Corps Expeditionary Medal, Haiti, 1929–31; American Defense Service Medal with base clasp; European-African-Middle Eastern Campaign Medal; Asiatic-Pacific Campaign Medal with three stars; World War II Victory Medal; National Defense Medal; Korean Service Medal with five stars; U.N. Korean Service Medal; Haitian Distinguished Service Medal with diploma; the Order of the Orange Nassau, Rank of Commander; Korean Order of Military Merit with Silver Star; and Korean Presidential Unit Citation with Oak Leaf Cluster.

General Oliver P. Smith died on 25 December 1977.

THOMAS, General Gerald Carthrae was born on 29 October 1894, at Slater, Missouri, and after local schools attended Illinois Wesleyan University. He was waiting for an appointment as 2dLt in the U.S. Army, but became impatient and he and two fellow football players enlisted as privates in the Marine Corps on 28 May 1917. In September 1917 Sergeant Thomas, with the 75th Co., 1/6, sailed for France, where he was selected to be the intelligence NCO for his battalion. He saw action with the 6th Marines at Verdun, Belleau Wood, and Soissons and was commissioned a second lieutenant on 26 September 1918, and assigned duties as a platoon leader with the 74th Co, 1/6, serving at Blanc Mont. Suffering from the flu, he was unable to take on the Meuse River campaign, but did make the long march into Germany. After participating in the occupation of Germany, he returned to the U.S. in July-August 1919.

He had pretty much made up his mind he would remain a Marine but when he was

Gerald Carthrae Thomas

back in the U.S. and some changes were effected, he reconsidered that decision. His opportunity for a regular commission was battered around by the famous (infamous?) Russell Board. Postwar Thomas had to consider whether he would remain a commissioned Marine. He was, however, saved and retained as a second lieutenant when a large number of senior Marine officers wrote letters supporting him. On 1 November he was on his way to Haiti to serve with the First Provisional Brigade of Marines. He was in action with the Cacos practically as soon as he arrived there. In May 1921 he was on his way back to the States, arriving at the MB, Quantico, on 10 August, and on the 3d of September he was promoted to first lieutenant. During that time he was at Quantico, he was detached for several months of duty with the guard company at the Disarmament Conference in Washington and also completed the Company Officers course at the MCS.

From 30 November 1923 to October 1925, he commanded the MD aboard the *Tulsa*, then on 2 November was stationed for two years at the MB, Navy Yard, Charleston, SC. Beginning on 9 September 1927, he was at Camp Holabird, MD, where he completed a course at the Army Motor Transport School. On 5 December 1928, after serving as Officer-in-Charge of Land Transportation at the MB, Parris Island, SC, he rejoined the 1st Brigade of Marines in Haiti and became Aide to the CO, Col. Mason Gulick. Returning to the United States in June 1931, on 4 September he entered the Army Infantry School at Fort Benning, GA, and graduated in June 1932 and then was made an instructor in the Basic School at the Philadelphia Navy Yard on the 15th. Capt. Thomas (1 November 1932) remained there until August 1934, when he was ordered back to Quantico as a student in the Senior course.

After completing that, he was ordered to China for duty with the MD at the American Embassy in Peiping, he and his family arriving on 21 June 1935. His job: skipper of Company B, plus sometime command of the Mounted Detachment. He made friends with his superior officers, including Col. Vandegrift and "Bobby" Erskine; the latter recommended him for the C&GSS at Fort Leavenworth. Selection helped Thomas to be promoted to major on 1 July 1937. He returned to the U.S. that month to attend the C&GSS, and after graduating in June 1938, he joined the staff of the MCS at Quantico on 23 June.

He was part of the umpiring team selected to observe the spring 1940 maneuvers of the 1st Brigade (an amphibious exercise) at Culebra. Lt.Col. Thomas (1 July 1940) was transferred to Cairo, Egypt, in May 1941 as a naval observer, then recalled to Quantico two months later to become Assistant Operations Officer of the 1stMarDiv. He was made Operations Officer of the division in March 1942, and two months later he sailed for the South Pacific in that capacity. At Guadalcanal he was appointed CoS of the division (see James) on 22 September, and was promoted to colonel on 1 October 1942.

When Vandegrift left the division on 7 July 1943 to take on the role of CG, IMAC, he took most of his staff with him, including Thomas as the Corps CoS. Brigadier General Thomas (7 December 1943) participated in the Empress Augusta Bay operation at Bougainville, then returned to the U.S. to join HQMC, where he was made Director of Plans and Policies in January 1944. He and MGC Vandegrift got caught up in the media storm over the casualties at Tarawa but both managed to weather it. Thomas got into his role which was to make decisions regarding where replacements were to come from. Mainly the Corps needed men on the line and less in service functions, and with the advent of selected draftees, he managed to find those men.

He remained at his desk until a fact-finding mission to China in July 1946. Next came the unification crisis with which he, his close friend, Lt.Col. "Bill" Twining and a few others were heavily engaged. That affliction lasted for several years, requiring the mixed covey of brains of the Corps which finally managed, with the help of Congress, to avoid being submerged into the U.S. Army.

In July 1947, Thomas was named CG of FMF, Western Pacific. After that unit was disbanded in March 1949, he became CoS of the Marine Corps Equipment Board at Quantico, later serving there as CG of the Landing Force Development Center. Major General Thomas (January 1951) assumed command of the 1stMarDiv in Korea in April 1951, serving in that capacity until returning to the U.S. in January 1952. The following month he was promoted to lieutenant general and designated by the President as Assistant Commandant of the Marine Corps. He served in that billet until June 1954, and the following month became Commandant of the Marine Corps Schools, Quantico. He retired from the Marine Corps and was promoted to his present rank on 1 January 1956. On 10 February 1954 he was awarded a degree of Doctor of Laws by his alma mater.

In 1951 the general earned the Army Distinguished Service Cross and Army Distinguished Service Medal while commanding the 1stMarDiv in Korea. During World War II (1942) he was awarded the Navy Distinguished Service Medal as Operations Officer of the 1stMarDiv; the Legion of Merit with Combat "V" as CoS of the 1st Marine Amphibious Corps in the Treasury-Bougainville operation. He was awarded a second Legion of Merit for outstanding service from January 1944 to November 1946, as Director of the Division of Plans and Policies at HQMC in Washington. Also, numerous campaign medals from World War I, World War II, the Korean War, and various expeditionary medals. He had earned a Silver Star and Purple Heart in France in World War I.

General Gerald C. Thomas, a veteran of more than 38 years of distinguished service, died 7 April 1984 at his Washington D.C. home.

TORREY, Major General Philip Huston was born on 18 July 1884, in Fort Douglas, UT, attending local schools, then Lehigh University between 1902 and 1903, followed by the University of Montana in 1904. He accepted a commission as a second lieutenant of Marines on 18 July 1905 and his first assignment was to the School of Application at the MB, Annapolis, MD, on 25 August. Torrey remained there until he joined the 1st Provisional Brigade of Marines at Havana, Cuba, on 1 October 1906. Torrey and most of his schoolmates were included in the 2804 Marines, officers and enlisted, that composed the brigade which was commanded by Col. Littleton W.T. Waller. Torrey and friends remained in that island until the revolt lost steam when on 31 December 1908, First Lieutenant Torrey (14 May 1908) and most of his fellows were en route back to the U.S.

He went directly back to Annapolis, but on 13 October 1909 he was assigned to duty at the Marine Officers' School, Port Royal, SC. He is listed as being there until the end of June 1911 and he was recorded as being on duty at the MB, Philadelphia, on 1 July. Actually he was with Major George C. Thorpe and 21 other Marine officers and 666 enlisted Marines: To protect American interests, they landed at Guantánamo Bay, Cuba, on 13 March 1911.

Upon his return, on 19 August 1912 he was assigned duty at the Naval Disciplinary Barracks, Port Royal, SC, remaining there until 15 April 1914, when he began serving aboard the *New York*. In April 1914 he landed at Vera Cruz, Mexico, with the ship's MD, returning aboard when the U.S. Army arrived to assume overall command. In April 1916 his sea duty ended and on 15 May he joined the MB at Norfolk, VA and was promoted to captain on 29 August 1916.

Promotions were coming rapidly at this time and on 22 May 1917 he was made a major. As major he was assigned to the MB, Quantico, on 16 July 1917 as an instructor of newly minted officers. He was a founder of the Marine Infantry School, begun on 12 January 1920 at Quantico.

His next overseas assignment was in Haiti, where he joined the First Brigade of Marines on 21 October 1920 remaining there until returning to HQMC on 25 August 1922. He was in Haiti during the Congressional inquiry into the affairs of the Marine Corps and other federal organizations in Haiti and Santo Domingo. Torrey remained at HQMC until 14 June 1926 when he arrived as the new CO at the MB, Naval Academy, Annapolis, MD. On 28 July 1929 he was back in Haiti, but now on the staff of the American High Commissioner, BG John Russell. He remained in that post until he joined the 1st Brigade (still in Haiti) on 23 December 1930.

Torrey returned to the States on 4 August 1931, joined the MB, Quantico, and on 1 September was promoted to lieutenant colonel. He attended (and graduated in June 1932) from the Field Officers' course at the MCS with this, other than his basic school, his first schooling as a Marine officer. Torrey's next assignment was to the NWC from which he graduated from the Senior course in May 1935. Col. Torrey's (1 November 1934) next assignment, after a suitable leave, was at the Puget Sound Navy Yard, arriving on 13 June 1935.

The following 31 October he joined the MB, San Diego, remaining at that post as CO of the 6th Marines until June 1937. From there he was back at Newport, RI on 29 June, to again attend the NWC and graduate from the Advanced course in May 1938. That June he was at Philadelphia and the following year at Quantico. Brigadier General Torrey (21 August 1939) ranked just after Holland Smith, and four grades ahead of Alexander Vandegrift.

Torrey was made Commandant of MCS in July 1939 and remained in that post until January 1941 when he assumed his next assignment as CG of Infantry Forces, First Marine Brigade, in January 1941. From June to August 1941 he led the 1st Joint Training Force, which included the brigade (later division) plus the 1st Infantry Division, in amphibious landings near New River, NC. When his brigade became the 1stMarDiv he was Acting CG, then CG of the Division on 14 June 1941, and his ADC was BG A.A. Vandegrift. Meanwhile, in November 1941, because he commanded the division, he was promoted to temporary major general.

For various reasons, mostly personal, his subordinates did not consider General Torrey to be efficient as CG of the 1st Division and MG Holland Smith, his CO, relieved him of command in March 1942. Smith believed that Torrey was not following his orders, and lacked a grasp of what was going on with the troops ashore.

His next assignment, from 16 April 1942 until 30 September 1942, possibly more to his ability, was at HQMC as Director of the Division of Reserve. Meanwhile he was made a permanent major general in April 1942. Torrey was Commandant of MCS from 1944 until 1946; he retired in August of that year.

Though I have no record of awards, he must have been eligible to wear medals for the Vera Cruz, Cuban, and Haitian interventions, plus the usual World War II medals.

Major General Philip H. Torrey died on 7 June 1968.

TURNAGE, General Allen Hal was born 3 January 1891 in Farmville, NC, where he attended local schools, then the University of North Carolina, before entering the Marine Corps as a second lieutenant on 20 August 1913. Following 17 months' instruction at the MCS at Norfolk, he joined the Second Marine Regiment, First Brigade (ABF), assembled at Philadelphia. On 30 July 1915 Admiral Benson (acting Secretary of the Navy) sent orders to the MGC (acting in Barnett's place was ADC Lejeune) to assemble an expeditionary force of 500 Marines to leave for duty in Haiti the *following day*. Lejeune selected five companies from the 2d Marine Regiment at Philadelphia and, on 31 July, they were aboard the *Connecticut* and sailed at 0900 with Col. Eli K. Cole in command.

Turnage participated in the expedition against hostile Cacos in Northern Haiti, then on 31 July was assigned to duty with the *Gendarmerie d'Haiti* until August 1918. During that period, he was first lieutenant on 29 August 1916, and captain on 26 March 1917. Smedley D. Butler later wrote that the "Cavalry Camp" was "pretty and well kept," then further complimented Turnage who "did a fine job of it. He is one of the best men I ever knew and his work out there showed it."

Almost immediately upon his return to the U.S., Major Turnage (1 July 1918) was sent to France, where he served as the CO, 5th Machine Gun Battalion, 5th Marine Brigade. The brigade and its units arrived too late to be committed as a unit and a few of the officers and men were used either as replacements in the 4th Brigade or more likely at AEF Headquarters. Turnage served in the occupation of Germany and came back in July-August 1919.

Following World War I, Turnage, like so many of his peers, was reduced in rank, he to captain. On 16 December Capt. Turnage went aboard the *Tennessee* to command the MD but remained aboard only a few months. He was at Quantico on 9 February 1920 as an instructor at the MOS. On 16 August 1922 he returned to Haiti and the 1st Brigade, serving with the *Gendarmerie d'Haiti* until September, returning to Quantico on the 26th graduating from the Field Officers' course.

He next drew a lengthy assignment at HQMC, arriving on 16 October 1926. His promotion to major came through on 29 June 1927. His next assignment, arriving on 10 June 1929, was sea duty as DMO aboard the *New Mexico* and on the staff of Battleship Divisions' Four. On 3 June 1930, he was aboard the *New York*, same post but now Division 3, and on 14 August 1931 he was aboard the *Texas*.

In April 1932 he went ashore and back to HQMC on 10 May. Lt.Col. Turnage (29 May 1934) was ordered to Philadelphia in June 1935 (arriving on 5 July); there he was appointed Director of the Marine Officers' Basic School at the Navy Yard. That lasted until June of 1937 when he assumed command on the 9th of that month of the 1st Battalion, 5th Marines, as Battalion CO and Regimental EO, respectively, at Quantico.

In May 1939 Col. Turnage (29 June 1938) was ordered overseas, where he served as CO of Marine Forces in North China, and CO of the MD, American Embassy, Peiping, beginning on 5 May. This was a

Allen Hal Turnage

rough period for the modest Marine presence in North China and Turnage was limited in what he could do about responding to incursions by the Japanese. He returned to HQMC in April 1941 and was serving as Director of the Division of Plans and Policies when World War II broke out.

In June 1942, now brigadier general as of 29 March 1942, Turnage was ordered to Camp Lejeune, NC, to take command of the base and its training center, which included organization and training of two Regimental Combat Teams for the 3dMarDiv. That October, Major General Turnage (28 September 1942) joined the newly formed 3dMarDiv as ADC, then becoming CG on Guadalcanal in September 1943. He led the Division in the landing at Empress Augusta Bay, Bougainville, on 15 October 1943, and in the recapture of Guam, beginning on 21 July 1944. He was awarded a Navy Cross (for 1 November) and a Distinguished Service Medal for his part in the satisfactory campaigns on Bougainville and Guam.

After two years with the 3dMarDiv, in September 1944 General Turnage was assigned to HQMC as Director of Personnel, and later, as Assistant Commandant of the Marine Corps. In May 1946, his alma mater, the University of North Carolina, awarded him the honorary degree of Doctor of Laws. His final assignment was as CG, FMF, Pacific.

General Turnage retired from active duty on 1 January 1948, and was advanced to four-star rank on retirement, effective on 4 October 1946, by reason of having been specially commended for heroism in combat.

In addition to the Navy Cross and Distinguished Service Medal, his decorations and medals include the Legion of Merit, Presidential Unit Citation, Guam, 1944; Navy Unit Commendation with two bronze stars, Bougainville, 1943, Guam, 1944; Haitian Campaign Medal, Haiti, 1915; Expeditionary Medal, Haiti, 1915–1917 and 1922–1924; Victory Medal with France Clasp and Maltese Cross, France, 1918; Second Nicaraguan Campaign Medal, Nicaragua 1932; China Service Medal, China, 1939; American Defense Service Medal with Base Clasp, China, 1939–1941; Asiatic-Pacific Campaign Medal with three bronze stars; American Campaign Medal; World War II Victory Medal; Haitian Distinguished Service Medal, Haiti, 1925; Nicaraguan Medal of Distinction with Diploma; Dominican Order of Military Merit, Class Two with White Insignia, Dominican Republic, 1930.

General Allen Hal Turnage died on 22 October 1971.

UNDERHILL, Lieutenant General James Latham was born 12 June 1891 in San Francisco, CA, where he attended local schools, then graduated from the University of California with a B.S. degree. Underhill was appointed a second lieutenant in the Marine Corps on 20 August 1913. His first assignment, beginning on 29 November, was to the MOS at the MB, Norfolk. He was in good company at the school: Other newcomers included Henry Larsen, Keller Rockey and Hal Turnage.

Underhill shipped out aboard the *Arkansas* and served with the Marines at Vera Cruz in April 1914. He returned to the States aboard the *Minnesota* in November, arriving at the Philadelphia Navy Yard to serve with the 1st Brigade (ABF) on the 15th. Underhill went aboard the *Connecticut* on 17 May 1916, then as First Lieutenant (29 August 1916) commanded the MD. With the war on, Underhill was promoted to captain on 26 March 1917 while still aboard ship.

He was transferred to Quantico to help train incoming men who would eventually become Marines. Major Underhill (26 March 1917) was placed in command of the 8th Separate (Replacement) Battalion in September 1918 and shipped to France aboard the *Pocahontas* on 20 October 1918, arriving in France on 3 November. Arriving too late to take part in the fighting, the replacements were blended into the badly depleted formations of the 4th Brigade. Underhill, an unwanted additional major, was sent home in December.

Reverting back to captain, he joined the Legation Guard at Managua, Nicaragua, on 22 March 1919, remaining there until May 1921, when he returned to the MB, Quantico, on 17 June. That October he became an instructor at MCS until June 1922 and then also graduated from the Field Officers' course. His next assignment was in the Quartermaster's Department beginning on 13 May 1924. On 5 August he was made Judge Advocate and QM at the MB, Cavite Naval Station, Philippine Islands. Major Underhill (September 1918) headed home and was assigned to the Marine Corps Base, San Diego, CA.

His stay at San Diego was relatively short. Trouble in China prompted the State Department to ask the Marine Corps to arrange for a brigade to be sent to North China on 21 March 1927. Underhill was with the 3d Brigade as plans and training officer, then CO of 3/6 in 1928. He returned to the States in October and to the MB, Quantico, in December that same year. He went back to the West Coast and arrived at the Naval Prison, Mare Island, CA on 27 December 1930, remaining there for several years.

He transferred to sea duty, as DMO, Battleship Division Three, on 18 February 1934. Soon after, on 29 May, he was promoted to lieutenant colonel. His shipboard duties terminated in January 1936 and on the 11th of that month he was at the Marine Base, San Diego. He returned to China for service in 1937 as EO, Sixth Marines, and succeeded to command the regiment on 13 January 1938 when its CO, Col. Thomas S. Clarke, was detached to the U.S. due to illness. Just after the regiment returned from China, he was in turn relieved by Lt.Col. Alphonse DeCarre the following 12 May. In June 1938 he was CO at the Naval Base, Portsmouth, NH, and on the 29th he was promoted to colonel. On 24 July 1939 he was at HQMC as EO of the Adjutant and Inspector's Department.

Brigadier General Underhill (28 March 1942) was assigned 14 March 1942 as CG of the Marine Corps Base, San Diego. In March 1943, BG Underhill was transferred to the command of Camp Lejeune, NC. In August he was placed in command of the East Coast Echelon of the 4thMarDiv and then was made the ADC. He was assigned to duty with VAC and was an observer at the Tarawa operation in November 1943. After serving a year as ADC of the 4thMarDiv, during which he participated in the Kwajalein operation, Underhill commanded the 25th Marines reinforced. He directed the landings on several smaller islands on which artillery was to be placed to support the main landing on Kwajalein.

After its occupation, he was made

James Latham Underhill

Island Commander of Tinian; his main responsibility was to create and develop a major air base on the island. He was also responsible for the care and feeding of the civilian population that had survived the fighting. He was awarded a Legion of Merit for this undertaking at Tinian. General Underhill remained there until November 1944 when he was made Deputy Commander, FMF, Pacific. In May 1944, he was promoted to major general to rank from 28 September 1942.

On 21 March 1945, he became Inspector General of the FMF, Pacific. He was serving as President of the Post War Reorganization Board at HQMC at the time of his retirement on 1 November 1946. General Underhill was accorded accolades for his efforts in absorbing many capable wartime reserve officers into regular commissions. He was promoted to lieutenant general at that time for having been specially commended for performance of duty in actual combat.

He held the Legion of Merit, Bronze Star Medal, Marine Corps Expeditionary Medal with one bronze star, Cuba 1917; Nicaragua 1919–21; Victory Medal, World War I, with France Clasp, France 1918; Yangtze Service Medal, China 1927; China Service Medal, China 1937–1938; Asiatic-Pacific Area Campaign Ribbon with three bronze stars, the Presidential Unit Citation; and the World War II Victory Medal.

Lieutenant General James L. Underhill died at the age of 100 on 7 October 1991 in Pacific Grove, Monterey, CA.

UPSHUR, Major General William Peterkins was born on 28 October 1881 in Richmond, VA, attending the local schools and graduating from the Virginia Military Institute in 1902. He attended Law School at the University of Virginia, between 1902 and 1903. His acceptance of a commission as a second lieutenant of Marines took effect on 16 January 1904. His first posting was to sea duty aboard the *Maine* on 28 December 1904 and it appears he was transferred aboard the *Kearsage* beginning on 31 March 1905. He was on the promotion list to first lieutenant effective 28 February 1905, which was rather rapid for those times.

His foreign shore duty included service with an expeditionary force to Havana, Cuba. The unit of 804 officers and enlisted Marines, rather large for those days, was partially culled from six ships' detachments; they landed on 1 October 1906. After the initial landing, the force retired to duty at Camp Evans, Deer Point, Guantánamo, Cuba, from 9 January to 8 February 1907, following which he was back aboard the *Kearsage*.

Upshur was at the MB, Norfolk, on 2 November 1907 and was detailed to expeditionary duty with a force of Marines led by Col. Eli K. Cole to the Isthmus of Panama from 19 June to 8 August 1908. The force of 19 officers and 706 enlisted Marines which was in Panama to enforce legitimate elections, left there aboard the *New Hampshire* and *Idaho* for the U.S. on 31 July. He was detailed to the recently reactivated MOS at Port Royal, SC, on 19 February 1909. This was the first schooling he received as a Marine officer. It appears, however, that rather he was an instructor during the period.

Arriving at Olongapo in the Philippine Islands on 17 December 1911 (other records show January 1912), he was assigned duty with the First Brigade of Marines. He was promoted to captain on 22 August 1912. He remained there until detached in February 1914 for duty to the MD, American Legation, Peking, China, where he served until 16 October 1914. Capt. Upshur returned to the States in October 1914 and after his annual leave assumed duty at the MB, Mare Island, CA on 14 November 1914. On 30 June 1915, he went to the Philadelphia Navy Yard and joined the First Brigade of Marines (ABF).

On 4 August 1915 Capt. Upshur assumed command of the 15th Mounted Company, Second Regiment, at Port-au-Prince, Haiti, where he participated in engagements against hostile Cacos bandits. During this action he was awarded the Medal of Honor. He and his subordinate, 1stLt Edward A. Ostermann, plus the famous Gunnery Sgt. Dan Daly, each on 24 October led a section of the 15th Company in three directions to drive off a large Cacos ambush group near Fort Dipitie. Other decorations for service in Haiti include the Haitian Campaign Medal and Marine Corps Expeditionary Medal. He hated the island soon after his arrival but when leaving in early 1917 he wrote to his father that he felt "a real regret at leaving this beautiful island and its black people."

Upon this country's entry into World War I, Major Upshur (26 March 1917) was again detailed for foreign shore duty, this time as CO of the 1st Battalion, 13th Regiment of Marines. They arrived in France in September, 1918 and most of them remained until August, 1919. The war was over in November and most of the Marines of the 5th Brigade did not get into the war, under orders of Gen. Pershing. They were instead spread around in France, some as replacements for the 4th Brigade, others with different duties. During this time he was in command of the American Military Prison, Casino des Lilas, Bordeaux and the American Guard Camp. He returned to the U.S. with the rest of the Marines during July-August 1919.

After a brief leave he was at the MB, Navy Yard, Philadelphia, on 2 October 1919. The following year, on 6 October 1920, he was at the MB, Quantico, as an administrative aide to BG Smedley D. Butler. In the main Civil War reenactment, Upshur was playing the part of Pickett and led the charge. In July and August 1921, he was on temporary duty at the Naval Station, St. Thomas, Virgin Islands, and on 30 July 1922 he went to the First Brigade in Haiti. That service terminated in June 1924 and he was selected to attend the C&GSS at Fort Leavenworth, KS, arriving 2 September and graduating the following 29 June 1925. He was, effective on 15 July, promoted to lieutenant colonel and back at the MB, Quantico.

From January to March 1929, he was on temporary duty as Chief Umpire, Fleet Training Exercise No. 5, at Culebra, Puerto Rico. On 2 July he was appointed FMO, Battle Fleet, aboard the *California*. On 4 June 1931 he reported to the NWC at Newport, RI, to attend and to graduate. The following year, Col. Upshur (27 July 1932) was a student on 15 August 1932 at the AWC in Washington. On 1 July 1933 he was at HQMC, remaining there until reporting to the Navy Department (19 April 1935), where he was on duty with the War Plans Division, Office of the Chief of Naval Operations, Navy Department, then back to HQMC on 1 May 1937. He assumed the role of Officer in Charge of the Marine Corps Reserve on 16 May and was promoted

William Peterkins Upshur

to brigadier general on 29 June 1938. Upshur was later mentioned as being "very active in all phases of the Reserve and his leadership contributed much to the high level of preparedness attained by the FMCR battalions by the close of 1939." The reserves were to be called into service and that command terminated on 18 August 1939.

On 20 September 1939 he was assigned as CG of the Marine Corps Base, and FMF, San Diego, and on the 1st of October was promoted to major general. Then to San Francisco on 9 December 1941 to become CG of the Department of the Pacific, which post he commanded until he was killed in an airplane crash near Sitka, Alaska, on 18 August 1943.

In September 1948 his remains were removed from his Alaskan burial plot and re-interred at the U.S. Naval Academy at Annapolis, MD. General Upshur's wife, Lucy M. Upshur, died in April 1952, and was also buried at Annapolis, MD.

Major General William P. Upshur, recipient of the nation's highest award, the Medal of Honor during the Haitian Campaign in 1915, also earned several campaign medals from his service in France, Haiti, and during World War II.

VANDEGRIFT, General and 18th Commandant Alexander Archer was born on 13 March 1887 in Charlottesville, VA. He attended local schools, then the University of Virginia, and was commissioned in the Marine Corps as a second lieutenant on 22 January 1909. Following instruction at the MOS, Port Royal, SC, and beginning on 29 December 1910, he served a tour of duty at the MB, Portsmouth, NH. On 26 May 1912 Vandegrift went on foreign shore duty at Camp Elliott, Canal Zone, as a member of Major Smedley D. Butler's battalion, based there waiting for an opportunity to land in Nicaragua, then as always in a state of ferment. Eventually receiving orders to go, Butler and his unit landed at Corinto, Nicaragua, on 14 August 1912.

Vandegrift seemed to have been a favorite of Butler, who on occasion would tease the quiet 2dLt, naming him "Sunny Jim" after an always smiling cartoon character of that time. In his writings he sometimes referred to Vandegrift as "James." Vandegrift participated in most of the activities, mostly pushing aside rebels, then the bombardment, assault, and capture of Coyotepe, a large hill position occupied by rebel forces in Nicaragua.

He next arrived at Vera Cruz, Mexico, from Panama on the early morning of 22 April 1914, landing under fire. "We jumped off early, hit some heavy street fighting but pushed on until some of our own naval five-inch shells took us under fire." He participated in the engagement and occupation of Vera Cruz, that month and remained there until later that year.

On 4 December 1914, following his promotion to first lieutenant (10 November), he joined the 1st Brigade, ABF, and attended the Advance Base course at the MB, Philadelphia. Upon completion of

Alexander Archer Vandegrift

schooling, he sailed for Haiti with the Brigade, arriving on 15 August 1915, and participated in action against hostile Cacos bandits at Le Trou and Fort Capois. Not long after his arrival, Capt. Vandegrift (29 August 1916) was once more in Butler's newly created *Gendarmerie d'Haiti* where his first task was to organize and train two 100-man companies. Major Vandegrift (1 July 1918) remained in Haiti until returning to MB, Quantico, on 13 December 1918 whereupon he was assigned duty with the Quartermaster Department and served briefly at Norfolk.

On 29 July 1919, at his request, he was back with the 1st Marine Brigade in Haiti. Vandegrift had suggested that instead of him that Holland Smith be his replacement at the QM Department, and later wrote that it was several years before Smith could laugh about it (or would even speak to him). Meanwhile, Vandegrift had retained his majority dated 4 July 1920.

The fighting in Haiti was quite fierce. Charlemagne Peralte was the leader of the Cacos and would cause some major headaches before Sgt. Hanneken and Cpl. Button finally put paid to him. Because of charges that the Marines were brutalizing the natives, the MGC Lejeune, accompanied by Smedley D. Butler, conducted an official on-site investigation in the fall of 1920. The latter stayed with Vandegrift and his wife for a few days. Vandegrift remained active in Haiti until April 1923 when he and wife Mildred returned to the U.S. and on 5 May he was back at the MB, Quantico.

He served for a time as CO of 1/5, then as CO of the regiment. During this period he participated in all that was going on there, including building the stadium and the Civil War reenactment campaigns. He completed the Field Officers' course and on 19 June 1926 arrived at the MB, San Diego as Assistant CoS.

In February 1927, he sailed for China where he served under Butler once again as Operations and Training Officer of the 3d Marine Brigade with Headquarters at Tientsin. His stay in China was fairly brief because in September 1928 he was ordered to HQMC where he became Assistant Chief Coordinator, Bureau of the Budget, on 14 January 1929. Following duty in Washington, he joined the MB, Quantico (31 August 1933), where he became Assistant CoS, G-1 Section, FMF. During this assignment, he was promoted to lieutenant colonel on 29 May 1934.

Ordered to China in June 1935, Lt.Col. Vandegrift served successively as EO and then CO of the MD at the American Embassy in Peiping when he temporarily replaced Col. Presley M. Rixey, who became ill and was sent to the coast. Later, after the very ill Rixey returned to the States, Vandegrift assumed the role of CO when promoted to colonel on 1 September 1936.

Col. Vandegrift reported on 7 June 1937 to HQMC, where he became Military Secretary to the MGC Thomas Holcomb. During this period he handled correspondence from senior, and some junior, officers to the MGC, which had a major impact on the direction which the Corps was to take in the following few years. In March 1940, he was appointed Assistant to the MGC, and Brigadier General Vandegrift (1 April 1940) was detached to the 1stMarDiv in November 1941 as the ADC to MG Philip Torrey. The latter was soon relieved of command and Major General Vandegrift (March 1942) sailed for the South Pacific Area that May as CG of the first Marine division to ever leave the shores of the United States.

On 7 August 1942, in the Solomon Islands, he led ashore the 1stMarDiv in the first large-scale offensive action against the Japanese. For outstanding service as CG of the 1stMarDiv during the attack on Guadalcanal, Tulagi, and Gavutu in the Solomon Islands, he was awarded the Navy Cross and, for the subsequent occupation and defense from 7 August to 9 December 1942, was awarded the Medal of Honor.

In July 1943, he assumed command of IMAC and on 1 November 1943 responsibility for the landing at Empress Augusta Bay, Bougainville, Northern Solomon Islands. Upon establishing the initial beachhead, he relinquished command and returned to Washington D.C. as the Commandant-designate. He was forced to briefly return to IMAC due to the demise of MG Barrett (see).

Nonetheless, on 1 January 1944, as a lieutenant general, he was sworn in as the 18th Commandant of the Marine Corps. On 4 April 1945, he was appointed general, with date of rank from 21 March 1945, the first Marine officer on active duty to attain four-star rank. While in that post he had many serious problems but, with capable subordinates, he managed to avoid the efforts of the U.S. Army to forcefully unite the Marine Corps with their venerable institution.

For outstanding service as Commandant of the Marine Corps from 1 January 1944 to 30 June 1946, Gen. Vandergrift was awarded the Distinguished Service Medal. He left active service on 31 December 1947 and was placed on the retired list 1 April 1949.

In addition to the Medal of Honor, Navy Cross, and Distinguished Service Medal, his decorations and medals included the Presidential Unit Citation with one bronze star; Navy Unit Commendation with one bronze star; Expeditionary Medal with three bronze stars; Nicaraguan Campaign Medal; Mexican Service Medal; Haitian Campaign Medal with one star; World War I Victory Medal with West Indies Clasp and one star; Yangtze Service Medal; American Defense Service Medal; Asiatic-Pacific Campaign Medal with four bronze stars; American Campaign Medal; and the World War II Victory Medal. He also received numerous foreign decorations.

General Alexander A. Vandegrift died after a long illness at age 86 on 8 May 1973 at the Naval Medical Center, Bethesda, MD. His interment date was 10 May 1973 at Arlington National Cemetery.

VOGEL, Major General Clayton Barney was born on 18 September 1882 in Philadelphia, PA, attending local schools, then Rutgers University, from which he graduated in May 1904. On 28 July 1904 he accepted a commission as a second lieutenant of Marines and on the 18th of August was a student at the School of Application, Annapolis, remaining there until 13 November 1905 when he was assigned to the MB, Pensacola, FL. He was transferred to the MB in Washington D.C. on 20 June 1906 with the task to prepare Marines going to the American Legation in Peking, China, as members of the recently appointed Marine Guard. He and his charges were shipped to China, arriving at Peking on 27 September 1906. First Lieutenant Vogel (25 February 1908) would remain there until 16 December 1908 when he left for HQMC.

He was ordered to the School of Application, now at Port Royal, SC, arriving on 30 March 1909; there he served as adjutant to Lt.Col. Eli K. Cole. Trouble was always brewing in the Caribbean and on 12 December 1909 Vogel was aboard the *Prairie*, with Cole's 2d Regiment of Marines heading for the Canal Zone. He and his regiment served at Camp Elliott, which eventually became the staging point for the later interventions in Nicaragua. The 2d Regiment was returned home 14 March 1910 to Port Royal but Vogel instead went to the MB, Washington, rejoining the 2d Regiment on 5 January 1911 aboard the *Dixie*. Not long after, Vogel was among the 22 officers and 666 enlisted Marines, commanded by Major George C. Thorpe, who landed at Guantánamo Bay on 13 March to protect American interests in Cuba.

He returned to the States with his

regiment and was assigned until 25 May 1912 as a Special White House Aide. Now Capt. Vogel (25 February 1915) would serve as skipper of the MD aboard the *Nebraska* beginning on 25 September 1915. Then on 16 December he arrived for duty with Philadelphia's First Brigade, ABF, which was subsequently shipped to Haiti.

His next assignment beginning on 20 March 1916 was as an Inspector with the *Gendarmerie d'Haiti*. While in Haiti he was promoted to major on 22 May 1917. On 5 December 1918 he was a patient at the Naval Hospital in Washington D.C but soon after was assigned to a spot on the Marine Corps Rifle Team. He distinguished himself during the National Rifle Matches at Caldwell, NJ, where "only the ever-present mosquitoes enjoyed those matches." He was next on recruiting duty in Philadelphia, beginning on 21 December 1918. On 12 July 1919 his majority was made permanent and in September 1919, he was assigned to command a detachment of Marines taking German prisoners of war to Germany. Upon his return, as of 15 December 1920, he was appointed to the command of the MB, Washington. While there he led his men on 28 January 1922 in a rescue at the fire in the Knickerbocker Theater.

On 2 July 1923 Major Vogel was reassigned as FMO, the Scouting Fleet, aboard the *Wyoming*, which post terminated in August 1925 and on the 10th he was at the MB, Quantico. During this period he also commanded the MD at the National Rifle Matches, held at Camp Perry, OH. He also managed to complete the Field Officers' course at the MCS, graduating in May 1926. On 2 July he was transferred to HQMC where he was assigned to duty at the Judge Advocate's Office, managing to complete a post-graduate course in law at Georgetown University. Lt.Col. Vogel (8 July 1928) remained on this duty until 12 April 1929.

His next move, on 1 May 1929, was when ordered to report as CoS of the Commandant of the *Guardia Nacional* in Nicaragua. Then on 24 October he reported as CO of the Northern District which post lasted until 18 November 1929 but he remained in Nicaragua until June 1930. Next he briefly served as CO of the MB, Hampton Roads, VA, until on 12 November 1930 he joined the *Garde d'Haiti* as CoS at Port-au-Prince. He remained in Haiti as Major General *Commandante* of the *Garde* until August 1934, when the Marines were finally withdrawn after nearly 20 years of occupation.

Back in the U.S., Col. Vogel's (29 May 1934) next assignment, as of 8 October 1934, was at HQMC in the Adjutant and Inspector's Office. He was appointed the Adjutant and Inspector of the Marine Corps on 1 March 1937 and promoted to brigadier general at that time. Vogel would remain in that post until 10 August 1939 when he assumed command of the 2d Marine Brigade, then at the MB, San Diego, and was also made CG of Camp Elliott, CA. General Vogel led the brigade in several amphibious training exercises in that area and worked tirelessly to bring his brigade up to a war footing. As was common for that time and place, it was often too little money and then much too late.

Major General Barney Vogel (1 March 1941) was made CG of the 2dMarDiv from February until November 1941, then CG of the Amphibious Corps, Pacific Fleet, until October 1942. While in that post he was responsible for the development of Camp Pendleton, Camp Elliott, and Camp Dunlap. Then, from October 1942 until August 1943, he became CG of the newly formed I Marine Amphibious Corps (IMAC), based at Noumea. While in this post, his many arguments with his superiors about difficulties became his downfall, and he was relieved by MG Barrett.

General Vogel returned to the U.S. and assumed command of the FMF, San Diego Area, from August 1943 until 30 April 1944.

Next he was CG of MB, Parris Island, from 1 May 1944 until January 1946 when he retired that month. He returned to the Philadelphia area and over the next few years engaged in many activities, mostly of a historic nature.

His decorations and awards were of the usual expeditionary nature: medals for duty in China, Haiti, Nicaragua, plus World War II campaign medals and Unit Citations.

Major General Clayton B. Vogel, age 82, died at the Naval Hospital, Philadelphia, on 26 November 1964.

WALKER, Lieutenant General John Thaddeus was born on 15 September 1893 in Azle, TX. He graduated from the Texas Agricultural and Mechanical College, College Station, TX, which school later (November 1948) conferred a "Doctor of Laws" degree upon him "in recognition of distinguished service to his country, his profession and his fellowmen."

He reported for active duty as a second lieutenant in the Marine Corps on 23 May 1917 and was promoted to first lieutenant on 11 August 1917. Walker arrived in France on 18 September 1917 and joined the 51st Co, 2d Battalion, 5th Marines, as a platoon leader.

While in France, Walker studied extensively in various U.S. military schools. Recalled in April 1918, he returned to the States and, beginning on 4 May, became an instructor in the Bayonet School at the MB, Quantico. Capt. Walker (1 July 1918) spent the rest of the war teaching that "trade" to enlisted Marines.

On 25 October 1920 Walker joined the Second Brigade of Marines in Santo Domingo, remaining until August 1922. During his tenure, the policy of containment seemed to be working but in 1921 a growing insurgency caused more problems for Marines. Then Walker was ordered to the MB, Norfolk, as Aide to the Commandant of the Navy Yard on 24 August 1922, remaining in that position until September 1925. On 2 September he arrived for duty at the MB, Quantico, and began classes in the MCS Company Officers' course, graduating the following spring.

On 15 July 1926 he boarded the *West Virginia* to command the MD, remaining until June 1928, then back ashore and leave. He arrived at the MB, Philadelphia Navy Yard, on 29 July 1928, remaining there until July 1932, and while there he served as an instructor for incoming officers at the Basic School. On 27 July 1932 he joined the *Garde d'Haiti*; according to the Commandant's Report, there were but 105 officers and enlisted Marines on duty with the *Garde* in 1932. The period of insurrection was over and within two years the Corps would be totally withdrawn. Major Walker (29 May 1934) was part of that withdrawal group, arriving in the States in August 1934.

On 4 September he was ordered to duty with the Division of Reserve at HQMC, where he remained until July 1937, when he was reassigned as a student at the Senior Officers' course, MCS, at Quantico. Upon completion of the course in May 1938, Lt.Col. Walker (1 December 1937) remained in that course as an instructor. Following the MCS's duty, on 29 June 1940 Walker arrived at the Marine Corps Base, San Diego, as Chief of the Planning Section. From there he was ordered in July 1941 as a Naval Observer to British Forces in and around Cairo, Egypt, returning to the States in December 1941.

Col. Walker (1 January 1942) joined the 2dMarDiv on 9 January, where he performed duties as Operations Officer until June when he assumed command of the Twenty-Second Marines and sailed with them for American Samoa the following month. He was a superb commander; his regiment was considered a spirited, competent unit. Walker led the regiment in the assault and capture of Engebi, Eniwetok Atoll, Marshall Islands, in February 1944, for which action he was awarded the Navy

Cross. Four days later the regiment, still under Walker's command, invaded Parry Island, destroying over 1000 Japanese defenders in desperate close-in fighting and capturing the island on which was based the Eniwetok Headquarters of the Japanese Army. His citation for the Navy Cross credited him with the successful overwhelming of the Japanese on the island within six hours. Rear Admiral Harry Hill wrote to the Commandant expressing his delight: "Col. J.T. Walker and the Twenty-Second Marines ... did a wonderful job and deserve all the praise which can be bestowed upon them."

Walker was named CoS to MG Shepherd of the First Provisional Marine Brigade in March 1944, then became temporary brigade commander on 10 April. He participated with the Brigade in the landing and subsequent recapture of Guam in July and August, earning the Legion of Merit.

Returning to the U.S. in December 1944, Walker was assigned as Assistant Director of Personnel at HQMC, which position he held until May 1945. Brigadier General Walker (retro back to 4 October 1942) was detached to the 2dMarDiv, then on Saipan. Now CG, he participated with the Division in the occupation of Japan and in February 1946 was temporary major general, effective back to 10 April 1942.

In April 1946, he was detached to the Marine Training and Replacement Command, San Diego Area, Camp Pendleton, where he was appointed Deputy Commander. Like many temporary wartime flag promotions, he had been reduced to brigadier general and in September 1946 he assumed duties as CG of the Third Marine Brigade (formerly 3dMarDiv) at Camp Pendleton This was a command he held until July 1947 when he was assigned as ADC of the 1stMarDiv at Camp Pendleton.

In February 1948, BG Walker was detached and ordered to duty as CG, Troop Training Unit, Amphibious Training Command, Pacific Fleet at Coronado, CA, now a temporary major general once again. Detached on 15 July 1949, he assumed duties as Director of Personnel on 31 August 1949. Walker retired in July 1954 as a lieutenant general.

In addition to the Navy Cross and Legion of Merit, Walker was awarded the Bronze Star, Japan 1945–1946; Navy Unit Commendation, Guam 1944; Victory Medal with Defensive Clasp, France 1918; Expeditionary Medal, Dominican Republic 1920–1922; American Defense Service Medal with Bronze Star; American Campaign Medal; Asiatic-Pacific Campaign Medal with two Bronze Stars; World War II Victory Medal; and Haitian Distinguished Service Medal with Diploma.

Lieutenant General John T. Walker died on 27 February 1955.

WALLACE, Lieutenant General William Jennings was born on 6 August 1895, in Church Hill, MD. He earned a B.S. from Washington College, Chestertown, MD, and was assigned to active service as a second lieutenant in the Marine Corps on 15 June 1918, but dated 15 August. On 16 August he was promoted to first lieutenant. Following a short tour of duty with the artillery of the Tenth Marine Regiment at the MB, Quantico, beginning on 13 September. Wallace went to foreign shore duty with the Second Provisional Marine Brigade in Santo Domingo on 7 April 1919, remaining until June 1921.

He returned to the U.S. and became a student Naval Aviator at the NAS, Pensacola, FL, and was appointed a Naval Aviator upon the successful completion of training and reported for flight duty to Brown Field, Quantico, on 28 December 1921. From here, he again went to foreign shore duty with the 1st Air Squadron, as part of the Second Marine Brigade in Santo Domingo, arriving on 7 November 1922. Their main role was to fly personnel or mail to the outposts occupied by small groups of Marines but engaged in very little ground support in attacks upon the rebel forces.

In July 1924 he returned to the States to become Test Flight Officer and Assistant Engineering Officer at the Marine Corps Base, San Diego, beginning on 16 August. In June of the following year, he attended the Air Service Advanced Flying School at Kelly Field, San Antonio, TX. Upon completion of training in the spring of 1926, he went back to the Marine Corps Base at San Diego where he served as a Division Commander until he sailed for Hsin Ho, China (April 1927), where he was a Squadron Commander serving the Third Brigade from 2 May. He and the rest of the aviation staff and flyers remained in China until 1929, then returned to the States.

Following their return to the States, they arrived at the NAS, San Diego, in December 1928 but Wallace was assigned on 2 September 1929 as a student in the Company Officers' course, MCS, Quantico. Upon graduation, Capt. Wallace (1 August 1930) was assigned successively to Aircraft Squadrons at San Diego on 29 August 1930, and on 5 October 1931 as Squadron Commander, VS-14M, Aircraft Battle Force, U.S. Fleet aboard the *Saratoga*. This was the first Marine squadron to be assigned duty aboard carriers (also see Farrell).

In August 1934, he was assigned as a student at the Air Corps Tactical School, Maxwell Field, Montgomery, AL, and upon graduation was ordered to duty at the MB, Quantico, arriving on 6 June 1935. There he performed duties as a Squadron Commander and as a successful student in the Senior course, MCS. Major Wallace (30 June 1936) then became aviation instructor in the Three Section of the MCS until he was detached in March 1941.

On 7 December 1941 Lt.Col. Wallace (1 March 1941) was EO of Marine Air Group Twenty-one at Pearl Harbor and participated in the defense of Ewa Field on the island of Oahu. His next assignment, as of 9 January 1942, was as CO of the Marine Aviation Detachment on Midway Island until April. Col. Wallace (21 May 1942) commanded MAG 23, which was later at Guadalcanal during the hectic summer and fall of 1942, for which he was awarded the Legion of Merit and Purple Heart Medal, having been wounded in action against the enemy.

Following that action, Wallace was sent home in February 1943 to become CoS of Marine Air West. This was followed after his promotion to brigadier general (5 December) by becoming the CG. In May 1944 he was back to the Pacific as CoS, Aircraft, FMF, Pacific. Later, from April to August 1945, he became the CG of the Air Defense Command and Fighter Command in Okinawa for which he was awarded the Distinguished Service Medal. His command's most difficult task was to squelch, as best they could, the very serious Japanese *Kamikaze* air attacks. Later his command was flying over Japan, even spraying city streets with their weapons.

Major General Wallace (retro back to 30 September 1942) assumed command of Marine Air West Coast in August 1945, until one year later, when he was ordered back as CG to Aircraft, FMF, Pacific. From that command he moved to Cherry Point, NC, in September 1947, when he became CG, Aircraft, FMF, Atlantic and then CG, Second MAW. He remained there until February 1948, at which time he was ordered to his assignment at HQMC to direct Marine Aviation and to become Assistant Commandant for Air which terminated in 1950. His last post was as CG, Aircraft, FMF, Pacific, based at El Toro, CA. He then retired in July 1952 as a lieutenant general.

In addition to the Distinguished Service Medal and the Legion of Merit, his decorations and medals include the Bronze Star Medal, Pacific Area, 1944; the Purple

Heart Medal, Guadalcanal, 1942; the Presidential Unit Citation with Star, Guadalcanal, 1942, and Okinawa, 1945; the Expeditionary Medal with Bronze Star, Dominican Republic, 1919–1921, China, 1927–1928; American Defense Service Medal; American Campaign Medal; Asiatic-Pacific Campaign Medal; and World War II Victory Medal.

Lieutenant General William J. Wallace died on 7 July 1977.

WALLER, Major General Littleton Waller Tazewell, Jr., was born in Norfolk, VA, on 18 September 1886, son and namesake of one of the Corps' most celebrated officers. He attended the Naval Academy at Annapolis, MD, but resigned as a midshipman on 6 March 1906. He accepted a commission as a second lieutenant of Marines on 17 September 1907. His first assignment was at the Navy Yard, Norfolk, VA, there being no Officers' basic school at that time. He spent a year aboard a ship (unknown) and returned to Norfolk in September 1908. On 31 December 1908 he arrived at Peking, China, to serve with the Marine Guard at the American Legation, leaving there in September 1910.

On 10 November 1910 First Lieutenant Waller (11 October) had returned to the MB, Norfolk, but he was soon again aboard a ship (unknown) for another ten months and then back to Norfolk on 18 September 1911. On 11 August 1912 he was at the MB, Mare Island, CA, until on 26 September 1913 he arrived at the MB, Philadelphia Navy Yard. That was the home of the 1st Expeditionary Regiment, then commonly known as the Advanced Base Force, where he was among the officers and men selected to intervene at Vera Cruz, Mexico, in April 1914. The Marines remained there for some months afterward to support the U.S. Army and on 4 January 1915 Waller went aboard the *Michigan* to join the MD. While aboard, he was promoted to captain on 29 August 1916 and became the "skipper" of the detachment.

With the war on, promotions went wild and Major Waller (22 May 1917) went overseas on 31 December as "skipper" of the 81st Company, 6th Machine Gun Battalion. His promotion to major had, however, forced him out of the company and battalion, and he was assigned to command the 7th Motorized Machine Gun Bn, 3d Infantry Division. However, with the death of Major Edward Cole at Belleau Wood in June, Waller was back with the 6th Machine Gun Bn as his replacement. He served with distinction at Soissons, St. Mihiel and at Blanc Mont, after which, on 24 October, he became the 2d Division Machine Gun Officer.

After serving in Germany on occupation duty, Waller returned to the U.S. in July-August 1919 with the rest of the 2d Division. After a leave he reported to HQMC on 21 October 1919 and on 28 August 1921 he was sent to the Depot of Supplies in Philadelphia. While there, Waller was awarded a Navy Cross for his actions in France. Major Waller, for a personal reason (or reasons), decided to resign his regular commission in 1925; he joined the Fleet Marine Corps Reserve (FMCR) and would thereafter attend drills. In the reserves he was promoted to lieutenant colonel effective back to 22 May 1917.

Lt.Col. Waller was ordered to active duty as a reserve colonel in June 1941. He was made officer in charge of target practice at HQMC, then director of personnel in February 1943. Brigadier General Waller (September 1942), the first reservist to become a flag officer, was also made Director, Marine Corps Reserve, on 1 October 1942, serving in that position until 1 May 1943. His next position was as CG of naval bases in the Fourteenth Naval District beginning in October 1944 until he retired as major general in June 1946.

Waller's decorations included the Navy

Cross, Purple Heart and Legion of Merit for the period, 15 September 1944 until 2 September 1945.

Major General Littleton W.T. Waller, Jr., died on 14 April 1967.

WATSON, Lieutenant General Thomas Eugene was born on 18 January 1892 in Oskaloosa, IA. He attended local schools, then Penn College, also in Oskaloosa, and on 11 November 1912 enlisted as a Marine Corps private, serving three years and 11 months, with two months' service at Vera Cruz. Watson was commissioned a second lieutenant in the Marine Corps on 30 August 1916. For the next three years, beginning with 16 November 1916, he was a member of the Second Provisional Brigade in the Dominican Republic and on several occasions participated in engagements with bandits in that country. It appears that his promotions skipped first lieutenant and he became Capt. Watson on 23 May 1917. He returned to the States in April 1919, and after brief leave his first assignment was at the MB, Mare Island, CA, arriving on 19 July. One year later he was again on foreign shore duty from 20 July 1920 with the *Policia Nacional Dominicana* of Santo Domingo. His captaincy was made permanent, effective on 31 August 1918.

In June 1924, Capt. Watson returned to the States and on 16 September was assigned to the Marine Corps Base, San Diego, CA, where he became CO of the Recruit Detachment and Officer-in-Charge, Drills and Instruction. Three years later, on 21 March 1927, he joined the Third Marine Brigade in China and saw service in Shanghai, Tientsin, and at the Marine air field at Hsin Ho. He returned to the U.S. in July 1928, and on 5 September was at the MB, Quantico, where he attended and graduated from the Field Officers' course. Like most graduates, he then began a period as instructor in the same course. While there, he was promoted to major on 26 December 1929.

From October 1930 he was U.S. Naval Attaché, Santo Domingo City, in the nation of Santo Domingo (now Dominican Republic). Back to the States in July 1931 and assigned to HQMC, as a member of the Commandants Department, then on 27 October, to the *Guardia Nacional* in Managua, Nicaragua, where he was Director of Operations and Central Area Commander, from 6 April until 31 August 1932. When he returned to the States in January 1933 he was again, beginning on 8 February, a member of the MGC's Department.

Lt.Col. Watson's (29 May 1934) next appointment was briefly as CO of the Naval Prison, Navy Yard, Mare Island, CA, then, on 19 February 1935, he assumed duties as CO, Second Battalion, Sixth Marines, and in July 1936, became Assistant CoS, Four Section, and Chief of the Planning Section, FMF.

On 24 June 1937 Watson was selected to serve on the Examining Board (for

Thomas Eugene Watson

promotions). In August 1937, he was designated as a student at the AWC in Washington D.C. and upon graduation was ordered to HQMC, where, on 30 July 1938, he became Chief of the War Plans Section, Division of Plans and Policies. On 1 July 1939 he was promoted to colonel. In November 1941, he assumed duties as EO of the Division of Plans and Policies.

On 8 April 1942 Col. Watson joined the Third Marine Brigade as CoS to BG Charles Barrett, and sailed for Samoa that month. The brigade's principal units were the 7th Marines and the 1st Battalion, 11th Marines, both from the 1stMarDiv. Brigadier General Watson (27 August 1942) assumed command of the Brigade on 23 August 1942.

In November 1943 he became CG of Tactical Group One which included the Twenty-Second Marine Regiment and certain Army Units and led this organization in the assault and capture of Eniwetok Atoll, Marshall Islands, from 6 February to 22 March 1944, for which he was awarded the Distinguished Service Medal.

Major General Watson, effective on 20 January 1944, became CG of the Second Marine Division in April 1944, and led that organization in active operations against enemy forces at Saipan and Tinian in the Marianas Islands for which he was awarded a Gold Star in lieu of a second Distinguished Service Medal. During the period 1 to 13 April 1945, the General led the Division as part of Task Group 51.2 in diversionary activities off the coast of Okinawa and as a floating reserve for the Tenth Army. Unfortunately, because of inter-organizational differences, the Second Division was not called upon to land on Okinawa, long considered a major judgmental error.

In August 1945, he returned to HQMC and became Director of Personnel, which position he held until detached in June 1946. He then assumed command of the Second Marine Division and also Camp Lejeune, NC. His final command, beginning on 1 January 1948, was as CG, FMF, Pacific, and just prior to retirement, he assumed the rank of lieutenant general.

Lt.Gen. Thomas Eugene Watson retired on 1 July 1950, after completing nearly 38 years in the Marine Corps.

In addition to the Distinguished Service Medal with Gold Star, his decorations and medals include the (enlisted service) Good Conduct Medal, 1912–16; Mexican Service Medal, 1914; Dominican Campaign Medal, 1916; Expeditionary Medal with Bronze Star, Dominican Republic 1916–19 and 1920–24, China, 1927–28; World War I Victory Medal with West Indies Clasp, Dominican Republic, 1918; Yangtze Service Medal, China, 1927; Second Nicaragua Campaign Medal 1931–33; American Defense Service Medal; Asiatic-Pacific Campaign Medal with four Bronze Stars; World War II Victory Medal; Dominican Military Medal of Merit with Diploma; and the Nicaraguan Medal of Distinction with Diploma.

Lt.Gen. Thomas E. Watson died 6 March 1966 in a U.S. government hospital in the Panama Canal Zone.

WHITEHEAD, Brigadier General Frank was born on 4 January 1888 in Camden, NJ. Whitehead enlisted in the Marine Corps in 1908 and served eight years and 11 months as an enlisted Marine with distinction until he accepted a commission as a first lieutenant on 24 July 1917. He was promoted to captain two days later. In the meantime, he was assigned to duty with the Fifth Marines and joined them in France on 31 December 1917. He served as "skipper" of the 67th Company, 1/5, in France during World War I at Verdun, Belleau Wood, Soissons, St. Mihiel, and Blanc Mont and was twice wounded in action, once at Belleau Wood on Hill 142 on 6 June 1918 and again at Blanc Mont on 4 October 1918. He was awarded a Distinguished Service Cross, later also a Navy Cross, plus a Silver Star citation and a French Croix de Guerre, Gilt. He remained with the 4th Brigade on occupation duty until returning to the U.S. in August 1919 where he remained at the MB, Quantico until transferred to HQMC on 27 July 1921. During this period, his permanent commission as captain was effective on 4 June 1920.

On 15 December 1923 Capt. Whitehead was shipped to the MB, Navy Yard, Pearl Harbor, as Post Quartermaster and remained there until February 1926. After a month's leave he was appointed Post QM at the MB, Navy Yard, Puget Sound, WA on 23 Mar 1926. That duty lasted until 13 August 1928 when he assumed duty at the recruiting station in Portland, OR. On 16 August 1929, he went aboard the Special Services Squadron ship the *Rochester* to command the MD. During this period, to aid the electoral process, he and his men served ashore in Nicaragua in the three months beginning in September through November 1930 and he was commended by the Chief of the Mission for his performance of duty. Shipboard service ended in July 1931, and he was back on duty at the MB, Quantico on 28 August 1931. While there he attended the Field Officers' course, graduating in June 1932.

On 15 June, Major Whitehead (20 April 1932) was assigned to the Navy Yard, New York, as Post QM, following which, on 20 June 1935, Lt.Col. Whitehead (27 July 1935) returned to HQMC. This duty lasted a year when, in June 1936, he was assigned to a course at the Army Industrial College, which he completed in June 1937. Then he was back at QM, having selected the QM administrative track for the balance of his career.

In July 1937 he was transferred to San Diego where he joined the Second Marine Brigade as QM and left for Shanghai, China, in August, not returning to the States until April 1938. Upon his return, Lt.Col. Whitehead, at the specific request of the Director of the Army Industrial College, was assigned duty with the college as an instructor on 13 June 1938. Col. Whitehead (8 July 1940) would remain teaching there until 1 February 1941, when, at the recommendation of the Under Secretary of War, he was detached by the President for duty with the U.S. Army. His assignment was as Commandant of the Army Industrial College, which post he retained until war was declared and the school was suspended in January 1942. He returned to the Marines Corps and was subsequently commended by the Under Secretary of War for the outstanding manner in which he had performed his duties.

From January to June 1942 Whitehead served in the Plans Division, Office of the Chief of Naval Operations, and from July to October 1942 in the Office of the Commander in Chief, U.S. Fleet. Then in October service with the Department of Plans and Policies, at HQMC until 1 May 1944.

Frank Whitehead

Whitehead was placed on the retired list and advanced to brigadier general for having been specially commended for the performance of duty in combat. He was, however, retained on active duty in Plans and Policies until 1 January 1946 when he was ordered home to inactive status.

General Whitehead's awards and decorations including the Navy Cross and Distinguished Service Cross, Silver Star, plus two Purple Hearts; also included, a Dominican Campaign Medal; Second Nicaraguan Campaign Medal; Good Conduct Medal; Expeditionary Medal; American Defense Medal; American Campaign Medal and both World War Victory Medals with clasps.

Brigadier General Frank Whitehead, 62, died on 21 July 1950 while a patient at the Bethesda Naval Hospital. He was buried with ceremony at Arlington Cemetery.

WILLIAMS, Major General Seth was born on 19 January 1880 in Foxboro, MA. He attended Norwich University between 1901 and 1903 during which, as with all Norwich students, he served as an enlisted man with the Vermont National Guard. He graduated and earned a B.S. from the College in June 1903. Williams accepted a commission as a second lieutenant of Marines on 30 June 1903. His first assignment, on 24 July, was to the MB, Annapolis, where he attended the School of Application.

First Lieutenant Williams' (3 March 1904) first foreign service was to the MB (later changed to the 1st Brigade), Olongapo, Philippine Islands, at which he arrived on 12 April 1904. His term in the Islands was over in June 1907 when he returned to the U.S. and after a leave, on 19 October he was on duty at the MB, Boston, MA. On 14 August 1908 he was promoted to captain and on 31 August 1908 had accepted an appointment with the Quartermaster Department and serving at the MB, Norfolk, VA. He would continue service in the QM Department until his retirement as Quartermaster General.

Williams remained at Norfolk until transferred in the same capacity to the MB, Puget Sound, WA on 30 December 1910 and ordered to temporary duty at the Depot of Supplies, San Francisco, CA on 18 January 1913. But on 28 February he was to return to the 1st Brigade of Marines in the Philippines. Something changed that plan and instead he wound up at the MB on Guam, with that post terminating in July 1915. He was back in the States and, after a leave, he was assigned to duty at HQMC, as Assistant QM on 1 November 1915.

Major Williams (18 October 1916) remained at HQMC until shipped overseas to join the AEF on 18 October 1918. While at HQMC he was the officer in charge of the successful building program at Quantico for which he would later receive recognition. He next served as QM for the 1st Battalion, 11th Marine Regiment, 5th Brigade in France and returned to the U.S. with the rest of the Marine contingents in Europe in July-August 1919 and upon arrival was back at HQMC. On 22 March 1920 he moved to the MB, Quantico.

Next came a big, important jump. He was assigned as QM to the MD, American Legation Guard, Peking, China, arriving on 19 September 1921. Then, upon return to the U.S., Lt.Col. Williams (17 April 1923) went as Quartermaster CO to San Francisco at Headquarters, Department of the Pacific, arriving on 22 October 1923. Meanwhile, the Secretary of the Navy issued him a Letter of Commendation for "services in building a complete cantonment for seventy-five hundred men of the United States Marine Corps at Quantico ... and at a time in charge of the purchase division of the Quartermaster's Office..."

In December 1926, Williams was assigned as Post QM, Parris Island, SC, arriving on 5 January 1927. His next move was as CO of the important Depot of Supplies, Philadelphia, arriving on 15 September 1928 and remaining there many years. While still at Philadelphia he was promoted to full colonel on 20 May 1931. It wasn't until 1 July 1936 that he moved back to HQMC.

On 1 December 1937 he was promoted to Marine Corps Quartermaster with the rank of brigadier general for a period of four years. He had been working rather closely with the Assistant Commandant, BG A.A. Vandegrift, in various planning programs and when a hurricane devastated Parris Island in 1940, he and Vandegrift went down there and created the "new" PI just in time for World War II. On 1 December 1941 Williams was promoted to QM with the rank of major general for four years. Vandegrift later told how Williams was an important ally in helping the 1stMarDiv to collect all the necessaries as they were going to New Zealand. During World War II Williams was the motivating force behind the gigantic building program resulting in the construction of Camp Lejeune, NC, Camp Pendleton, and Camp Elliott, both in California. Williams was permanently made a major general, effective back to 20 March 1942, when he retired in February 1944.

In addition to his Letter of Commendation, General Williams was awarded the Haitian Distinguished Service Medal with Diploma for his services as purchasing agent for the *Garde d'Haiti.*

Major General Seth Williams died on 29 July 1963 at age 83, a little over 19 years after retirement.

WOODS, Lieutenant General Louis Earnest was born 7 October 1895 in Fredonia, New York. He attended Syracuse University, Syracuse, New York, and was commissioned a second lieutenant in the Marine Corps on 6 February 1917. On 23 May he was promoted to captain and on 3 September he attended a course of instruction at the School of Application, MB, Norfolk. He went to sea duty on board the *Georgia* and remained aboard until April 1919. On 30 October he transferred to the *Pittsburgh* to command the MD; except for a period of four months, he remained aboard until ordered ashore in September 1921. In the meantime, after the World War I turmoil, his rank was confirmed as captain on 4 June 1920. On 6 October he was on duty at the recruiting office in Pittsburgh, PA. During that period he applied for training as an aviator.

On 6 June 1922, after attending the Aviation School, Pensacola, FL, he was designated a Naval Aviator and from 12 July, and for the next two years, he was a pilot stationed at Marine Air Station, Quantico. On 8 July 1924 he was ordered to foreign shore duty in Haiti, where he joined as EO of Observation Squadron Two, First Marine Brigade, at Port-au-Prince. The overall situation there was rather quiet and he was back in the States in July 1926.

Shortly after his return, on 25 October 1926, he arrived at HQMC for duty in the Aviation Section of the Major General Commandant's Department. Except for a one-year course of instruction at the Air Corps Tactical School, Langley Field, VA, beginning on 24 August 1929 ending 15 September 1930, he remained at HQMC until August 1933, until he was detached to overseas duty once again in Haiti. There he joined the First Marine Brigade as EO, Observation Squadron Nine-M, at Port-au-Prince on 11 September 1933. The withdrawal of Marines from Haiti in August 1934 found him at the MCS, Quantico, from 14 August (first as a student, Senior course) and later, until June 1937, as Chief of the Aviation Section of the Schools. Major Woods' (29 May 1934) moved up in the lineal list to #67 of 155 majors. This was the era when the Marine Corps moved to selection as opposed to seniority and on 30 June 1936 he was up to lieutenant colonel.

During the next three years, beginning on 30 June 1937, he was EO, and then CO, of the Second MAG at the NAS, San Diego, CA. In June 1940, he became a student in the Senior course, NWC, Newport, RI and upon graduation in May 1941, joined the First MAW as CoS on 20 June. Col. Woods (1 October 1941) accompanied the Wing to the South Pacific in September 1942, where he participated in the occupation and defense of Guadalcanal as part of the famed CACTUS Air Force. He and they prevailed through one of the stormiest periods in Marine Corps history. During the battle, Woods was promoted to brigadier general on 25 September 1942 and for his outstanding contributions to the success of the Guadalcanal operation, Woods was awarded a Distinguished Service Medal. He returned to the U.S. and assumed duties as Director, Division of Aviation, HQMC, in June 1943, receiving a Gold Star in lieu of a second Legion of Merit. On 10 September 1944 he was promoted temporarily to major general.

He went to the war in the Pacific for the second time when he assumed command of the Fourth MAW based in the Marshall-Gilbert Area and was Commander, Shore Base Force, and was awarded the Legion of Merit for his outstanding service in this area. He left this position to become CG of the Tactical Air Force, Tenth Army and the Second MAW on Okinawa, for which he was awarded a Gold Star in lieu of his Third Legion of Merit.

In November 1945, he assumed command of the First MAW at Tientsin, China, and received an Oak Leaf Cluster in lieu of a fourth Legion of Merit for his meritorious performance of duty in providing air support for all Allied Forces in North China.

He returned to the United States to become Commander, Marine Air West Coast in August 1946 and when that organization was deactivated in September 1947,

Louis Earnest Woods

General Woods was named CG of the First MAW which had just returned to the United States. He was detached to Cherry Point, NC on 1 August 1949, where he remained until his retirement as a lieutenant general on 1 July 1951 after 34 years' service.

In addition to the Distinguished Service Medal and Legion of Merit with two Gold Stars and one Oak Leaf Cluster, his decorations and medals include the Presidential Unit Citation with two stars, Guadalcanal 1942, Okinawa 1945; Victory Medal, 1918; Expeditionary Medal Haiti 1924; American Defense Service Medal; American Campaign Medal; Asiatic-Pacific Campaign Medal with five Bronze Stars; World War II Victory Medal; Haitian Order of Honor and Merit, rank of Chevalier, with Diploma; Commander of the Most Excellent Order of the British Empire; and the Order of the Cloud and Banner with Grand Gordon (Chinese decoration).

Lieutenant General Louis E. Woods, one of the Marine Corps' outstanding aviators, died 20 October 1971 in Washington D.C.

WORTON, Major General William Arthur was born on 4 January 1897, in Boston, MA. He attended Boston Latin High School, then Harvard University, which awarded him a B.A., and Boston University Law School, which awarded him an L.L.B. He joined the Massachusetts Naval Militia in 1917 and was soon commissioned a second lieutenant of the MNM Marines. On 29 March 1917, he reported for active duty as a reserve first lieutenant of Marines and was assigned to the 6th Marines, then at Quantico, as a platoon leader in the 79th Company, 2d Battalion, commanded by Major Thomas Holcomb.

After the entire regiment arrived in France, the 6th was brigaded with the 5th Marines and 6th Machine Gun Bn to become the 4th Brigade and went into the lines near Verdun for a two-month period. They were next at what would become known as Belleau Wood. There, on 6 June 1918, he was badly wounded and gassed while advancing on the village of Bouresches. After hospitalization he was returned to the U.S. in September. In the meantime he had been promoted to captain effective 1 July 1918.

He must have been fully recovered because, after a brief leave, on 13 November he was sent to join the 2d Brigade in Santo Domingo. Remaining there until returning to the States in December 1920 and to his next assignment at the Naval Prison, Portsmouth, NH, on 17 December. On 28 November 1922 he had taken up a post with the MB, at the Naval Torpedo Station, Keysport, WA.

On 13 December 1923 he was on duty with the MD, American Legation, Peking, China, the first of a long connection with that nation. This trip terminated in December 1925 and his next posting began that month at the MB, Quantico. However, dates were altered (must presume he had alternate posting for several months) and the record shows his duty there beginning instead on 7 May 1926. While at Quantico he attended the MCS and graduated from the Company Officers' course.

On 2 May 1927 he joined the 3d Brigade in China, but returned to the States in September 1928 and on 26 November was at the NAS, San Diego. On 22 July 1929 he boarded the *Oklahoma* to command the MD and while aboard he put in for duty in China once again but the Commandant turned him down. He went "behind the scenes" and some political pressure from the Secretary of the Navy changed MG Ben Fuller's mind.

Worton was back at the MD, American Legation, Peiping, China on 8 September 1931, as, according to his oral history, a Chinese Language Student. He later said that he spent six hours every day for three years studying the Chinese language and he would remain in China for most of the 1930s. His experiences were the stuff that novels are made of. Meanwhile he was awarded the Purple Heart Medal. In 1935 Major Worton (29 May 1934) was listed as being a Japanese (?) language interpreter. He was also listed as being in San Francisco in July 1935. What is not usually known, however, is that he was assigned to the ONI and given a special "discharge" so he could establish himself as a "businessman" in Shanghai. In reality it was an unofficial leave of absence; and he was told that if he should get into trouble he was entirely on his own. At any rate, he engaged in espionage against the Japanese, and in fact recruited and sent into Japan several agents to spy on the Japanese navy. His own story is that he believed that after one year his value had exceeded further involvement and requested that he be relieved of further duties. Worton went back to San Francisco where he was "deprogrammed" by ONI agents. He left behind an unshakable and well-established system which continued working efficiently until after the war.

Major Worton is listed as being at Quantico in July 1936 and was Marine Officer, Scouting Force, on 7 June 1937, followed by promotion to lieutenant colonel that 1 September. He was back at Quantico on 22 July 1939 and in June 1940 a graduate of the Senior course. On 31 May 1941 he and his 2d Battalion, 6th Marines, were shipped east to occupy Iceland, thereby relieving the British. While there, the Marines became subordinate to the U.S. Army command which service arrived in Iceland somewhat later. This duty terminated for Col. Worton (1 January 1942) on 22 March 1942 and for a period of time, post–Iceland, he was in England as a military observer.

When the 5thMarDiv was being organized, Col. Worton was selected to be its CoS, serving in that capacity until transferred as ADC to the 3dMarDiv then engaged on Guam. He was promoted to brigadier general, although this didn't happen until late 1944. His next assignment was as the CoS of the III Marine Amphibious Corps from June 1945 until September 1946. He was the man who was appointed the first CG, Marine Garrison Forces, Pacific, and established his headquarters at the MB, Pearl Harbor. With a few staff officers, he led the advance party into China, going directly into Shanghai, China, to meet with General Wedemeyer, the area commander.

Worton's CoS, Col. Charles C. Brown, another old "China Hand" and qualified Chinese language interpreter, made all necessary arrangements for the two Marine divisions soon to arrive in North China. In June 1946 Worton, who had been CoS of the Corps, became the ADC of the 1stMarDiv. On 26 August he was relieved by BG Alfred Noble and returned to Pearl Harbor as CG Marine Garrison Forces, Pacific.

In February 1947 he was ordered to Washington to the Office of the Chief of Naval Operations. It was during this period, when the Unification crisis was at its most dangerous for the Marine Corps, that he was able to provide inside information to the famous "Chowder Society" to enable them to prepare counter-activities. In September he assumed command of the Troop Training Unit, Amphibious Training Command, Atlantic Fleet, located at Little Creek, VA.

On 13 May 1949 he assumed a berth with the 1stMarDiv at Camp Pendleton, from which he retired in June 1949 and was promoted to major general at that time. In November 1955 he was one of a select group of Marines present at the erection of a plaque at Belleau Wood in honor of the 4th Marine Brigade.

His awards include the Legion of Merit awarded by the U.S. Army for services in North China; the Bronze Star medal with a Gold Star in lieu of a second medal for his service on Guam; the Purple Heart for his wounds at Belleau Wood; numerous campaign medals; and several foreign decorations, like the Legion of Honor, Officer (French); the Cloud and Banner (Chinese), and the Military Order of Merit (Dominican).

Major General William A. Worton died at La Jolla, CA, on 26 July 1973 and was buried in Arlington National Cemetery with full honors.

WRIGHT, Major General Raymond Race was born on 5 February 1892 in Council Bluffs, IA. He was appointed to the Naval Academy and upon graduation on 5 June 1915 selected a commission as a second lieutenant of Marines. His first assignment was on 8 July 1915 at the School of Application, Norfolk, VA. Wright was on the lineal list just behind DeWitt Peck and Archie Howard, but before Pedro del Valle. Exiting the school a first lieutenant as of 29 August, he went aboard the *Utah* to join the MD on

17 October 1916. While aboard he was promoted to captain on 26 March 1917. He most likely was with the ship when it was part of the British Grand Fleet, based at Bantry, Ireland. Although a somewhat debatable record purports to show that he served in Santo Domingo in 1916 and Haiti from 1916 to 1921, I could find nothing official that verified that data.

He returned to the U.S. in November 1918 and on 9 November he decided to pursue a career in the Paymaster's Department, and was assigned duty at HQMC. On 15 November 1920 he went with the former Commandant, BG George Barnett, to San Francisco for duty with the newly created Department of the Pacific. That position ceased when he was transferred to service with the 1st Brigade in Haiti on 27 February 1923 (he was no longer listed in the Paymaster's Department, but I believe he was still an assistant paymaster) and was back in the States in September 1924.

His next posting was at HQMC beginning on 24 September and he was officially back with the Paymaster's Department followed one year later, on the 23d of September 1925, as Assistant Paymaster, Philadelphia. On 9 December 1926 he was at the MB, Quantico, where he attended and graduated from the Field Officers' course and on 27 June 1927 was once again Assistant Paymaster at Philadelphia.

Arriving on 31 March 1928, he was appointed as Brigade paymaster of the Second Marine Brigade in Nicaragua, remaining at that post until April 1930. While there he was promoted to major on 16 May 1929. Following Nicaragua on 1 May 1930 he went back to the Department of the Pacific, staying there until May 1933. His next stop, beginning on 1 June 1933, was at the recruiting office in San Francisco. Beginning on 9 June 1935, Lt.Col. Wright (29 May 1934) was assigned to study at the NWC, Newport, RI, from which he graduated in June 1936. Then he was back at HQMC and remained there, but now was named Assistant Paymaster of the Marine Corps. He was promoted to colonel on 1 June 1939, later back dated to 1 April 1939.

Col. Wright (1 April 1939) was on 29 September 1939 stationed at the Department of the Pacific, San Francisco. He became Brigadier General Paymaster of the Corps Wright for four years on 1 January 1942. At the end of that month he was transferred back to HQMC, remaining there until August 1946. In the meantime he had been promoted to Major General Paymaster of the Corps on 22 June 1945. Wright retired from the Marine Corps in December 1946.

His decorations included the Legion of Merit for his services between February 1942 to January 1946, World War I and World War II Victory medals, plus the usual campaign medals for expeditionary services in Santo Domingo, Haiti and Nicaragua.

Major General Raymond R. Wright died on 19 February 1964.

Appendix A.
Summary of Generals

Name	Birthplace	Origins	Specialty
Ames, Evans O.	MA		
Barrett, Charles D.	KY		
Blake, Robert	WA		
Bourke, Thomas E.	MD	enlisted USA	
Brewster, David L.S.	DC		Naval Aviator (until 1922)
Brice, William O.	SC	enlisted USA	Naval Aviator
Campbell, Harold D.	VT	Norwich Univ	Naval Aviator
Cates, Clifton B.	TN		
Cauldwell, Oscar R.	IN	USNA	
Clement, William T.	VA	VMI	
Creesy, Andrew E.*	MA	USNA	
Cumming, Samuel C.	JP	VMI	
Curtis, Merritt B.**	CA		
Cushman, Thomas J.	MO	enlisted USMC	Naval Aviator
DeCarre, Alphonse	DC		
Del Valle, Pedro A.	PR	USNA	
Denig, Robert L.	NY		
Edson, Merritt A.	VT		Naval Aviator (until 1926)
Erskine, Graves B.	LA	enlisted LA NG	
Farrell, Walter G.	CA	enlisted IL NG	Naval Aviator
Fegan, Joseph C.	TX		
Fellows, Joseph H.	DC		
Geiger, Roy S.	FL		Naval Aviator (until 1943)
Gregory, Maurice C.	IO		
Hall, Elmer E.*	ID	enlisted USMC	
Harrington, Samuel M.	MD		
Harris, (Thomas) Field	KY		Naval Aviator
Hart, Franklin A.	AL	enlisted AL NG	
Hermle, Leo D.	NE		

*Quartermaster. **Paymaster.

Appendix A

Name (alpha)	Birthplace	Origins	Specialty
Hill, Walter N.	MA		
Hill, William P.T.*	OK		Naval Aviator (1919)
Holcomb, Thomas	DE		
Howard, Archie F.	KS	USNA	
Howard, Samuel L.	DC	USNA	
Hunt, Leroy P.	NJ		
Jacobsen, Arnold W.*	OH		
James, William C.	SC	Citadel	
Johnson, Byron F.	KS		Naval Aviator
Jones, Louis R.	PA	enlisted USMC	
Keyser, Ralph S.	VA	enlisted USA	
Kingman, Matthew H.	IO	VMI	
Larkin, Claude A.	WA	enlisted USMC	Naval Aviator
Larsen, Henry L.	IL		
Little, Louis McC.	NY		
Long, Earl C.	NJ		
Marston, John	PA		
McKittrick, William L.	SC	Citadel	Naval Aviator
Merritt, Lewie G.	SC	Citadel	Naval Aviator
Miller, Ivan W.	OH	USNA	Naval Aviator
Miller, Lyle H.	MI		
Mitchell, Ralph J.	CT	USNA	Naval Aviator
Moore, James T.	SC	Citadel	Naval Aviator
Moses, Emile P.	SC		
Mulcahy, Francis P.	NY		Naval Aviator
Nimmer, David R.	MO	enlisted USMC	
Noble, Alfred H.	MD		
Ostermann, Edward A.	OH	enlisted USA	
Peck, DeWitt	CA	USNA	
Pepper, Robert H.	DE		
Pfeiffer, Omar T.	OH		
Pickett, Harry K.	SC	Citadel	
Price, Charles F.B.	GE	Pennsylvania Military College	
Puryear, Bennet, Jr.*	VA		
Putnam, Russell B.**	LA		
Rea, Leonard E.*	NY		
Riley, William E.	MN		
Robinson, Ray A.	CA		
Rockey, Keller E.	IN		
Rogers, Ford O.	TX		Naval Aviator
Rogers, William W.	IN	enlisted USMC	
Rowell, Ross E.	IO		Naval Aviator
Rupertus, William H.	DC	Rev Cutter School	

*Quartermaster. **Paymaster.

Summary of Generals

Name	Birthplace	Origins	Specialty
Sanderson, Charles R.*	DC		
Sanderson, Lawson H. McP.	WA		Naval Aviator
Schilt, Christian F.	IL	enlisted USMC	Naval Aviator
Schmidt, Harry.	NB		
Shepherd, Lemuel C., Jr.	VA	VMI	
Silverthorn, Merwin H.	MN	enlisted USMC	
Smith, Holland McT.	AL		
Smith, Joseph T.	CA		
Smith, Julian C.	MD		
Smith, Oliver P.	TX		
Thomas, Gerald C.	MO	enlisted USMC	
Torrey, Philip H.	UT		
Turnage, Allen H.	SC		
Underhill, James L.	CA		
Upshur, William P.	VA	VMI	
Vandegrift, Alexander A.	VA		
Vogel, Clayton B.	PA		
Walker, John T.	TX		
Wallace, William J.	MD		Naval Aviator
Waller, Littleton W.T., Jr.	VA	USNA	
Watson, Thomas E.	LA	enlisted USMC	
Whitehead, Frank*	NJ	enlisted USMC	
Williams, Seth*	MA	Norwich Univ	
Woods, Louis E.	NY		Naval Aviator
Worton, William A.	MA		
Wright, Raymond R.**	IO	USNA	

	Brigadier Generals:	14
	Major Generals:	43
	Lieutenant Generals:	24
	Generals:	17
	Total	98
Origins	Enlisted USMC	11
	Enlisted other	9
	USNA	10
	VMI	5
	Citadel	5
	Military schools	4
	other	54
Served as	Quartermaster	7
	Paymaster	3
	Naval Aviators	23

*Quartermaster.   **Paymaster.

Appendix B.
Generals by Birthplace

Washington, D.C.
Brewster, David L.S.
DeCarre, Alphonse
Fellows, Joseph H.
Howard, Samuel L.
Rupertus, William H.
Sanderson, Charles R.
Maryland (five)
Bourke, Thomas E.
Harrington, Samuel M.
Noble, Alfred H.
Smith, Julian C.
Wallace, William J.

South Carolina
Brice, William O.
James, William C.
McKittrick, William L.
Merritt, Lewie G.
Moore, James T.
Moses, Emile P.
Pickett, Harry K.
Turnage, Allen H.

Virginia
Clement, William T.
Keyser, Ralph S.
Puryear, Bennet Jr.
Shepherd, Lemuel C., Jr.
Upshur, William P.

Vandegrift, Alexander A.
Waller, Littleton W.T., Jr.

California
Curtis, Merritt B.
Farrell, Walter G.
Peck, DeWitt
Robinson, Ray A.
Smith, Joseph T.
Underhill, James L.

Massachusetts
Ames, Evans O.
Creesy, Andrew E.
Hill, Walter N.
Williams, Seth
Worton, William A.

New York
Denig, Robert L.
Little, Louis McC.
Mulcahy, Francis P.
Rea, Leonard E.
Woods, Louis E.

Iowa
Gregory, Maurice C.
Kingman, Matthew H.

Rowell, Ross E.
Wright, Raymond R.

Ohio
Jacobsen, Arnold W.
Miller, Ivan W.
Ostermann, Edward A.
Pfeiffer, Omar T.

Texas
Fegan, Joseph C.
Rogers, Ford O.
Smith, Oliver P.
Walker, John T.

Indiana
Cauldwell, Oscar R.
Rockey, Keller E.
Rogers, William W.

Louisiana
Erskine, Graves B.
Putnam, Russell B.
Watson, Thomas E.

Missouri
Cushman, Thomas J.
Nimmer, David R.
Thomas, Gerald C.

Appendix B

New Jersey
Hunt, Leroy P.
Long, Earl C.
Whitehead, Frank

Pennsylvania
Jones, Louis R.
Marston, John
Vogel, Clayton B.

Washington
Blake, Robert
Larkin, Claude A.
Sanderson, Lawson H. McP.

Alabama
Hart, Franklin A.
Smith, Holland McT.

Delaware
Holcomb, Thomas
Pepper, Robert H.

Illinois
Larsen, Henry L.
Schilt, Christian F

Kansas
Howard, Archie F.
Johnson, Byron F.

Kentucky
Barrett, Charles D.
Harris, (Thomas) Field

Minnesota
Riley, William E.
Silverthorn, Merwin H.

Nebraska
Hermle, Leo D.
Schmidt, Harry.

Vermont
Campbell, Harold D.
Edson, Merritt A.

Connecticut
Mitchell, Ralph J.

Florida
Geiger, Roy S.

Idaho
Hall, Elmer E.

Michigan
Miller, Lyle H.

Oklahoma
Hill, William P.T.

Tennessee
Cates, Clifton B.

Utah
Torrey, Philip H.

Germany
Price, Charles F.B.

Japan
Cumming, Samuel C.

Puerto Rico
Del Valle, Pedro A.

Selected Bibliography

United States Government Publications

American Battle Monuments Commission. *American Armies and Battlefields in Europe.* Washington, D.C.: U.S. Government Printing Office, 1938.

Annual Register Reports of the Navy Department for the Fiscal Years 1900–1960. Washington, D.C.: U.S. Government Printing Office, by dates.

Annual Reports of the Navy Department for the Fiscal Years 1917–1920. Washington, D.C.: U.S. Government Printing Office, 1918–1921.

Annual Reports of the Navy Department for the Fiscal Years 1921–1950. Washington, D.C.: U.S. Government Printing Office, 1922–1951.

Annual Report of the Secretary of War 1919. Washington, D.C.: U.S. Government Printing Office, 1919.

Bailey, Major Alfred Dunlop. *Alligators, Buffaloes, and Bushmasters: The History of the Development of the LVT Through World War II.* Washington, D.C.: History and Museums Division, Headquarters, U.S. Marine Corps, 1986.

Blanc Mont (Meuse-Argonne-Champagne). Monograph No. 9, reprint. Pike, NH: Brass Hat, 1994.

Clifford, Kenneth J., ed. *The United States Marines in Iceland, 1941–1942.* Washington, D.C.: Historical Division, Headquarters, U.S. Marine Corps, 1970.

Condit, Kenneth W., and Edwin T. Turnbladh. *Hold High the Torch: A History of the 4th Marines.* Washington, D.C.: Historical Branch, G-3 Division, Headquarters, U.S. Marine Corps, 1960.

The Genesis of the American First Army. Washington, D.C.: Historical Section, 1938.

History of U.S. Marine Corps Operations in World War II, 5 vols. Washington, D.C.: U.S. Government Printing Office, n.d. (circa 1958–1968).

[McCahill, William.] *The Marine Corps Reserve: A History.* Washington, D.C.: Division of Reserve, Headquarters, U.S. Marine Corps, 1966.

McClellan, Edwin N. *The United States Marine Corps in the World War.* Washington, D.C.: U.S. Government Printing Office, 1920.

Navy Yearbook 1920 and 1921. Washington, D.C.: U.S. Government Printing Office, 1922.

Order of Battle of The United States Land Forces in the World War. Reprint, vols. 1 and 2 of 5 vols. Washington, D.C.: U.S. Government Printing Office, 1988.

Pershing, John J. *Final Report of Gen. John J. Pershing.* Washington, D.C.: U.S. Government Printing Office, 1920.

Report of the First Army, American Expeditionary Force, Organization and Operations. Fort Leavenworth, KS, 1923.

Shaw, Henry I., Jr. *The United States Marines in the Occupation of Japan.* Washington, D.C.: Historical Branch, G-3 Division, Headquarters, U.S. Marine Corps, 1962 edition.

United States Army. *Records of the Second Division (Regular)*, 10 vols. Washington, D.C.: Army War College, 1927.

United States Army in the World War 1917–1919. Vols. 1, 3, 4 and other volumes. Washington, D.C.: Historical Division, 1948.

United States Navy. *Annual Report of the Secretary of the Navy for the Fiscal Years 1918-1919-1920*. Washington, D.C.: 1918, 1919, 1920.

United States Marine Corps World War II Monograph Series (By Publishing Date)

1947. Stockman, James R. *The Battle for Tarawa*. Historical Section, Division of Public Information, Headquarters, U.S. Marine Corps.

1948. Rentz, John N. *Bougainville and the Northern Solomons*. Historical Section, Division of Public Information, Headquarters, U.S. Marine Corps.

1949. Zimmerman, John L. *The Guadalcanal Campaign*. Historical Division, Headquarters, U.S. Marine Corps.

1950. Hoffman, Carl W. *Saipan: The Beginning of the End*. Historical Division, Headquarters, U.S. Marine Corps.

1950. Hough, Frank O. *The Assault on Peleliu*. Historical Division, Headquarters, U.S. Marine Corps.

1951. Hoffman, Carl W. *The Seizure of Tinian*. Historical Division, Headquarters, U.S. Marine Corps.

1952. Hough, Frank O., and John A. Crown. *The Campaign on New Britain*. Historical Branch, Headquarters, U.S. Marine Corps.

1952. Rentz, John N. *Marines in the Central Solomons*. Historical Branch, Headquarters, U.S. Marine Corps.

1954. Bartley, Whitman S. *Iwo Jima: Amphibious Epic*. Historical Branch, G–3 Division, Headquarters, U.S. Marine Corps.

1954. Heinl, Robert D., and John A. Crown. *The Marshalls: Increasing the Tempo*. Historical Branch, G–3 Division, Headquarters, U.S. Marine Corps.

1954. Lodge, O.R. *The Recapture of Guam*. Historical Branch, G–3 Division, Headquarters, U.S. Marine Corps.

1955. Nichols, Chas. S., Jr., and Henry I. Shaw, Jr. *Okinawa: Victory in the Pacific*. Historical Branch, G–3 Division, Headquarters, U.S. Marine Corps.

Personal Papers and Unpublished Memoirs

Barnett, George. "Soldier and Sailor Too." N.p. [1923?].

Bellamy, David. "Personal diary, 23 October 1917–22 August 1919." N.p., n.d.

Cordes, Onnie J. *The Immortal Division*. N.p., n.d., about 57 pages typewritten a few photos.

Draucker, James H. *Telling it Like it Was*. N.p., n.d., about 50 typewritten pages. Circa 6 April 1917 through August 1919.

Moore, William B. *Letters to His Mother*. 31 March 1918 through August 1919. About 35 pages.

Paris, Gus. "Hold Every Inch of Ground," unpublished biography of Logan Feland. Owensboro, KY: n.d.

Soares, Denzil I. *Diary of Pvt. Denzil I. Soares. April 1918–April 1919 U.S.M.C.* N.p., n.d., about 20 pages in diary form with chronological entries.

Thomas, Eugene R. *Letters to His Mother*. Begins with a letter dated Mother's Day 1918. He was a Marine corporal clerk at division headquarters.

Thompson, Troy T. *Private Edward Clyde Thompson—A Marine's Accounting of World War I*. N.p., n.d., c. 2003, mostly diary entry style with added material. Entries are substantial and begin on 11 April 1917.

Zischke, Peter H. *Recollections of My Father Herman A. Zischke, etc.* Orinda, CA: 2004. Includes memoirs and additional material put together by his son. About 100 pages.

Published Reminiscences and Biographies

Asprey, Robert B. See Vandegrift, Alexander A.
Brannen, Carl Andrew, edited by Rolfe L. Hillman, Jr., and Peter F. Owen. *Over There, A Marine in the Great War*. College Station: Texas A&M University Press, 1996.
Collins, Harry, with David Fisher and George B. Clark. *The War Diary of Corporal Harry Collins*. Reprint, Pike, NH: Brass Hat, 1996.
Cooke, Elliot D. *"We Can Take It, We Attack": Americans vs. Germans*. Pike, NH: Brass Hat, 1992. One-volume reprint of 1936 edition (2 volumes).
Cooper, Norman V. *A Fighting General. The Biography of Gen Holland M. "Howlin Mad" Smith*. Quantico, VA: Marine Corps Association, 1987.
Curley, W.J.P., Jr. *Letters from the Pacific, 1943–1946*. Privately printed, 1959.
Daniels, Josephus. *The Cabinet Diaries of Josephus Daniels, 1913–1921*. Lincoln: University of Nebraska Press, 1963.
Del Valle, Pedro A. *Semper Fidelis: An Autobiography*. Hawthorne, CA: Christian Book Club of America, 1976.
Derby, Richard. *"Wade in, Sanitary!" The Story of a Division Surgeon in France*. New York: G.P. Putnam and Sons, 1919.
Finney, Ben. *Once a Marine—Always a Marine*. NY: Crown, 1977.
Fitzpatrick, Tom. *A Character that Inspired: Major General Charles D. Barrett, USMC*. Fairfax, VA: Privately printed, 2003.
Gordon, George V. *Leathernecks and Doughboys*. 1927. Reprint, Pike, NH: Brass Hat, 1996.
Gulberg, Martin G. *A War Diary*. 1927. Reprint, Pike, NH: Brass Hat, 1989.
Harbord, James G. *Leaves from a War Diary*. New York: Dodd Mead, 1925.
_____. *The American Army in France 1917–1918*. Boston: Little, Brown, 1936.
Hemrick, Levi. *Once a Marine*. New York: Carlton, 1968.
Hoffman, Jon T. *Chesty: The Story of Lieutenant General Lewis B. Puller, USMC*. New York: Random House, 2001.
_____. *Once a Legend: "Red Mike" Edson of the Marine Raiders*. Novato, CA: Presidio, 1994.
Hunt, George P. *Coral Comes High*. NY: Harper and Brothers, 1946.
Isely, Jeter A., and Philip A. Crowl. *The U.S. Marines and Amphibious War: Its Theory and Its Practice in the Pacific*. Princeton, NJ: Princeton University Press, 1951.
Jackson, Warren R., George B. Clark, ed. *His Time in Hell, a Texas Marine in France*. Novato, CA: Presidio, 2001.
Kean, Robert W. *Dear Marraine, 1917–1919*. N.p., 1976.
Krulak, Victor H. *First to Fight: An Inside View of the U.S. Marine Corps*. Annapolis, MD: Naval Institute, 1984.
Leahy, Edward. *In the Islands*. Tucson, AZ: Hat's Off, 2002.
Lejeune, John A. *Reminiscences of a Marine*. Philadelphia: Dorrance, 1930.
Letcher, John Seymour. *One Marine's Story*. Verona, VA: McClure, 1970.
Liggett, Hunter. *AEF Ten Years Ago in France*. New York: Dodd, Mead, 1928.
Ludendorff, Erich von. *Ludendorff's Own Story, Vol. 2*. New York: Harper Bros., 1919.
Mackin, Elton E., and George B. Clark, ed. *Suddenly We Didn't Want to Die*. Novato, CA: Presidio, 1993.
Matthews, Allen R. *The Assault*. New York: Simon and Schuster, 1947.
Miller, Thomas G. *The Cactus Air Force: The Story of the Handful of Fliers Who Saved Guadalcanal*. New York: Harper & Row, 1969.
Millett, Allan R. *In Many a Strife: General Gerald C. Thomas and the U S. Marine Corps, 1917–1956*. Annapolis, MD: Naval Institute, 1993.
_____ and Jack Shulimson, eds. *Commandants of the Marine Corps*. Annapolis, MD: Naval Institute, 2004.
Morgan, Daniel E. *When the World Went Mad*. 1931. Reprint, Pike, NH: Brass Hat, 1992.
Pershing, John J. *My Experiences in the World War*. 2 vols. New York: E A. Stokes, 1931.
Ranlett, Louis Felix. *Let's Go!: The Story of A.S. No. 2448602*. Boston: Houghton Mifflin, 1927.

Rendinell, Joseph E., and George Pattullo. *One Man's War: The Diary of a Leatherneck.* New York: Sears, 1928.
Robillard, Fred S. *As Robie Remembers.* Bridgeport, CT: Wright Investors Service, 1969.
Rottman, Gordon L. *U.S. Marine Corps World War II Order of Battle: Ground and Air Units in the Pacific War, 1939–1945.* Westport, CT: Greenwood, 2002.
Schimidt, Hans. *Maverick Marine: General Smedley D. Butler and the Contradictions of American Military History.* Lexington: University Press of Kentucky, 1987.
Sellers, James McB. *World War I Memoirs of Lieutenant Colonel James McBrayer Sellers, USMC.* Pike, NH: Brass Hat, 1997.
Smith, Holland M. *Coral and Brass.* New York: Charles Scribner's Sons, 1949.
Smythe, Donald. *Pershing, General of the Armies.* Bloomington: Indiana University Press, 1986.
Thomas, Lowell. *Old Gimlet Eye: The Adventures of Smedley D. Butler.* New York: Farrar & Rinehart, 1933.
Twining, Merrill B., with Neil Carey. *No Bended Knee.* Novato, CA: Presidio Press, 1996.
Vandegrift, Alexander A., and Robert B. Asprey. *Once a Marine.* New York: W.W. Norton, 1964.
Vandiver, Frank E. *Blackjack: The Life and Times of John J. Pershing,* vol. 2, College Station: Texas A&M University Press, 1977.
Venzon, Anne Cipriano, ed. *General Smedley Darlington Butler: The Letters of a Leatherneck, 1898–1931.* Westport, CT: Praeger, 1992.
Williams, Robert Hugh. *The Old Corps: A Portrait of the U.S. Marine Corps Between the Wars.* Annapolis, MD: Naval Institute, 1982.
Willock, Roger. *Unaccustomed to Fear: A Biography of the Late General Roy S. Geiger, U.S.MC.* Princeton, NJ: privately published, 1968.
Wise, Frederic M., and Meigs O. Frost. *A Marine Tells It to You.* New York: J.H. Sears, 1929.

Citations, Awards and Decorations

Blakeney, Jane. *Heroes, US. Marine Corps, 1861–1955.* Washington, D.C.: 1957.
Citation Orders, General Headquarters, American Expeditionary Forces. *Citation Orders 1 through 10, 3 June 1919–31 August 1920.* France and Washington, D.C.: n.d.
Clark, George B. *Decorated Marines of the Fourth Brigade in World War I.* Jefferson, NC: McFarland, 2007.
____, ed. *Major Awards to US. Marines in World War One.* Reprint, Pike, NH: Brass Hat, 1992.
____. *United States Marine Corps Medal of Honor Recipients.* Jefferson, NC: McFarland, 2005.
Decorations, United States Army, 1862–1926–. Washington, D.C.: War Department, Office of the Adjutant General, 1927.
General Orders 40, July 5, 1918; G.O. 44, July 12, 1918; G.O. 88, December 31, 1918. Headquarters Second Division, American Expeditionary Forces.
Kerrigan, Evans E. *American War Medals and Decorations.* New York: Viking, 1971.
Navy. *Medal of Honor, 1861–1949.* N.p., n.d., c.1950
Office of the Adjutant General. *Decorations United States Army, 1862–1926.* Washington, D.C.: Government Printing Office, 1927.
Smith, Scott D. *Awards of the French Croix de Guerre to Marines during the World War.* Twentynine Palms, CA: n.d., c. 1995.
Stringer, Harry R., ed. *Heroes All!* Washington, D.C.: Fassett, 1919.
____. *The Navy Book of Distinguished Service.* Washington, D.C.: Fassett, n.d., c. 1921.

Official and Semi-Official Unit Histories

Akers, Herbert H. *History of the Third Battalion, Sixth Regiment, U.S. Marines.* Hillsdale, MI: Akers, MacRitchie and Hurlburt, 1919.
American Battle Monument Commission. *2d Division Summary of Operations in the World War* Washington, D.C.: U.S. Government Printing Office, 1944.

Brown, Ronald J. *A Few Good Men: The Story of the Fighting Fifth Marines*. Novato, CA: Presidio, 2001.
Clark, George B. *The Second Infantry Division in World War I: A History of the American Expeditionary Force Regulars, 1917–1919*. Jefferson, NC: McFarland, 2007.
____, ed. *A Brief History of the Sixth Regiment U,S. Marine Corps July, 1917-December; 1918*. Reprint, Pike, NH: Brass Hat, 1992.
____, ed. *History of the Fifth Regiment Marines (May 191 7—December 31, 1918)*. Reprint, Pike, NH: Brass Hat, 1995.
Curtis, Thomas J., and Lothar R. Long. *History of the Sixth Machine Gun Battalion*. Reprint, Pike, NH: Brass Hat, 1992.
History of the Second Battalion, Fifth Marines. Quantico, VA: Marine Barracks, 1938.
History of the Sixth Regiment, US. Marines. Tientsin, China: n.p., 1928.
History Third Battalion, Sixth Marines. N.p., n.d.
Jones, William K. *A Brief History of the 6th Marines*. Washington, D.C.: Headquarters, USMC, 1987.
Mitchell, William A. *The Official History of the Second Regiment of Engineers and Second Engineer Train, United States Army in the World War*. San Antonio, TX: San Antonio Print, 1920.
Second Division and its participation in the Great War. Reprint, Pike, NH: Brass Hat, 1993.
The Second Division, Syllabi of the Histories of Regiments and Separate Organizations. Coblenz, Germany: Coblenzer Volkszeitung, 1919.
Sherrod, Robert. *History of Marine Corps Aviation in World War II*. Washington, D.C.: Combat Forces, 1952.
Spaulding, Oliver Lyman, and John Womack Wright. *The Second Division American Expeditionary Force in France, 1917–1919*. New York: Hillman Press for the Second Division Association, 1937.
Strott, George G. *History of Medical Personnel of the United States Navy, Sixth Regiment Marine Corps, American Expeditionary Forces in World War 1917—1918*. Reprint, Pike, NH: Brass Hat, 1995.
____. *The Medical Department of the United States Navy with the Army and Marine Corps in France in World War I*. Washington, D.C.: U.S. Navy, 1947.
Thomason, John W., Jr., and George B. Clark, ed. *The United States Army Second Division Northwest of Chateau Thierry in World War I*. Jefferson, NC: McFarland, 2006.

Selected Other Books

Alexander, Joseph H. *Edson's Raiders. The 1st Marine Raider Battalion in World War II*. Annapolis, MD: Naval Institute, 2001.
____. *Utmost Savagery: The Three Days of Tarawa*. Annapolis, MD: Naval Institute, 1995.
Asprey, Robert B. *At Belleau Wood*. New York: G.P. Putnam and Sons, 1965.
Aurthur, Robert A., Kenneth Kohlmia, and Robert T. Vance. *The Third Marine Division*. Washington, D.C.: Infantry Journal, 1948.
Brown, Ronald J. *A Few Good Men: The Fighting Fifth Marines: A History of the USMC's Most Decorated Regiment*. Novato, CA: Presidio, 2001.
Burrus, L.D. *The Ninth Marines: A Brief History of the Ninth Marine Regiment*. Washington, D.C.: Infantry Journal, 1946.
Calder, Bruce J. *The Impact of Intervention: The Dominican Republic During the U.S. Occupation of 1916–1924*. Austin: University of Texas Press, 1984.
Cass, Bevan G. *History of the Sixth Marine Division*. Washington, D.C.: Infantry Journal, 1948.
Catlin, Albertus W. *With the Help of God and a Few Marines*. New York: Doubleday, 1919.
Clark, George B. *Devil Dogs: Fighting Marines of World War I*. Novato, CA: Presidio, 1999.
____. *The Six Marine Divisions in the Pacific*. Jefferson, NC: McFarland, 2006.
____. *Treading Softly: U.S. Marines in China, 1819–1949*. Westport, CT: Praeger, 2001.
____. *With the Old Corps in Nicaragua*. Novato, CA: Presidio, 2001.
Clifford, Kenneth J. *Amphibious Warfare Development in Britain and America from 1920–1940*. Laurens, NY: Englewood, 1983.

_____. *Progress and Purpose: A Developmental History of the U.S. Marine Corps, 1900–1970.* Washington, D.C.: History and Museums Division, U.S. Marine Corps, 1973.

Conner, Howard M. *The Spearhead: The World War II History of the 5th Marine Division.* Washington, D.C.: Infantry Journal, 1950.

Cowing, Kemper F., and Courtney R. Cooper. *"Dear Folks at Home": The Glorious Story of the United States Marines in France as Told in their Letters from the Battlefield.* Boston: Houghton Mifflin, 1919.

Croziat, Victor J. *Across the Reef: The Amphibious Tracked Vehicle at War.* London: Arms and Armour, 1989.

Fleming, Charles A. *Quantico: Crossroads of the Corps.* Washington, D.C.: Headquarters, U.S. Marine Corps, 1978.

Fuller, Stephen M., and Graham A. Cosmas. *Marines in the Dominican Republic, 1916–1924.* Washington, D.C.: History and Museums Division, U.S. Marine Corps, 1974.

Hallas, James H., ed. *The Devil's Anvil: The Assault on Peleliu.* Westport, CT: Praeger, 1994.

_____. *Doughboy War: The American Expeditionary Force in World War I.* Boulder, CO: Lynne Rienner, 2000.

_____. *Killing Ground on Okinawa: The Battle for Sugar Loaf Hill.* Westport, CT: Praeger, 1996.

_____. *Squandered Victory: The American First Army at St. Mihiel.* Westport, CT: Praeger, 1995.

Heinl, Robert D. *Soldiers of the Sea: The U.S. Marine Corps, 1775–1962.* Annapolis, MD: United States Naval Institute, 1962.

Hough, Frank O. *The Island War: The United States Marine Corps in the Pacific.* Philadelphia: J.B. Lippincott, 1947.

Isely, Jeter A., and Philip A. Crowl. *The U.S. Marines and Amphibious War: Its Theory and Its Practice in the Pacific.* Princeton, NJ: Princeton University Press, 1951.

Johnston, Richard W. *Follow Me! The Story of the Second Marine Division in World War II.* New York: Random House, 1948.

Langley, Lester D. *The Banana Wars: An Inner History of American Empire 1900–1934.* Lexington: University Press of Kentucky, 1983.

Macaulay, Neill. *The Sandino Affair.* Chicago: Quadrangle, 1967.

McCrocklin, James H., compiler. *Garde D'Haiti, 1915–1934.* Annapolis, MD: United States Naval Institute, 1956.

McMillan, George. *The Old Breed: A History of the First Marine Division in World War II.* Washington, D.C.: Infantry Journal, 1949.

Metcalf, Clyde H. *A History of the United States Marine Corps.* New York: G. P. Putnam and Sons, 1939.

Millett, Allan R. *Semper Fidelis: The History of the United States Marine Corps.* New York: Macmillan, 1980.

Munro, Dana G. *The United States and the Caribbean Republics, 1921–1933.* Princeton, NJ: Princeton University Press, 1974.

Musicant, Ivan. *The Banana Wars: A History of United States Military Intervention in Latin America from the Spanish-American War to the Invasion of Panama.* New York: Macmillan, 1990.

Paul, Doris A. *The Navajo Code Talkers.* Bryn Mawr, PA: Dorrance, 1973.

Proehl, Carl W., ed. *The Fourth Marine Division in World War II.* Washington, D.C.: Infantry Journal, 1946.

Schmidt, Hans. *The United States Occupation of Haiti, 1915–1934.* New Brunswick, NJ: Rutgers University Press, 1971.

Schuon, Karl. *U.S. Marine Corps Biographical Dictionary.* New York: Franklin Watts, 1963.

Thomason, John W., Jr. *Fix Bayonets!* New York: Scribner's 1925.

United States Marine Corps. *A Review of the Organization and Operations of the Guardia Nacional de Nicaragua.* By Direction of the Major General Commandant of the United States Marine Corps. N.p., n.d., c. 1936.

Venzon, Anne Cipriano, ed. *The United States in the First World War: An Encyclopedia.* New York: Garland, 1995.

Index

Numbers in *bold italics* indicate pages with photographs.

American Legation, Peking (Peiping) 23, 32, 36, 40, 42, 47, 48, 54, 58, 59, 62, 67, 68, 72, 74, 80, 91, 98, 101, 104, 112, 118, 122, 130, 152, 156, 161, 174
Ames, MG Evans O. *17–18*
BB *Arkansas* 112, 144, 156
Arlington National Cemetery 20, 25, 56, 67, 70, 88, 106, 120, 123, 125, 131, 136, 141, 143, 149, 162, 171, 175
Army War College (AWC) 13, 22, 30, 32, 36, 42, 55, 62, 63, 65, 69, 88, 99, 100, 159, 169
Azores 23, 66, 134

Barnett, MGC George 29, 67, 81, 154, 175
Barrett, MG Charles D. *18–20*, 35, 56, 94, 103, 109, 113, 118, 162, 164, 169
Battlefields: Belleau Wood 19, 20, 175; Blanc Mont 11, 27, 31, 169; Marbache 27, 74, 116, 141, 144; Meuse Argonne 19, 29, 83, 115; St. Mihiel 20, 27, 29, 169; Soissons 20, 27, 29, 169; Verdun 27, 28, 31, 169
Bearss, BG Hiram I. 35, 74
Belleau Wood 19, 20, 175
Blake, MG Robert *20–22*
Blanc Mont 11, 27, 31, 169
Bougainville 17, 22, 26, 32, 56, 60, 91, 103, 118, 152, 156, 161
Bourke, LG Thomas E. *22–23*, 124
Brewster, BG David L.S. *23–25*
Brice, Gen William O. 6, *25–27*
Brown Field 25, 28, 38, 49, 54, 89, 90, 94, 97, 100, 133, 135, 165
CR *Buffalo* 54, 127
Butler, MG Smedley D. 17, 32, 35, 50, 54, 69, 74, 88, 91, 94, 104, 108, 112, 120, 131, 137, 146, 155, 159, 160
Button, Cpl William R. 122, 160

"Cactus Air Force" 41, 95, 129, 135, 179
BB *California* 17, 20, 29, 58, 103, 127, 144, 159
Camp Dunlop, CA 163
Camp Elliott, CA 23, 141, 162, 163, 172; early 53, 86, 98, 104, 112, 146, 160
Camp Lejeune 23, 24, 63, 67, 78, 86, 92, 104, 109, 120, 122, 156, 157, 169, 172
Camp Pendleton 48, 52, 109, 111, 146, 151, 163, 165, 172, 175
Campbell, MG Harold D. *27–28*, 71
Cape Gloucester 109, 131, 140, 150
Cates, GenC Clifton B. *28–31*
Cauldwell, MG Oscar R. *31–32*, 71
Cavite, PI 49, 53, 88, 110, 114, 126, 131, 156
Cherry Point 26, 39, 79, 91, 94, 97, 134, 136, 166, 173
China 5, 6, 9, 10, 11, 19, 20, 23, 24, 30, 32, 34, 37, 73, 78, 79, 87, 104, 120, 134, 139, 140, 161, 168, 174, 175
Chosin Reservoir 60, 140, 150
Clarke, Col Thomas S. 113, 157
Clement, LG William T. *32–34*
Cole, Col Eli K. 8, 13, 98, 155, 158, 162
BB *Connecticut* 155, 156
Corregidor 33, 73
Coyotepe (and Barranca) Hill 54, 98, 160
Creesy, MG Andrew E. *34–35*
Cuba 39, 42, 43, 50, 59, 64, 69, 76, 77, 84, 86, 102, 103, 105, 107, 112, 114, 127
Cumming, MG Samuel C. *35–37*, 49
Curtis, BG Merritt B. *37–38*
Cushman, LG Thomas J. *38–39*, 60, 93

Daly, GySgt Daniel J. 105, 159
DeCarre, MG Alphonse *39–41*, 92

BB *Delaware* 58, 83
Del Valle, LG Pedro *41–43*, 70, 95, 109, 176
Denig, BG Robert L. *43–45*
Dixie (transport) 87, 162
Doyen, Col Charles A. 10, 143

Edson, MG Merritt A. *45–47*, 75
Elliott, MGC George F. 75
Empress of Augusta Bay 152, 156, 161
Eniwetok Island 139, 165, 169
Erskine, Gen Graves B. *47–49*, 104

Farrell, MG Walter G. *49–50*, 79, 93, 166
Fegan, MG Joseph C. *50–52*
Fellows, BG Joseph H. *52–53*
BB *Florida* 50, 129
Ft. Benning Infantry School 13, 31, 35, 37, 48, 59, 61, 76, 86, 95, 118–19, 149, 152
Ft. Leavenworth C&GS 13, 32, 36, 55, 71, 100, 107, 113, 119, 152, 159
France 11, 18, 19, 20, 21, 27, 28, 29, 31, 69, 74, 79, 83, 86, 115, 116, 141, 144, 149, 169, 174, 175
Fuller, MGC Ben 96, 174

CR *Galveston* 98, 107, 144
Geiger, Gen Roy S. 28, *53–56*, 97, 112, 129, 148
Gilbert Islands 135, 146, 173
Gregory, BG Maurice C. *56–57*
Guadalcanal 30, 41, 42, 46, 60, 71, 75, 78, 92, 100, 102, 110, 130, 133, 152, 156, 161, 166, 173
Guam 21, 23, 43, 55, 65, 86, 104, 109, 134, 140, 145, 156, 165, 175
Guantánamo 8, 46, 57, 65, 67, 78, 97, 98, 101, 103, 128, 131, 139, 147, 153, 158, 162
Guardia Nacional 11, 44, 48, 56, 59, 75, 77, 90, 91, 100, 147, 163, 168

189

Haiti 5, 6, 9, 11, 15, 35, 36, 163, 172, 175
Hall, BG Elmer E. *57–58*
Halsey, Adm William F. 103, 119
Hanneken, Sgt Herman H. 122, 160
Harllee, Capt William C. 19, 43
Harrington, BG Samuel M. *58–59*
Harris, LG Field *59–60*
Hart, Gen Franklin A. *60–63*, 64
Hawaii 23, 27, 28, 38, 44, 44, 136, 175
Hermle, LG Leo D. *63–64*
Hill, BG Walter N. *64–66*
Hill, MG William P.T. *66–67*
Holcomb, GenC Thomas 33, 45, 52, *67–70*, 78, 88, 92, 110, 115, 144, 161, 174
CR *Houston* 33, 142
Howard, MG Archie F. 34, *70–71*, 175
Howard, LG Samuel L. 39, *72–74*, 107
Hunt, Gen LeRoy P. *74–76*, 120

Iceland 64, 75, 92, 150, 175
BB *Idaho* 58, 139, 158
Iwo Jima 23, 30, 62, 64, 121, 123, 126

Jacobsen, MG Arnold W. *76–77*
James, BG William C. *77–78*
Johnson, MG Bryon F. *78–79*
Johnson, Sect Louis 31, 150
Jones, MG Louis R. *79–81*

Keyser, MG Ralph S. 19, 69, *81–82*
Kingman, BG Matthew 39, 72, *82–84*
Korea 27, 31, 39, 60, 109, 136, 140, 150, 153
Krulak, Capt Victor 46, 67
Kwajalein 36, 48, 93, 146, 157

Larkin, LG Claude 79, *84–85*
Larsen, LG Gen Henry L. 39, 72, 82, *85–86*, 156
Lee, BG Harry 19, 69, 71
Lejeune, MGC John A. 5, 13, 45, 69, 70, 81, 127, 139, 154, 161
CV *Lexington* 25, 50, 60
Little, MG Louis McC. *86–88*
Long, MG Earl C. *88–90*

MacArthur, LG Douglas 31, 33, 34, 75, 131
Mail Guard duty 32, 75, 120
Marbache 27, 74, 116, 141, 144
MarFairWest 85, 93, 100, 133
Marianas Islands 24, 145, 169
Marine Corps: Adjutant and inspector 58, 63, 83, 86, 106, 157, 163; Department of the Pacific 7–8, 29, 37, 49, 52, 66, 76, 183; Depot of Supplies 8, 46, 57, 77, 115, 118, 131, 167; Equipment board 30, 59, 86, 99, 153; Headquarters (HQMC) 5, 20, 21, 22, 24, 183; Naval attaché 42, 50, 55, 60, 62, 79, 85, 101, 128, 135, 148, 149, 168; Operations and training 30, 42, 55, 62, 69, 72, 88, 121, 144, 148; Paymaster Dept. 37–38, 42, 67, 71, 116, 137, 138, 175; Plans and policies 20, 27, 90, 103, 108, 121, 126, 150, 152, 153, 156, 169, 170, 171; Publicity ("Denig's Demons") 44, 127; Quartermaster Dept. 12, 35, 44, 48, 53, 56, 66, 77, 89, 101, 111, 114, 117, 125, 172; Reserves 30, 52, 62, 142, 150
Marine Corps bases: Camp Dunlop, CA 163; Camp Elliott, CA 23, 141, 162, 163, 172; Camp Lejeune 23, 24, 63, 67, 78, 86, 92, 104, 109, 120, 122, 156, 157, 169, 172; Camp Pendleton 48, 52, 109, 111, 146, 151, 163, 165, 172, 175; Guantánamo 8, 46, 57, 65, 67, 78, 97, 98, 101, 103, 128, 131, 139, 147, 153, 158, 162
Marine Corps posts, foreign: American Legation, Peking (Peiping) 23, 32, 36, 40, 42, 47, 48, 54, 58, 59, 62, 67, 68, 72, 74, 80, 91, 98, 101, 104, 112, 118, 122, 130, 152, 156, 161, 174; Cavite, PI 49, 53, 88, 110, 114, 126, 131, 156; Olongapo, PI 18, 44, 51, 67, 73, 101, 131, 159, 171; Samoa 20, 28, 32, 86, 95, 113, 146, 165; Tientsin 73, 78, 79, 87, 104, 120, 134, 139, 161, 168, 173
Marine Corps schools (MCS) 6–7, 12, 13, 17, 21, 23, 24, 26, 174; Port Royal 18, 23, 28, 50, 53, 58, 66, 79, 88, 94, 114, 136, 138, 147, 153, 159, 160, 162, 167
Marine Pacific operations: Bougainville 17, 22, 26, 32, 56, 60, 91, 103, 118, 152, 156, 161; Cape Gloucester 109, 131, 140, 150; Corregidor 33, 73; Empress of Augusta Bay 152, 156, 161; Eniwetok Island 139, 165, 169; Gilbert Islands 135, 146, 173; Guadalcanal 30, 41, 42, 46, 60, 71, 75, 78, 92, 100, 102, 110, 130, 133, 152, 156, 161, 166, 173; Guam 21, 23, 43, 55, 65, 86, 104, 109, 134, 140, 145, 156, 165, 175; Iwo Jima 23, 30, 62, 64, 121, 123, 126; Kwajalein 36, 48, 93, 146, 157; Marianas Islands 24, 145, 169; Marshall Islands 56, 62, 126, 134, 145, 164, 169; Midway Island 112, 166; Okinawa 22, 33, 43, 47, 56, 76, 79, 81, 102, 125, 136, 140, 150, 167, 169, 173; Peleliu 28, 55, 130, 136, 148, 150; Roi-Namur 32, 62, 80, 138; Saipan 48, 62, 80, 126, 138, 145, 169; Solomon Islands 26, 43, 71, 85, 96, 100, 135, 136, 162; Tarawa 23, 46, 58, 64, 93, 148, 152, 158; Tinian 36, 48, 62, 75, 78, 126, 138, 145, 158, 169; Wake Island 111, 112, 124
Marshall Islands 56, 62, 126, 134, 145, 164, 169
Marston, MG John, III 41, 64, *91–92*
McKittrick, MG William L. *90–91*, 92
Merritt, MG Lewie G. 39, *92–93*
Meuse Argonne 19, 29, 83, 115
BB *Michigan* 91, 167
Midway Island 112, 166
Miller, MG Ivan "W" *93–94*
Miller, BG Lyle H. 39, 72, *94–96*
BB *Missouri* 34, 43, 53, 55
Mitchell, LG Ralph J. *96–97*
Moore, LG James T. *97–98*
Moses, MG Emile P. *98–99*
Mulcahy, LG Francis P. *99–101*, 128

BB *Nevada* 31, 122
Neville Board 11, 110, 146
BB *New Mexico* 72, 86, 92, 117, 155
New Zealand 17, 30, 41, 42, 75, 86, 103, 140, 148, 172
New Zealand Air Force 26, 96
Nicaragua 6, 9, 11, 15, 21, 24, 38, 40, 42, 45, 46, 50, 176; Coyotepe (and Barranca) Hill 54, 98, 160; *Guardia Nacional* 11, 44, 48, 56, 59, 75, 77, 90, 91, 100, 147, 163, 168
Nimmer, MG David R. *101–102*
Noble, Gen Alfred H. 25, 71, *102–104*
Northern Bombing Grp 54, 99, 124

Okinawa 22, 33, 43, 47, 56, 76, 79, 81, 102, 125, 136, 140, 150, 167, 169, 173
BB *Oklahoma* 84, 108, 137, 174
Olongapo, PI 18, 44, 51, 67, 73, 101, 131, 159, 171
Ostermann, MG Edward A. *104–106*, 159

Panama (Canal Zone) 9, 11, 21, 45, 50, 54, 68, 71, 87, 98, 105, 131, 143, 158, 160, 169; Camp

Index

Elliott (early) 53, 86, 98, 104, 112, 146, 160
Gunboat *Panay* 46, 77
Patch, MG Alexander M., USA 41, 92
Pearl Harbor 23, 28, 38, 175
Peck, MG DeWitt 71, *106-108*, 175
Peleliu 28, 55, 130, 136, 148, 150
Pendleton, Col Joseph 42, 98, 116
BB *Pennsylvania* 21, 85
Pepper, LG Robert H. *108-109*, 111-112
Peralte, Charlmagne 49, 54, 122, 133, 161
Pershing, Gen John J. 69, 79, 94
Pfeiffer, MG Omar T. *109-111*
Pickett, MG Harry K. *111-112*
CR *Pittsburgh* 101, 172
Policia Nacional 11, 51, 61, 71, 168
Port Royal 18, 23, 28, 50, 53, 58, 66, 79, 88, 94, 114, 136, 138, 147, 153, 159, 160, 162, 167
Prairie (transport) 127, 162
Price, LG Charles F.B. 46, 95, *112-114*, 130
Puryear, MG Bennet, Jr. *114-115*
Putnam, BG Russell B. *115-116*

Rea, MG Leonard E. *116-118*
BB *Rhode Island* 87, 147
CR *Richmond* 35, 42
Riley, LG William E. *118-120*
Robinson, Gen Ray A. *120-122*
CR *Rochester* 24, 45, 61, 170
Rockey, LG Keller E. 23, 71, 72, 82, *122-124*, 156
Rogers, MG Ford O. 6, *124-125*
Rogers, MG William W. *125-126*
Roi-Namur 32, 62, 80, 138
Roosevelt, Franklin D. 14, 52, 101, 130
Roosevelt, Theodore 13, 87
Rowell, LG Ross E. 39, 55, *126-129*
Rupertus, MG William H. 39, *129-131*, 150
Russell, MGC John H. 9, 14, 18, 88, 108, 127, 154; Neville Board 11, 110, 146; Russell Board 11, 45, 110, 146, 152
Russell Board 11, 45, 110, 146, 152

St. Mihiel 20, 27, 29, 169
Saipan 48, 62, 80, 126, 138, 145, 169
Samoa 20, 28, 32, 86, 95, 113, 146, 165
Sanderson, BG Charles R. *131-132*
Sanderson, MG Lawson H. McP. *132-134*
Sandino, Augusto 24, 46, 48, 96, 123, 126, 128, 137

Santo Domingo 5, 6, 9, 11, 15, 19, 22, 24, 27, 175; *Policia Nacional* 11, 51, 61, 71, 168
CV *Saratoga* 6, 25, 166
Schilt, Gen Christian 28, *134-136*
Schmidt, Gen Harry 126, *136-138*
CR *Seattle* 61, 63
Shepherd, GenC Lemuel C. 19, 30, 36, 60, 71, *138-141*
Silverthorn, LG Merwin H. *141-143*
Small Wars Manual 46, 59
Smith, Gen Holland McT. 12, 36, 46, 47, 101, *143-146*, 148, 154, 161
Smith, MG Joseph T. *146*
Smith, LG Julian C. 23, 46, 64, 114, *146-149*
Smith, Gen Oliver P. 60, *149-151*
Soissons 20, 27, 29, 169
Solomon Islands 26, 43, 71, 85, 96, 100, 135, 136, 162

Tarawa 23, 46, 58, 64, 93, 148, 152, 158
BB *Tennessee* 77, 137, 155
Tentative Landing Operations Manual 14-15, 28, 71, 103, 122
BB *Texas* 42, 80
Thomas, Gen Gerald C. *151-153*
Tientsin 73, 78, 79, 87, 104, 120, 134, 139, 161, 168, 173
Tinian 36, 48, 62, 75, 78, 126, 138, 145, 158, 169
Torrey, MG Philip H. 101, *153-154*, 161
Truman, Harry 30, 140, 150
Turnage, Gen Allen H. 39, 56, 72, 82, 103, *154-156*

Underhill, LG James L. 72, *156-158*
U.S. Army schools: Army War College (AWC) 13, 22, 30, 32, 36, 42, 55, 62, 63, 65, 69, 88, 99, 100, 159, 169; Ft. Benning Infantry School 13, 31, 35, 37, 48, 59, 61, 76, 86, 95, 118-19, 149, 152; Ft. Leavenworth C&GS 13, 32, 36, 55, 71, 100, 107, 113, 119, 152, 159
U.S. Marine units: *Air Groups*: MAG Two 36, 135, 179; MAG Eleven 10, 12; *Air Wings*: 1st MAW 24, 47, 69, 86, 92, 137, 179, 180; 2d MAW 12, 24, 91, 92, 95, 129, 135; 3d MAW 36, 69, 76; 4th MAW 135, 180; "Cactus Air Force" 41, 95, 129, 135, 179; *Amphibious Corps*: Atlantic Fleet 35, 48; Pacific Fleet 145, 163; *Brigades*: 1st Marine Brigade 9, 15, 25, 53,
67, 76, 87, 103, 106, 117, 137, 143, 144, 148, 166; 2d Marine Brigade 9, 15, 19, 21, 24, 27, 52, 58, 78, 80, 83, 86, 90, 96, 100, 111, 116, 122, 124, 125, 128, 134, 137, 146, 163, 174; 3d Marine Brigade 9, 15, 17, 25, 30, 32, 36, 74, 78, 80, 82, 84, 80, 108, 121, 137, 139, 146, 157, 161, 174; 4th Marine Brigade 19, 28, 43, 63, 65, 69, 174; 5th Marine Brigade 15, 19, 45, 57, 60, 88, 94, 98, 101, 111, 112, 120, 132, 154, 159, 171; *Corps*: IMAC 20, 24, 35, 55, 71, 89, 103-4, 117, 142, 153, 162, 163, 169; IIIMAC 43, 55, 102, 124, 142, 148, 175; VAC 35, 48, 52, 89, 109, 126, 138, 145, 146, 148, 157; *Divisions* (including some regiments): 1st MarDiv 21, 30, 35, 42, 46, 59, 73, 75, 78, 80, 104, 109, 117, 130, 140, 145, 150, 152, 153, 154, 161, 169, 175; 2d MarDiv 23, 41, 43, 46, 58, 64, 92, 114, 121, 123, 145, 148, 150, 163, 164, 169; 3d MarDiv 17-18, 21, 32, 48, 103-4, 119, 121, 140, 145, 156, 165, 175; 4th MarDiv 30, 36-37, 62, 64, 80, 126, 138, 157; 5th MarDiv 23, 64, 121, 123, 175; 6th MarDiv 33, 34, 71; *Flying Fields*: Brown Field 25, 28, 38, 49, 54, 89, 90, 94, 97, 100, 133, 135, 165; Cherry Point 26, 39, 79, 91, 94, 97, 134, 136, 166, 173; MarFairWest 85, 93, 100, 133; Northern Bombing Grp 54, 99, 124
U.S. Navy: BB *Arkansas* 112, 144, 156; BB *California* 17, 20, 29, 58, 103, 127, 144, 159; BB *Connecticut* 155, 156; BB *Delaware* 58, 83; BB *Florida* 50, 129; BB *Idaho* 58, 139, 158; BB *Michigan* 91, 167; BB *Missouri* 34, 43, 53, 55; BB *Nevada* 31, 122; BB *New Mexico* 72, 86, 92, 117, 155; BB *Oklahoma* 84, 108, 137, 174; BB *Pennsylvania* 21, 85; BB *Rhode Island* 87, 147; BB *Tennessee* 77, 137, 155; BB *Texas* 42, 80; BB *Utah* 78, 175; BB *West Virginia* 33, 76, 146, 164; BB *Wyoming* 41, 42, 59, 72, 106, 144, 146, 147, 163; Chief of Naval Operations (CNO) 20, 71, 110, 123, 142, 159, 170, 175; Commander in Chief (CinC) 102, 108, 110, 119, 170; CR *Buffalo* 54, 127; CR *Galveston* 98, 107, 144; CR *Houston* 33, 142; CR *Pittsburgh* 101, 172; CR *Richmond* 35, 42; CR *Rochester* 24, 45, 61, 170;

CR *Seattle* 61, 63; CV *Lexington* 25, 50, 60; CV *Saratoga* 6, 25, 166; *Dixie* (transport) 87, 162; Gunboat *Panay* 46, 77; Naval War College (NWC) 13, 32, 37, 51, 60, 71, 84, 88, 95, 98, 99, 100, 101, 119, 142, 147, 154; Office of Naval Intelligence (ONI) 21, 128, 174; *Prairie* (transport) 127, 162
Upshur, MG William P. 105, 128, *158-160*
BB *Utah* 78, 175

Vandegrift, GenC Alexander A. 55, 78, 101, 109, 110, 117, 120, 130, 131, 150, 152, 154, *160-162*, 172
Vera Cruz 9, 19, 65, 85, 89, 91, 112, 116, 129, 131, 137, 147, 153, 156, 160, 167, 168
Verdun 27, 28, 31, 169
Virgin Islands 22, 36, 65, 85, 97, 100, 103, 125, 135, 146, 159
Vogel, MG Clayton B. 71, *162-164*

Wake Island 111, 112, 124
Walker, LG John T. *164-165*
Wallace, LG William J. 25, 94, *165-167*
Waller, MG Littleton W.T., Jr. 68, 83, *167-168*
Watson, LG Thomas E. 46, 78, *168-169*
BB *West Virginia* 33, 76, 146, 164
Whitehead, BG Frank *169-171*
Williams, MG Seth *171-172*
Woods, LG Louis E. *172-174*
Worton, MG William A. *174-175*
Wright, MG Raymond R. 71, *175-176*
BB *Wyoming* 41, 42, 59, 72, 106, 144, 146, 147, 163

www.ingramcontent.com/pod-product-compliance
Lightning Source LLC
Chambersburg PA
CBHW081558300426
44116CB00015B/2931